Research Methodology
in
POLITICAL SCIENCE

Research Methodology in POLITICAL SCIENCE

Chetan Agarwal
Vijay Sharma

Commonwealth

Research Methodology in Commerce

Edition : 2025

ISBN 978-81-311-0333-3

Published by :
COMMONWEALTH PUBLISHERS
4831/24, Prahlad Street,
Ansari Road, Darya Ganj,
New Delhi - 110002
Ph. : 23275511, 23257835
Fax : 91- 011- 23257835
e-mail : commonwealthbooks@gmail.com

Laser Typesetting by :
Arnav Computers
Delhi

Printed at :
Roshan Offset Printers
Delhi

Preface

Political science has suffered from being methodologically and theoretically naive. Growing out of history, law and public administration it has not developed, within a tradition of social science. Compared to economics or psychology, politics has paid little attention to methodology and there is apparently little consensus concerning the methods to be employed when undertaking political research. Unlike sociology, politics has little sense of its theoretical or historical roots, and there is a lack of a shared sense of what politics is, or what the subject of political analysis should be. A reflexive revolution seems recently to have engulfed the discourse and discipline of political science.

This book is an introduction to the theory and practice of empirical research methods in political science. Among the topics covered in this book are theory, empirical reasoning, development of testable and verifiable research questions, and operationalisation of key concepts. Numerous examples and case studies as well as important aspects of the research process are illustrated.

The book is designed to provide an appreciation of political science research and the use of various methods to arrive at objective conclusions and to allow student to consume social science literature in various academic fields. After reading this book, students will have a basic grasp of general methods, models, and statistical tools. They will not only learn why research methods are important but also how to use them.

Authors

Contents

1

Nature of Political Science

Human social life is not a tranquil experience. People seem able to argue and disagree over most things—education, nuclear weapons, the National Health Service, race, gender, the European Union, genetic engineering, the north-south divide, the future of Northern Ireland, and so on *ad infinitum*. Differences are voiced in arguments in pubs and clubs and MPs are elected to continue the arguments in Parliament. Even religious leaders enter the fray; the Church of England's 1985 report, *Faith in the City,* was a damning indictment of inner-city decay and neglect.

Not only do people argue, they resort to violence. Today we see demonstrations, race riots, attacks on the police, attacks by the police and bitter strikes. We see blood and death as people fight for their rights, the rights of others or even the rights of animals. Some are prepared to die. In 1913 Emily Wilding

Davison fatally flung herself under the hooves of the King's horse in the Derby and other women threatened to starve themselves to death in Britain's prisons because they wanted the right to vote. In February 1995 animal rights campaigner Jill Phipps was martyred beneath the wheels of a lorry carrying veal calves for export. People, and even the government, will also kill for their beliefs, as planted bombs and shoot-to-kill policies testify. Throughout all, the unblinking eye of the mass media watches, reports and incites.

These widely-disparate patterns of behaviour, involving matters great and small, serious and trivial, originating at home or abroad, involving ordinary people and the high and the mighty, which may be enacted within the great state institutions of Westminster, Whitehall and the Inns of Court, or in streets and factories, share little in common except for one thing: along with countless other such examples they would be recognised as *events in politics.* It is clear that if we are to study this subject seriously it is necessary to make some order of a world of bewildering complexity; to try to distil the essence of the activity known as *politics.* This is by no means easy; scholars continue to dispute the definition of politics.

Politics arises from certain basic facts of human existence: that people generally choose (indeed find it necessary for survival) to live together and that they differ in myriad ways in their opinions as to how the community should be organised and the nature of the decisions it makes. The source of conflict may either be the simple fact that individuals are self-interested and greedy, never able to feel content with their lot, or that they hold differing views on big moral questions. Disputes are inevitable because the world's resources are finite (no one can have all he or she wants) and the range of opinion on moral questions is limitless.

However, when we come to address directly the fundamental question 'What is politics?' we find it impossible to give a simple answer. Politics can be seen variously as concerned with the art of *compromise,* the exercise of *authority,* the acquisition of *power* and as a form of devious *deception.* It is not the case that any one of these categories of definition is correct and the others wrong, but rather that politics is a manysided concept, only to be understood if viewed from various angles.

Politics as the 'Art of the Possible'

Politics as 'the art of the possible' is a well-known but enigmatic definition (authorship of which is attributed variously) and retains its relevance because it encapsulates a particular view of politics as a process of participating and finding agreement which has been attractive to western minds since the time of the famous Ancient Greek philosopher Aristotle (384-322 BC). Amongst modern thinkers it is most eloquently expressed by Bernard Crick:

> Politics is not just a necessary evil; it is a realistic good. Political activity is a type of moral activity; it is a free activity, and it is inventive, flexible, enjoyable, and human.

However, if such a view were rigidly adhered to, there would be little material for political scientists to study in the real world of violence, murder, duplicity and self-interest. Yet this definition remains important for several reasons.

— It defines the pure essence of politics.

— It stands as an ethical ideal.

— It provides a measure against which real-world systems may be judged.

The view of politics as a compromising and conciliatory activity might suggest that it is opposed to the idea of sovereignty and rule by a central authority. This is wrong because differences cannot be reconciled without some overarching authority, even if this is no more than the idea of *agreement* (or contract) reached between the parties. This leads to a second definition.

Politics as Authority

David Easton, an influential American political scientist, argued that politics was concerned with the 'authoritative allocation of values. Authority is the right of some person or institution (king or government) to make decisions affecting the community. A woman with a gun, or a man with a large wallet, may be able to get their own way but will not have authority if those obeying do so with a sense of grievance. Such rule is unstable; those subjected may be expected to revolt when they glimpse their chance. Authority is derived from legitimacy.

Legitimacy When a government enjoys legitimacy people will obey because they believe it right to be ruled in this way. This is a key to the success of any political system, and explains why military dictatorships taking power by force are soon seeking the appearance of democratic civilian rule.

Forms of authority The great sociologist Max Weber distinguished three kinds of authority: *rational legal* (bestowed by normative rules, such as constitutions and election); *traditional* (conferred by history, habit and custom—like a hereditary monarchy); and *charismatic* (where the personal qualities of the leader inspire the confidence, and even adulation, of the masses).

Of course, to say that a government enjoys legitimacy does not necessarily imply that it is a *good* government; legitimacy merely resides in popular consciousness. Hence political regimes will devote considerable time and energy not to making policies for the people's education, welfare, and so on, but to the shaping of attitudes—the process of legitimation. We shall see that a great deal of British political life serves this end. For example, when Elizabeth II was crowned by the Archbishop of Canterbury the British people witnessed a tradition whereby the monarchs of old sought to present their earthly power as a manifestation of the will of God.

While it is clear that the exercise of authority is part of politics, this presents a rather legalistic and simplistic picture. Governments cannot always expect to possess legitimacy; in a complex society there will be elements opposed to the government of the day, questioning and challenging it and even seeking to destroy it. Governments can aim to maintain themselves by deception of the masses and by force. This leads to an analysis of one of the most central concepts in politics—power.

Politics as Power

American political scientist Harold Lasswell gave the discipline a memorable catch-phrase in the title of his book *Politics: Who Gets What, When, How?* Here the essence of politics is power, and those who get most of what is going are the powerful. Power can be defined as the ability to achieve some desired effect, regardless of the opposition. Authority is one form of power, but a glance at the world today quickly reveals that many regimes are based on cruder forms such as wealth, gender, physical might and violence.

Concentration on pure power takes us beyond the trappings of government into shadowy corners behind the throne. The authority of the government is often nothing more than an empty legal *(dejure)* title; the real *(de facto)* power to get what is wanted, when it is wanted, lies elsewhere. Although some are content to study only the trappings of the state, it should be a central task of political analysis to track down the real source of power, to find the constitutional Mr Big, though the trail can often resemble the Yellow Brick Road to the elusive end of the rainbow.

Politics as Deception

A popular use of the term 'political' denotes devious, shifty behaviour generally aimed at securing personal advantage—usually position or office. Many of Shakespeare's plays dwell on the intrigue in politics so that Enoch Powell could say in a 1950s BBC series: 'The stage used to be called the

Court, now they call it a Cabinet, but all the characters are in Shakespeare... Only the costumes date.' Such activity can take place at the micro level (within government organisations), as well as the macro level (between rulers and the ruled).

Deception in micro-politics It was probably in this sense that the word 'politics' first appeared in English, as a term of disapproval applied to the activities of those engaged in faction, intrigue and opposition to established governments. People who are 'politicking' are usually understood to be plotting against rivals. The term is often applied to the behaviour of individuals in large organisations, where those engaged in politics (from planning to oust the chairman to gaining a larger desk) are unlikely to be contributing to the organisation's collective goal. Much activity of this kind takes place within the corridors and tearooms of the Palace of Westminster, and in the clubs and bedsits around about. Indeed the British Cabinet itself was originally a secretive group of ministers scheming together as a *cabal.*

> One has to be a bit of a lowbrow, a bit of a murderer, to be a politician, ready and willing to see people sacrificed, slaughtered for the sake of an idea.
>
> —Henry Miller (1891-1980; American writer), Writers *at Work*

This view is often linked with the ideas of the Italian Renaissance thinker Niccolo Machiavelli; to be labelled 'Machiavellian' is usually taken as insulting. However, Machiavelli's essential point was that intrigue and plotting were justified by the greater purposes of government. In other words, he believed the old adage that the ends justify the means: 'when the act accuses, the end excuses'. This leads to deception at the level of macro-politics.

Deception in macro-politics This is by far the more important in the outcomes of politics and was captured by the great nineteenth-century prime minister Benjamin Disraeli in the aphorism that politics was 'the art of governing mankind through deceiving them'. Legitimation itself can be seen as a form of deception. The perceptive English political essayist Walter Bagchot placed particular stress on deception of the masses as a key to successful government. Today, as the term 'spin doctor' enters common parlance, one is presented with a great mist of deceptive activity (including official secrecy) and the attempt to shine a searchlight through it is one of the principal duties of the political scientist.

> I have lots of enemies.... Hurd has always been against me, told the lady [Margaret Thatcher] not to make me Minister for Trade—which she very splendidly repeated to me on the evening of my appointment. Arsehole. He's looking more and more like Aldridge Prior.
>
> Alan Clark on ministerial rivalries, *Diaries* (I Feb. 1991)

> The erosion of public confidence in the holders of public office is a serious matter. In so far as a culture of moral vagueness, a culture of sleaze has developed, we seek to put an end to it.
>
> The Nolan Committee on Standards in Public Life, quoted in the *Guardian*.

As we conclude this discussion on the nature of politics, it should be apparent that all our definitions are inextricably interwoven. There is no doubt that society harbours many conflicting interests which must be reconciled, often by the exercise of authority, and the process is clouded by evidence of great inequality of power and much devious behaviour.

Individuals and groups disagree over ends and means in most walks of life. There are countless institutions that can resolve such conflict, including religious groups, trade unions, clubs, schools, universities, business firms, families, and so on. Does this mean that these are political institutions? Some academics do in fact study the politics of small communities, usually taking a psychological perspective, but the particular focus of attention for the political scientist is the state—a very special, unique, and profoundly important social formation.

The State

A state is a community formed for the purpose of government. The Ancient Greeks talked of the city-state (sometimes termed the polity, from the Greek *polis)* and today we speak of the nation-state, a relatively recent formation. Philosophers dispute the nature of the state, the German Hegel giving it a particularly metaphysical significance as the highest expression of ethics; only through allegiance to, and service in, the state could individuals fully realise themselves. Generally the state is taken to be a community with the following characteristics.

— A clearly defined territory.

— A legitimate government.

— Sovereignty within its territory.

— An existence recognised by other states in international law.

— A 'persona', in which name it is able to make treaties and have obligations and rights independent of any actual person. Thus we speak of the state doing this and that: prosecuting people (state prosecution), providing welfare (welfare state), being sinned against (crimes against the state), keeping secrets (state secrets), educating citizens (state education), and so on.

— Perpetual succession—rulers may change but the state continues to exist, with no alteration to its commitments and responsibilities.

— Universality—all those living within the jurisdiction of the state (there are some exceptions for diplomats) are subject to its rules. Unlike other associations (say, sports clubs or a church), members do not have the right to opt out of state jurisdiction (unless they emigrate, though in this case they would soon come under some other state).

— The right to use force and coercion against members. Weber saw this as the most singular characteristic of the state, distinguishing it from all other organisations. If other agencies, say bouncers outside a disco, teachers, or even parents, use force, they may find themselves subject to the law, but the state can legally imprison, harass, and sometimes kill. From this it becomes starkly obvious that operating the state apparatus confers great and threatening power.

Today some argue that a process of globalisation through economics and technology and the horror of modern weaponry make the concept of the nation-state dangerously outmoded. With the increasing role of international associations and transnational groupings, the borders of modern states are becoming softened. Moreover, human rights and security concerns lead states or groups of states to demand rights of inspection over others.

The state and society The notion of the state may be differentiated from that of society; the former is constructed and based upon law, while the latter arises naturally from the free association of people (sometimes termed civil society). In the state, individual members stand as citizens with legally prescribed rights and obligations, but no such conditions attach to them as members of society, where they are constrained more by economic and ethical norms. The same distinction was made by the German sociologist Ferdinand Tonnies, who spoke of *Gesellschaft* (a community formed by artificial, human contract) and *Gemeinschaft* (a community arising from bonds of affection or kinship). The national community is both state *and* society, a fact that is a source of friction. While all citizens are legally equal, as members of society they can be decidedly unequal. When the legal equality of citizenship is markedly at variance with the real level of societal equality, there will be the potential for political tension.

Government

The idea of government lies at the heart of political science. Indeed no society has ever been found that did not have some kind of government. It can take various forms: it may be *constitutional*, *absolutist* (unlimited by laws), *primitive* (a chieftain's rule over a tribe), *on pluralist* (consisting of several institutions sharing the role). Following Aristotle, it is customary to group forms of government in terms of the number of rulers, thus distinguishing monarchy (rule by one person), aristocracy (rule by an enlightened few) and democracy (rule by all the people—the *demos*). However, each of these may be said to tend in practice towards a corrupt variant: tyranny, oligarchy and mob rule.

Government and self-interest The fatal deterioration of the forms of government is usually attributed to the corrupting influences of power, which may lead those holding it to act in their own interests rather than that of the community. The historian Lord Acton observed memorably:

> Power tends to corrupt, and absolute power corrupts absolutely. Great men are almost always bad men.

The selfish tendency of human beings is a hard truth that forms the starting point for much political thought. The key issue is reconciling the common good with the need for government. Scottish philosopher David Hume believed that 'every man ought to be supposed a knave and to have no end other than private interest', arguing that it was crucial for a state to devise a form of government that would inhibit the corrupting tendencies.

> A republican and free government would be an obvious absurdity, if the particular checks and controuls *[sic]*, provided by the constitution, had really no influence, and made it not in the interest, even of bad men, to act for the public good.

The Philosophical Radicals of the nineteenth century took the individual pursuit of self-interest as the key to understanding human behaviour. This idea was very influential in shaping many of our modern institutions.

Government and politics Government will necessarily entail politics, even in primitive societies where institutions have taken only the most rudimentary form. In developed societies, politics is often seen as being about the formal working of the machinery of government—taking control of it, influencing its decisions, reforming it, changing those in office, and so on. However, it is important to remember that politics does not belong exclusively to the world of institutions. From the boardrooms of industry to the clubs, pubs and launderettes—politics is found wherever people gather and express their anger, hopes and anxieties, and assess their potential to influence events.

State and the Government

The state and the government are conceptually distinct. In the UK, the position of the Queen, who plays no effective part in government yet is head of state, underlines the distinction. For practical purposes the British government is usually regarded as the collection of around a hundred secretaries of state, ministers, junior ministers and their various assistants drawn from Parliament. In contrast, the state can be seen to comprise a much wider set of institutions (the civil service, the Bank of England, local authorities, health authorities, various quasi-autonomous bodies, nationalised industries, the judiciary, the military and the police). Some would go further and include the mass media, the institutions of the capitalist economy and trade unions.

Politics and Non-politics

It will be apparent that if politics is about reconciling diverse interests it must have many manifestations; indeed no area of life can be seen as intrinsically non-political. Some people find this thought peculiarly disturbing and it is common to hear calls to 'take education (or health, or the siting of power stations, and so on) out of polities'. If something is to be taken out of politics, where is it to go? We have seen that politics is a process whereby differences and conflicts are resolved through conciliation, the exercise of authority and power. However, politics is by no means the only way of resolving such differences; there are three particularly important alternatives.

— The *economic market place* allows the forces of supply and demand to set prices and determine who gets what.

— Through *rational decision-making* experts weigh up the pros and cons of a case to arrive at the 'best' solution.

— *Violence* enables the unsatisfied, dispossessed or greedy to attempt to take what they want by physical force.

All these are present in Britain today, though each has limitations.

The market. The eighteenth- and nineteenth-century classical economists believed the market to be a wondrous mechanism for bringing buyers and sellers together at a mutually acceptable price resulting in the optimum allocation of resources within society. However, this raises difficult ethical problems. In the first place it is undemocratic, favouring the economically strong against the weak because it does not *redistribute* resources; it gives only unto him or her that already hath (that is, can afford the price). Thus, rather than taking matters out of politics, it creates a new basis for dissatisfaction and conflict. Secondly, not all allocations can be determined by the laws of supply and demand. Matters such as the level of sex and violence on television, the decision whether to send troops to Iraq, the degree of religious toleration to be allowed within society, or the age of consent for homosexuals lie in a territory of value-judgement and morality where the market is quite silent. When governments try to bring the market into areas such as education and health care many people are deeply disturbed. Indeed, because the human capacity to disagree over value-judgements is potentially limitless, there are infinitely more areas of dispute to be settled by politics than by the market.

Rational decision-making. The idea of making communal decisions on the basis of rational criteria seems very attractive; it is the argument for the use of experts (town planners, architects and the like). Organisational theorist Herbert Simon believed that state decision-makers should arm themselves with all the available information, calculate the outcomes of all possible courses of action, and choose the best policy for the community. However, in practice certain intractable problems beset such processes.

— The principle is essentially elitist and paternalistic, based on the notion that certain people know what is best for the masses.

— It is difficult to decide who the experts should be; obviously election cannot be the answer.

— In reality, experts can never be sure that they have all the information necessary to make the 'right' decisions.

— Experts may be tempted to place their own personal interests before those of the community.

— Experts frequently disagree with each other.

Rational decision-making also carries with it connotations of a threatening 'Big Brother' style of bureaucratic rule as depicted in George Orwell's novel *1984.* Both fascist and totalitarian communist governments can be accused of trying to govern by putting experts in charge, while the call to replace politics with managerialism is ever-present in Britain.

Violence. In the real world there can be little doubt that making and enacting collective decisions for communities is often accomplished by various forms of physical force and state violence. Two world wars, the Nazi extermination of the Jews, the treatment of blacks in South Africa, the silencing of dissidents in Eastern Europe, the brutality of the Tiananmen Square massacre or the ethnic cleansing in former Yugoslavia can leave no one in any doubt of this harsh reality. Historically Britain has been a very violent nation and the Suez invasion, Northern Ireland and the Falklands war have revealed modern politicians still willing to seek violent solutions to political problems. After the Falklands war, Mrs Thatcher employed the language offeree on the home front, speaking of the 'enemy within'. This turned out to be the miners, who were to find themselves embroiled in a physical confrontation with the police and security services.

As an alternative to participating in conventional political processes, guerrilla warfare is increasingly chosen by groups wishing to gain their ends or make their voices heard. Today nobody is immune; several thousand civilians have been killed over Northern Ireland, hijacks and atrocities such as the Lockerbie air disaster can occur anywhere, and in 1989 the Ayatollah Khomeini set a chilling precedent with his *fatwa* on author Salman Rushdie because his book *The Satanic Verses* gave religious offence. Most dramatically of all, the events of 11 September 2001 sent reverberations throughout the political system, challenging norms and testing conventions. It was said that things could never be the same again. However, like the market and the rational decision-making model, violence is not very effective at resolving problems. Violence breeds more violence and, when the fighting has ceased, the parties must sit round the conference table to seek a durable solution. This has been the case in both the Northern Ireland and Arab-Israeli conflicts, despite the high price paid in blood.

Characteristics of Political Science

Throughout the history of western civilisation there runs a great tradition of political thought with a pantheon of giant figures who have applied their minds to profound questions relating to politics. The subject is also the stuff of much great drama, literature and art. Aristotle described politics as the 'Master Science' and it is not difficult to see what he meant. All we do in our lives, in society, the sciences and arts, will be influenced by politics; it is through politics that the totality of social existence is orchestrated.

Political scientists do not wear white coats, peer through microscopes or fill up test tubes. Is political science really a science? Can it produce the systematic, ordered, predictive propositions associated with a subject such as physics? This is not a new question. The work of Aristotle, which involved him in a famous classification of the constitutions of the many Greek city-states, was just as systematic and 'scientific' as his work in the natural sciences. However, the advent of Galileo and Newton in physics led to developments that seemed to transport the physical sciences into new realms of precision, uniformity and prediction.

Yet some social scientists have tried to build a body of political theory—laws of society and politics resembling those of the physical sciences. Karl Marx was one of these.

Under the influence of *logical-positivism* (a school of philosophy holding that only statements capable of being disproved can be meaningful), the post-war era saw renewed efforts by political scientists to steer the discipline towards rigorous theoretical propositions by the use of careful techniques and methods of empirical observation. In this effort to ape the objective observational methods of the 'hard' sciences they sought to ally the discipline more closely with anthropology and psychology. This movement was termed behaviourism and one of its results was a preoccupation with the observable, or more particularly, the quantifiable. The problem with this was that many of the studies (from attitude surveys to voting statistics) were often tedious and sometimes essentially trite. They did not address the really big questions of politics, such as: What is power? Where does it really lie? Why do states go to war? Why do people die of starvation amidst abundance?

Others, including Max Weber, were sceptical of the idea that people and organisations could be studied in this way. Human beings reason and interpret the world, and the proposition that they are best treated as unthinking molecules in a test tube is dubious, if not ludicrous. He argued that the study of human affairs should take account of reason, motives and emotions in order to afford a deeper level of understanding, which he termed *verstehen.*

Today few would deny Weber's argument. Ironically, as the hard sciences push further into the unknown they encounter less rather than more precision and are obliged to construct 'uncertainty principles', 'fuzzy logic' and 'chaos theories' reflecting the vagaries that have long confronted the social scientist. Yet behaviouralism has left a beneficial legacy in that political scientists can no longer allow their minds to dwell for too long in the stratosphere of abstraction and metaphysics, like medieval scholastics who disputed how many angels could balance on the point of a needle.

Hence, the modern discipline of political science combines many approaches and includes a number of interrelated subdisciplines with various focuses and methodologies.

— *Political theory* examines theories of political institutions, including the law, the state, systems of representation, forms of government, and so on

— *Political philosophy* searches for highly generalised answers to major questions such as the meaning of freedom, justice, equality and rights. Ultimately political philosophy addresses the biggest questions of all: what is the nature of the 'good life' and what must the state do to promote this?

— *Political ideology* is concerned with ideas about the way the state should be organised.

— *Political economy* examines the state in the economic system. It leads us to the power of economic forces and the working of the global economy.

— *Political sociology* looks more towards the social world for an understanding of politics. It is concerned with how political attitudes are formed and how they are influenced by those with power. It also studies social stratification, including class formation and elites.

— *Political institutions* lead students to the formal machinery of the state, a key site of much political activity.

— *Policy studies* focus on the policy-making process of government and are centrally concerned with the analysis of power.

— *Comparative government* searches for generalisations about politics derived from widespread examination of groups of countries. Conceptually straightforward, it can be immensely daunting in practical terms.

— *International relations* studies the ways in which states relate to each other in war and in peace.

Interdisciplinary Perspective

Not only does political science comprise the subdisciplines outlined above, it is itself multidisciplinary; magpie-like, it draws upon a wide range of other disciplines. The social sciences study one single, complex reality and the different disciplines are artificial territories staked out to facilitate microscopic study of particular aspects. However, this can hinder understanding if we adopt a blinkered view.

Many of the forces acting upon the political system are *economic* in origin, whether originating from the stock exchange or the plight of the homeless. To understand the British constitution we require a *legal* perspective, although this must be seasoned with an understanding of the balance of power, which breathes life into the formal constitution. The discipline of *sociology*, concerned with education, culture, class, racism and gender—all of which fuel much political activity—must also have a central place. Underlying all is the *historical* dimension. It is almost impossible to comprehend the present without understanding patterns of development. We do not take an historical perspective by way of neat chronological introduction; we do so because the politics of today is only an ephemeral bloom on the tree of the past.

There is also an important *geographical* dimension to politics. At home there are issues of territorial management and in the world there is a global economy populated by more and less developed countries as well as giant corporations, many of them richer than states. Beyond the world economy is a political order reflecting the balance of military power, political alliances and a global ecological system innocent of national boundaries, underscoring the interdependence of states in the modern world. Only by rejecting the narrow disciplinary approach can the study of politics aspire to the title the 'master science'.

Governance Perspective

The existence of interstate groupings, particularly the development of the European Union (EU), has led some scholars to focus on the concept of multi-level governance. In the case of the UK, bodies such as NATO, the World Bank and the EU imply a level of governance above the state. In addition there are transnational corporations, which are themselves virtual institutions of governance, and international non-government organisations (NGOs) pursuing social goals such as the relief of child poverty, peace or environmental protection.

Below the Westminster government there are new provincial assemblies, regional institutions (and pressure for elected regional assemblies) in England, a complex structure of elected and non-elected local authorities, composed of yet more tiers, public-private partnerships and a network of private organisations and groups with varying degrees of power over the lives of citizens. Hence, it no longer makes sense (if it ever did) to study state governments in isolation as if they are in complete command of their destinies.

In this world, state boundaries become blurred and hierarchical relationships slacken or disappear entirely, to be replaced by more subtle processes of negotiation, bargaining, exchange and compromise. Thus the EU does not necessarily command state governments and state governments do not necessarily command local governments. Regional and local authorities, or even private companies, can bypass nation-states to treat directly with international bodies.

Governance, as used in this context, becomes more than a synonym for the act of governing It aims to characterise the processes of contemporary politics in a more realistic way. Approaches taking the formal institutions of government as the fount of all power (examining what is sometimes termed the 'Westminster model') appear outmoded and misleading.

Peering behind the facade

The political scientist must be attentive to the real world before all else and, like Machiavelli, seek to peel away the facade in search of a deeper reality for, as observed above, much in politics is about deception. Writers in the orthodox liberal-democratic tradition betray a tendency to describe what they see as a beautiful stately home. Like overawed paying visitors, they are content to admire the ornate outer facade and the fine draperies and furniture inside but remain too timid to push beyond the red ropes into the living quarters.

Orthodox writing on British politics purports to take an objective position, without a commitment to any political ideology. The cogs and cams of the system are detailed in much the same way as the internal combustion engine might be. The implication of this approach is that the state itself is an apolitical machine, not favouring any particular interest within society, which a government takes over like the driver of a car. This belief is a central plank in the theory of British liberal democracy. However, the idea of the neutral state, easily controlled by anyone in the driving seat, may be contested. To Marxists and others it serves the interests of capital and wealth. Hence, writers implying it to be impartial are actually making a political (anti-left) statement. Rather than peeling away the facade they are contributing to the process of concealment.

Key points

— A common definition of politics is the resolution by

compromise and conciliation of the inevitable conflicts in any community.

— Politics necessarily entails the concept of authority, an accepted or legitimate form of power.

— It is possible to speak of politics in the context of any organisation but political scientists mainly study the state.

— The state is a community with a territory within which it enjoys legal sovereignty.

— The government of the day may be in control of the state, but is conceptually distinct from it.

— The decisions made through politics can be made by other means but the idea that politics can be removed from life is an illusion.

— The study of politics should be concerned with looking behind the formal facade of government to understand where power lies; to understand who gets what, when and how.

2

History of Studies in Political Science

The history of political science serves as a context within which we make sense of the nature and role of our discipline. Narratives about the past development of British and American political science help to frame debates, choices, and identities within the contemporary discipline in Britain. What do recent studies on the history of political science tell us about the character of political science in Britain and America? What do they suggest about the relation of the British study of politics to British identities more generally? Our review of recent work concentrates on three issues: (1) how historical studies of political science relate to approaches and identities within the contemporary discipline; (2) how they relate to the past, i.e. whether their historical vision is marred by presentism; (3) whether they look beyond the boundaries of the discipline.

It is now forty-five years since Bernard Crick published *The American Science of Politics*. Crick's view of American political science did much to set the terms in which many British political scientists understand themselves. In this view, American political science has fallen prey to a false scientism that seeks universally applicable general theories, a scientism that arguably masks its actual role as an American ideology, an ideology that Crick suggested bore a striking resemblance to the totalitarianism it purported to oppose. The British study of politics is viewed, in contrast, as sensitive to historical and cultural particulars; it embodies the defence of politics against the ideology of scientism. The unquestioned influence of Crick's work makes it all the more striking that so little work has been done in Britain on the history of political science in the last forty years. What is morc, thc rise of thc history of political science as a distinctive sub-genre in America might appear to belie the dichotomy of American scientism and a British sensitivity to history. What does recent work in the history of political science tell us about the character of political science in Britain and America? What does it tell us about the relation of British political science to English and British identities?

The impact of Crick's work illustrates how the history of political science serves as a context within which we make sense of the nature and role of the discipline. It is, at least implicitly, a source of our disciplinary identity. Even so, there are, of course, students of politics who believe that the history of the discipline has little to offer current practitioners. Political scientists might dismiss disciplinary history as of mere antiquarian interest if they consider the discipline to be a cumulative science dealing in general patterns and relationships that recur within a given domain. Equally, political theorists might dismiss it as a distraction from the epic ideas that constitute the perennial subject matter of philosophical speculation. Despite such exceptions, many students of politics believe that knowledge of history and politics are closely related. We have already remarked on the role this belief has played in the self-understanding of many British students of politics. Similarly, several of the most prominent contemporary movements in American political science are avowedly historical: neostatists and historical institutionalists have presented themselves, for several decades, as offering historically sensitive alternatives to the formalist excesses of behavioralism and, more recently, rational choice theory. Those political scientists who avow that knowledge of history and politics are closely related have shown surprisingly little interest in historicising their own discipline. The belief that the political scientist must also be in part a historian of politics surely makes most sense as part of a broad and consistently applied historicism. Such historicism goes beyond exploring how the content and character of politics changes over time, as political actors build upon and remake the legacies of the past. It also reflexively extends its historicist perspective to the knowledge and practices of political scientists themselves. Just as political actors work from a background of historically given practices and beliefs that they interpret and refashion in their actions, so do political scientists. A key role is played in both settings by narratives of the past that serve to frame debate and choices in the present. These narratives may remain stable for some time. They may be perpetuated over successive cohorts. They may even come to appear almost self-evident. One such narrative is that of genteel 'British decline', a narrative that was widespread among British political elites through the twentieth century. Another is that of a genteel 'British study of politics', a related narrative that is equally widespread among British political scientists, and one that took comfort in Crick's opposition to American scientism.

We want to review several recent publications that illustrate the current state of work on the history of political science in Britain and America. Our review will concentrate on three issues. First, we are concerned with how historical studies of political science relate to the approaches and identities found within the discipline. Do they provide them with historical support, or do they offer a revisionist challenge to them? Of course the roles they play depend not only on their own content but also on the audiences who read them. Their impact can thus vary across time or place. We might suggest, for example, that Crick's study challenged those American scholars who sought to craft a science of politics on the model of the natural sciences, while reassuring British scholars that they did well to stick with their established practices and resist the lures of the American alternative. If this first issue directs attention to how historical studies relate to the presuppositions of a given audience, a second issue concerns how they relate to the past. A recurring worry is that studies may succumb to 'presentism'. They may narrate the past in a fashion that engages present-day debates at the expense of pursuing an adequate understanding of that very past. Such presentism need not involve a conscious promulgation of myths. It may also involve a selective recounting of decontextualised slivers of the intellectual past. Or it may describe the past in terms of anachronistic concepts that misshape its texture and significance. While efforts to make the past speak to current debates can result in a problematic presentism, they need not do so. To the contrary, Crick's study illustrates, at least in our opinion, the possibility of a lively engagement with present-day concerns that builds upon historical understanding rather than bypassing or foreclosing it.

Our third issue is how historical studies treat political science as a discipline. Some of these studies take the discipline as a coherent intellectual unit suited to characterisation in the aggregate. Others do far more to cover terrain beyond the discipline's institutional boundaries, as well as to explore differences within these boundaries. Crick's study again nicely illuminates our concerns here. While it is sometimes read as giving an aggregate account of the American discipline, Crick himself disavowed such a goal; he emphasized that he offered a 'critical history of an idea in a particular country, not of a discipline or profession'. Crick traced the origins and conditions of the idea of a science of politics modelled on the natural sciences. In doing so, he directed his attention beyond the boundaries of political science, for he mainly turned to sociologists to trace the roots of this idea. The American discipline does not appear in Crick's study as a coherent intellectual unit characterised in the aggregate by such scientism; it appears instead as an institutional site that has been increasingly penetrated by scientism at the expense of older modes of thought. Crick's genealogy set out to defend these older traditions against the rise of scientism, not to submerge this contrast beneath a monolithic image of the discipline.

British Histories

Although British students of politics often define themselves as more historically sensitive than their American counterparts, they have shown little interest in the history of political science. When they do produce work on the history of political science, it often consists of luminaries looking back on their own lives and those of their teachers and predecessors in an attempt to trace the intellectual and institutional origins of the discipline and to assess the progress it has made. The most prominent recent example of such work is perhaps the British Academy centenary monograph on *The British Study of Politics in the Twentieth Century* edited by Jack Hayward, Brian Barry, and Archie Brown. Although some essays in the volume are exceptions, the overall tone is of luminaries celebrating the past. Such work usually produces a naturalising perspective in which political science appears as constituted by a pre-given empirical domain – politics – and a shared intellectual agenda – to make this domain the object of empirical study. It inspires histories that focus on the establishment of an autonomous discipline, that tell of an initial optimism evolving into a more stolid professionalism, and that highlight the emergence of professional norms and institutions. Instead of playing a revisionist role, it often reinforces received disciplinary identities, such as that of a historically sensitive British study of politics. It tends to a selective presentism that celebrates established scholars and ideas, such as S. E. Finer in comparative politics or the English School in international relations, while giving scant attention to participants in other traditions who, while institutionally within the discipline, are not part of the memories that frame contemporary identities therein.

An instructive alternative to this naturalising perspective is provided by the historicism of Julia Stapleton and her doctoral supervisor, Stefan Collini. Stapleton's recent book, *Political Intellectuals and Public Identities in Britain since 1850*, illustrates many of the more significant contrasts. Stapleton's meticulously researched and argued book describes the strong tradition, albeit one in decline, of intellectuals drawing sustenance from the sense of an English or British identity. It extends her earlier argument that political thought has played a role on a par with that of literature as vehicle and guardian of national identity.

Political Intellectuals sets out from an examination of the Victorian roots of this tradition of the national intellectual. Stapleton shows how the tradition arose as British intellectuals sought to respond to issues they believed were posed by the rise of democracy and especially the Second Reform Act. National intellectuals aspired to take charge of the national culture so as to counteract the dangers they associated with democracy, notably demagogic manipulation and social divisiveness. They had a broadly shared sense of a British identity that they tried to promote and reproduce through publicly accessible scholarship. A. V. Dicey, James Fitzjames Stephen, Leslie Stephen, J. R. Seeley and others all promulgated a vision of a unified Britain characterised by a strong moral sense, a love of liberty, a respect for justice and fair play, and a stout manliness. Interestingly, Stapleton does not remark on the implicit contrast between the homogeneous visions of these national intellectuals and the divided nature of the democracy they sought to counteract. Might it be that they belonged to a homogeneous clerisy that was under threat from the rise of other classes and groups?

Stapleton then proceeds to provide a terrific analysis of the fate of the tradition of the national intellectual in the inter-war years. She distinguishes here between two overlapping tendencies. Some intellectuals responded to the global issues of the time – fascism, communism, and one should add economic depression – with grand theory. A. D. Lindsay, T. S. Eliot, John Strachey and Alfred Zimmern appear as intellectuals who adopted more cosmopolitan visions or prophetic tones; they made sharp criticisms of their fellow nationals' inherited practices, local identities and everyday experiences.

Other intellectuals responded to similar dilemmas by reasserting a national perspective against just such grand theory. Arthur Bryant, John Betjeman, G. M. Trevelyan, A. L. Rowse and others fostered those ideas of an English or British character that played such a hugely important role in marshalling civilians during World War Two and informed large parts of the national consciousness of middlebrow, middle England in the post-war era. Stapleton tackles here thinkers who are rarely explored by political theorists. While her own work also usually concentrates more on rather high intellectual culture than on social movements, Stapleton here locates the conservatives who are in many ways the heroes of this book by engaging in a more cultural style of history, exploring the National Book Association and a host of relatively modest, quiet, and obscure intellectuals. It appears to be conservatives, who in the context of the twentieth century, are most in need of rescue from the enormous condescension of posterity. In rescuing them, Stapleton joins those students of politics who emphasize, often in the wake of Thatcherism, the persistently conservative nature of the British people. But whereas most of these others are cosmopolitan social democrats trying to explain what otherwise seems too abrupt a halt to the forward march of labour, Stapleton comes close to celebrating visions of middlebrow decency, village cricket, parish churches, and warm beer. She begins and ends her book by explicitly juxtaposing the tradition of the national intellectual who is embedded in local identities with the multicultural cosmopolitan beliefs that she believes dominate Britain today. We have suggested that the historicism of Stapleton and Collini generates a different stance toward the discipline of political science from that of the naturalising perspective. They are wary of postulating some given empirical domain or shared intellectual agenda as a defining feature of a discipline. They thus have turned the constitution of a discipline from an assumption or even a fulfilment into a problem. 'Disciplines are unstable compounds', as Collini recently put it, since 'what is called a "discipline" is in fact a complex set of practices, whose unity, such as it is, is given as much by historical accident and institutional convenience as by a coherent intellectual rationale'.

Therefore, we might argue that the creation of an apparently given empirical domain and a shared intellectual agenda arise as the contingent victory of particular intellectual traditions that often legitimate themselves precisely by telling the history of the discipline as if their own assumptions were unproblematic. When historicists such as Collini and Stapleton portray disciplines as unstable, they draw attention to the dangers of an excessive focus on the idea of a discipline. Disciplinary histories risk privileging the category of the discipline as if its institutional presence – the Political Studies Association or membership within departments of politics – demarcated boundaries to the flow of ideas, or explained the ways in which ideas have developed within such boundaries. In contrast, Collini and Stapleton show an admirable interest in the mutual exchanges between political science and, say, literature and history. Here *Political Intellectuals* explores the impact of T. S. Eliot, Rowse, and Bryant on Englishness and politics. What is more, because historicists treat disciplines as problematic, they often use other aggregate categories to convey generalisations that cover multiple authors. Historicism encourages us, we might suggest, to deploy concepts such as tradition, language or discourse; while these traditions might parallel the institutions of a discipline, they also might parallel the contours of particular sub-fields, or cut across disciplinary and sub-disciplinary boundaries. Here *Political Intellectuals* explicitly traces what Stapleton calls a 'tradition' of national intellectuals, an aggregate concept that covers, as we have seen, various poets, historians, philosophers, journalists and others, as well as the occasional teacher of politics.

Stapleton's *Public Intellectuals* illustrates how historicism can lead to narratives of the history of political science that stand in contrast to those generated by a more naturalising perspective. Her historicism reflects, we would suggest, that of the approach to intellectual history associated with Quentin Skinner, J. G. A. Pocock and Collini, that is to say, those who have been labelled the Cambridge School. Its 'informing spirit' is perhaps what Collini has described as 'the attempt to recover past ideas and re-situate them in their intellectual contexts in ways which resist the anachronistic or otherwise tendentious and selective pressures exerted by contemporary academic and political polemic'. Perhaps, though, it is time that we began to disaggregate the notion of a Cambridge School since the intellectual historians who are purportedly covered by this term differ from one another in important respects. In particular, we here might distinguish Skinner's advocacy of a distinctive method and republican politics from a strand of intellectual history, also much favoured by Cambridge folk, that embodies a Whiggish preference for style and parliamentarianism: whereas Skinner defends his method and politics in principled, abstract, and even universal terms, Collini and Stapleton exhibit a Whiggish distrust for abstractly stated principles, preferring to locate their insights and politics in local practices. Collini dismisses 'coordinated programmes', 'programmatic manifestos', 'methodological programmes', and 'tight conceptual schemes' by suggesting that they are rationalistic fads that artificially impose inappropriate generalities on our practice. He champions 'a certain deliberate eclecticism', 'a matter of tone and level of treatment', 'common preoccupations', 'similar dispositions', where the content of such things is presumably left unspecific precisely because of a Whiggish distrust of general principles. Stapleton, likewise, presents *Political Intellectuals* as a defense of local and concrete, rather than abstract and universal, commitments. She appears to identify with her national intellectuals, who mine local traditions and identities to find the wisdom therein.

A Whiggish proclivity appears in various emphases in the narratives told by Collini and Stapleton. It appears, first, in a preference for high culture. Their work concentrates on public intellectuals and Oxbridge academics who themselves remained influenced by Whiggism, while giving relatively little attention to such other figures as autodidacts, socialists, and utopian visionaries. While Whiggish views are most clearly articulated by Collini with regard to matters of method, in Stapleton's work they take on a more clearly politically substantive form. At times she appears to share the almost supercilious disdain towards democracy and ordinary citizens that she and Collini ascribe to those about whom they write. Her sympathy seems to lie with those aristocratic Whigs and liberals in academia and politics who we allegedly need. Stapleton applauds her national intellectuals whose self-appointed 'custodial role' was 'to introduce aristocratic virtues into democracy'. As we suggested earlier, there is a tension between the claim to speak for a nation and the conviction that aristocratic Whigs and liberals in academia and politics should 'assert their independence from the popular movements and sectarian interests of a modern democratic society'. Does speaking for the nation actually mean defending an aristocratic ethos against the rise of the plebian masses? If so, does this mean the plebian masses are a danger to a nation of which they presumably are not a part?

The Whig orientation of Collini and Stapleton appears, secondly, in the nostalgia that pervades their work. Because Whiggism and aristocratic liberalism fell into precipitous decline early in the twentieth century, those who still remain faithful to them almost always look back with nostalgia to a time when they stood firm before the onset of modern democracy. Stapleton thus identifies a 'malaise' in political theory in the 1920s largely with the decline of liberalism. She echoes Keynes's complaint that liberalism was eclipsed by socialism, which he dismissed as 'a force led by "sentimentalists and pseudointellectuals"'.

There appears to be a longing here for the more austere, manly liberalism – dare we say, muscular Christianity – of late Victorian liberals. Nostalgia for Whiggism and aristocratic liberalism appears in a somewhat different vein in Collini's writings, where it is often tempered with an ironic detachment, perhaps reflecting recognition that such beliefs and ideals are markedly out of synch with modern politics. It is difficult perhaps to be passionate about ideas one knows to be inadequate for our times. Collini and Stapleton exhibit an attachment to Whiggism or aristocratic liberalism, finally, in their preoccupation with Englishness and the content they ascribe to it. Englishness is, Stapleton suggests, 'restrained rather than belligerent, inclusive rather than exclusive, and social rather than political in emphasis'. She concludes with a pean to the English virtues of moderation and toleration as ways of accommodating difference:

> Earlier political theorists in Britain were alive to the importance of national and cultural difference, and emphasized the benefits of contact and fusion. However, they were wary of politicising 'difference', believing in an English/British model of the state that had kept such matters largely under political wraps... They sensed well enough the dangers of fragmentation and conflict that would inevitably accompany the ascendancy of groups whose aims were limited and whose methods were belligerent... They confined their enthusiasm for 'difference' to the relatively mundane level of 'liberal pluralism' – the right to maintain an identity that has been largely constructed out of resources internal to it, but within a wider public configuration in which it can expect to find few echoes... The sense of caution, distrust of excessive particularism and wider public role for public intellectuals that such a devotion to England/Britain inspired is worth remembering, even at this late juncture for 'old Britain'.

What, though, of other types of Englishness, from the National Front to pro-Europeans? Why is the 'true' Englishness that found in Whiggism and aristocratic liberalism? Stapleton might reply that history reveals England to have been dominated by such Whiggism. But this reply would require some justification, especially as she herself argues that much of the relevant parts of Whiggism arose as a defense of an aristocratic ethos against the popular movements of modern democracy.

Even as Collini and Stapleton offer us sophisticated, historicist alternatives to a naturalising perspective on the history of political science, so their Whiggish sympathies lead them to recount narratives that exhibit nostalgia for a high culture of liberal learning. Stapleton evokes such nostalgia in her evident sympathy for intellectuals who propounded the familiar narrative of an 'English exceptionalism' that exhibits 'opposition to the "abstract", intellectualist values which were often deemed responsible for the political travails abroad'. This narrative clearly overlaps with those by which British political scientists often make sense of themselves in contrast to their American counterparts.

What should we make of this overlap? Is it possible that British political scientists understand themselves in terms set by a Whig account of English exceptionalism? After all, the British study of politics is defined as methodologically eclectic, moderate and sensitive to local contexts; it is contrasted with the dogmatism, scientism and rationalism of an American political science that is supposedly enthralled by rigid conceptual structures and programmatic manifestos. It is interesting to note here that Stapleton's nostalgia seems to extend from the intellectual tradition of Whiggism to an idealised Westminster Model of British government. She appears, like so many British political scientists, to endorse Sir Ernest Barker's pleasure in a parliamentary system in which issues are resolved as in a debating chamber. She evokes a time 'before parliament became simply a seal on policies which had been worked out previously by specialist ministers, civil servants and interest groups'.

American Histories

The history of political science in Britain is limited in several senses, all of which are highlighted by a comparison with the state of affairs on the other side of the Atlantic. The first limitation is of number. Historical studies that address the past of American political science in one fashion or another have appeared regularly for decades. There has been a plethora of such studies published in the last year alone. The second limitation concerns the variety of scholars producing such studies. Work on Britain has consisted in retrospectives by disciplinary luminaries and historicist studies by intellectual historians. In America, these two approaches are supplemented by a growing sub-genre of studies written from within the discipline but by scholars outside of its limelight. The third limitation appears in the overlap between Stapleton's and the disciplinary luminaries' visions of a distinctive British approach to the study of politics. While Stapleton's study diverges from the luminaries' naturalising perspective – she carefully avoids presentism and she helpfully aggregates intellectual conversations across disciplines – her study echoes their image of the past and it thereby supports a received disciplinary identity rather than challenging it. In contrast, American studies provide us with diverse images of the past, some with revisionist implications and some without.

The most recent of the 'State of the Discipline' volumes that appear every decade or so under the auspices of the American Political Science Association may suggest that luminaries of the American discipline have little interest in the history of political science. But this trend is not without exceptions. To the contrary, one of the volume's co-editors, Ira Katznelson, has recently published a study of post-World War II scholarship, Desolation and Enlightenment: Political Knowledge After Total War, *Totalitarianism, and the Holocaust*. Unlike other studies by luminaries, Katznelson's book does not take the discipline as its aggregate intellectual unit. Instead it crafts and deploys the 'political studies enlightenment'. This category groups together a cross-disciplinary set of scholars, notably Hannah Arendt, Karl Polanyi, David Truman, Richard Hofstadter, Harold Lasswell, Charles Lindblom and Robert Dahl. Katznelson presents these scholars as sharing a common response to the dilemmas posed by total war, totalitarianism, and the holocaust; they all turned 'to the social sciences and history in an effort to deepen and guard the tradition of Enlightenment'. He locates this response in contrast to that of 'rejectionists' who responded to these dilemmas by rejecting the Enlightenment.

Desolation and Enlightenment is decidedly presentist in approach – we might even say proudly so, if we were sure it was a self-conscious authorial choice. Katznelson makes very little effort to establish the historical intentions of the figures incorporated within his 'political science enlightenment'. He does not document, for example, whether they understood their own agenda as one of reviving 'the Enlightenment'. Instead he concentrates on representing their works as exemplary for those who might take up just such an agenda today in response to contemporary postmodern skepticism. We would suggest that Katznelson's study pivots upon a belief that today's historical institutionalists should take a leading role in this agenda, and a worry that they are hindered in doing so by their dismissive images of the scholarship that arose in the wake of World War Two. In the 1970s and 1980s, dismissive images of this scholarship helped to make attempts to combine an analytical temperament with broad historical perspective, and to make the state a center of attention, appear exciting and novel. Katznelson now puts aside, and at times explicitly challenges, the images that supported this sense of novelty among his fellow historical institutionalists. He thereby offers a new vision of the intellectual past, a vision in which the members of his 'political studies enlightenment' emerge as nothing quite so much as proto-historical institutionalists.

Katznelson fleshes out his new vision in the second and third chapters of *Desolation and Enlightenment*. These chapters strike us as a mixed bag. The third chapter addresses scholars, largely political scientists, at Columbia and Yale, and it is the highlight of the book. Katznelson deftly signals that behavioural – era figures such as Truman, Lasswell and Dahl shared the concern of today's historical institutionalists with viewing the dynamics of the modern liberal state in historical and analytical perspective. Moreover, since the scholars discussed in this chapter interacted and influenced one another, Katznelson's grouping of them proves historically informative. Alas, the elements that make this third chapter work are absent from Katznelson's problematic second chapter, which focuses on Polanyi's *The Great Transformation* and Arendt's *The Origins of Totalitarianism.* Katznelson's reading of these books as pursuing analytical social science in a manner akin to that favoured by historical institutionalists is strained at best. There is scant ground for interpreting these works with the categories of today's historical institutionalism. There is scant ground, too, for grouping Polanyi and Arendt alongside the other members of Katznelson's 'political studies enlightenment.' Both Polanyi and Arendt, each in their own way, steer well clear of the modernist epistemology and liberal presuppositions that constitute the continuities between today's historical institutionalists and behavioural-era scholars that Katznelson captures so well elsewhere in his book.

The presentism of Katznelson's book makes it a prime example of exactly the kind of studies that John Gunnell has sought to supplant. Gunnell has been a leading figure in promoting disciplinary history as an emerging sub-genre of specialised research within American political science. He champions the goal of a body of researchers, committed to anti-presentist standards, and producing historical studies with an increasing degree of autonomy from the heated ebb and flow of agendas in the contemporary discipline. Gunnell's particular version of anti-presentism receives an extended articulation in the appendix to his new book,

Imagining the American Polity: Political Science and the Discourse of Democracy (2004). Although some aspects of Gunnell's vision are contested by other contributors to the sub-genre that he has done so much to promote, what is most noteworthy in contrast to the British scene is simply that this sub-genre exists within the disciplinary institutions of political science. Gunnell rightly identifies Crick's book as having played a foundational role in shaping the conversation of this sub-genre. His own new book offers, we would suggest, an attempt to shift that conversation onto a new set of topics. *Imagining the American Polity* breaks clear of the long shadow cast by Crick's book, and more broadly, of the behavioural-era debates during which it appeared. Gunnell does this by pointedly taking changing conceptions of democracy, rather than scientism, as the orientating concern of his scrupulously researched study. This move involves more than just a change of theme. Gunnell's study seeks to establish that inter-war and post-war developments in the American discipline are narrated better in terms of a contest over the meaning of democracy than in terms of the rise of scientism. His book is especially informative and persuasive with regard to the interwar period. A pre-occupation with scientism has narrowly focused most prior study of this period onto the Chicago school. *Imagining the American Polity*, in contrast, covers far more of the discipline as it tracks the debate over new pluralist conceptions of democracy and the related crafting of a distinctive American notion of liberalism. It offers telling evidence in support of its reading of these movements as far more central to the mainstream of interwar disciplinary debate and development than the scientism then flourishing in Chicago.

Gunnell's novel, a compelling account of the interwar period, makes his book a landmark study of the history of American political science. An overplaying of his hand leads, however, to some weaknesses in the book's relatively briefer treatment of later developments. Gunnell almost inverts the presentist tendency to project later concepts and contentions back onto earlier scholars in that he projects interwar concepts and debates forward a little too hastily. Scholars from the behavioural-era to today are presented as echoing interwar intellectual moves, regardless of whether they are indebted to those earlier discussions or not. Gunnell's concern to find echoes is far from as egregiously de-historicising as most presentist predecessor hunting, but it does submerge somewhat the contexts, concerns, and conceptual nuances of more recent scholarship.

If we step back to consider Gunnell's book alongside Katznelson's, we find it striking that, despite their divergence with regard to presentism, there are noticeable parallels between them with regard to the issue of revisionism. Both authors challenge common images of the discipline's past. Katznelson queries the reputed ahistorical, anti-institutionalist character of behavioural-era work. Gunnell suggests that interwar debates over democracy and liberalism, not the supposed 'revolution' of the behavioural-era, mark the most significant transformation that American political science has ever undergone.

Yet in neither work does this contestation over the past support much in the way of a sharp revisionist challenge to approaches prominent among American political scientists today. Katznelson's work does offer historical institutionalists something of a new identity, but the potential shifts involved remain largely at the level of legitimating rhetoric; they entail no major shift in the way research is practised or its purpose conceived. Gunnell's work does connect with present scholarly debates, but primarily by way of questioning whether they are as novel as they are sometimes taken to be, a query that, as valid as it certainly is, does not articulate a clear agenda for a major change of approach.

For an example of how the historical study of political science can lead to a challenging revisionist stance, we would recommend a third new book, Ido Oren's Our Enemies and US: America's Rivalries and the Making of Political *Science*. Oren frames his study in relation to the paradoxical self-image of American political science: the discipline sees itself as, at once, both 'an objective science independent of its national origin and historical context,' and as committed to 'freedom and democracy'. The explicit aim of Oren's book is to undermine this self-image. Oren queries how committed to freedom and democracy the American discipline has been in practice, and above all, challenges its claim to objectivity. He argues that the discipline is ideological in the sense that it is 'human thought that avoids reflection upon the circumstances in which it is embedded or the interest it serves'. He supports this interpretation with historical mini-narratives that seek to establish a recurring association between the content of disciplinary discourse and shifts in American foreign policy. Oren's mini-narratives explore political science before and after America's entry into conflicts with imperial Germany, Nazi Germany, Fascist Italy and Soviet Russia. They suggest that characterisations of these countries swung from being uncritical or even positive to become sharply negative. There is, we would suggest, some room to quibble over whether Oren's pattern is quite as good a fit in each of these cases as he makes out. Thus, for example, disciplinary discourse critically treating Germany and Russia as 'totalitarian' has origins before the onset of World War II, let alone the Cold War with which Oren associates it. However, while some such qualifications might be needed to add a bit more historical nuance to Oren's compact account, the basic thrust of his interpretation strikes us as largely right and its implications for the contemporary field well worth pondering. Particularly engaging is Oren's attention to major changes in the way that American political scientists have defined democracy with its content curiously shifting over time so as to emphasize similarities between the US and its allies, and contrasts with its rivals. As Oren points out, these shifts have some major implications for how we understand the kind of knowledge constructed from American data sets, such as the finding of a 'democratic' peace.

Oren's attention to changing conceptions of democracy sets up his book as an excellent companion to Gunnell's *Imagining the American Polity*. The two books illustrate the vibrancy of the growing sub-genre of disciplinary histories being written by American political scientists. They also point to some of the space for methodological debate within this sub-genre. Not only is Oren's book more revisionist than *Imagining the American Polity*, it also diverges from the 'internalist' stance favoured by Gunnell, who is wary of locating disciplinary shifts relative to broad external contexts. The fact that both books overlap in their concern with changing views of democracy provides readers with an excellent opportunity to reflect upon how differences in approach relate to substantive conclusions. However, rather than weighing in here with our own views on the long running, and rather tiresome, debate over internal versus external approaches, we would like to direct attention to a further issue. Whatever their differences, Oren and Gunnell both employ a move that is perhaps too dominant in the sub-genre they contribute to. Both adopt the discipline as their primary unit of intellectual aggregation. They thus frequently make claims characterising the discipline as a whole; sometimes going so far as to suggest a quasi-agency in which 'political science' does or responds to things as a singular actor. Such an approach can encourage a retrospective downplaying of past diversity within political science. It can also encourage historical narratives that give short shrift to the role of extra-disciplinary intellectual exchanges in the development of political science.

As in Britain with the work of Collini and Stapleton, so in America, it is intellectual historians who most often write studies that are both non-presentist and trans-disciplinary in their approach. Two new books provide excellent examples: S. M. Amadae's *Rationalising Capitalist Democracy: The Cold War Origins of Rational Choice Liberalism* and Nils Gilman's *Mandarins of the Future: Modernisation Theory in Cold War America*. Both of these books grew out of dissertations supervised by the leading American intellectual historian, David Hollinger. It is perhaps unsurprising, therefore, that they display marked similarities of approach. Both authors devote careful attention to the work of individual scholars while also self-consciously employing aggregate categories. Both offer an overview of the post-war development of an important trans-disciplinary theoretical agenda: Amadae tracks rational-choice theory, while Gilman explores modernisation theory. Both span the space between the work of individual scholars and these aggregate agendas by attending to various institutional sites of interaction. Amadae identifies the RAND Corporation as the most important site for the crafting of rational-choice theory, while also exploring the Public Choice Society and the political science department at the University of Rochester. Gilman's account of modernisation theory focuses on Harvard's Department of Social Relations, MIT's Center for International Studies, and the Social Science Research Council's Committee on Comparative Politics. When Amadae and Gilman interpret the work of individual scholars, they thus do so, not primarily in relation to disciplinary affiliations, but in relation to aggregate theoretical projects and institutional sites of intellectual interaction. The result in each book is a fascinating narrative of just the kind of trans-disciplinary developments that largely elude histories framed around disciplines. While political scientists interested in the history of their field might, at first sight, overlook *Mandarins of the Future* and

Rationalising Capitalist Democracy because they are only partly devoted to political science, it is precisely their trans-disciplinary approach that makes both these books vital supplements to the kind of disciplinary histories offered by scholars such as Gunnell and Oren.

Amadae and Gilman alike concentrate on the 1950s and 1960s. Mind you, they do not limit their attention to those decades. When they look forward from them, Gilman closes with chapters on the 'collapse' and 'aftermath' of modernisation theory, while Amadae closes with one on the 'consolidation' of rational-choice theory. The different long-term fate of these two post-war theoretical projects has distinctive ramifications for each book. In particular, the continuing vigor of the rational-choice project enables Amadae's work to take on dimensions not available to Gilman. Making deft use of her skills as an intellectual historian, Amadae directly engages some of the haze of contesting perceptions at play today in the continuing debate over rational-choice theory. The third part of her book is devoted to careful rebuttals of the view that rational-choice theory is a continuation or revival of older approaches. Against such a view, Amadae argues that rational-choice theory diverges at key points from both the classical liberalism of Adam Smith, and the marginalist approach to economics inaugurated in the late nineteenth century. Her book provides a persuasive case for seeing rational-choice theory as a distinctively post-WWII creation. And her retracing of the theory's interdisciplinary origins outside of mainstream economics challenges contemporary assertions about the imperialism of economics. *Rationalising Capitalist Democracy* ably illustrates the potential of non-presentist historical inquiry to bring valuable clarity to present-day debates.

Perhaps no book is without some weaknesses. We would suggest that the most notable flaw in Amadae's book concerns the way that she deploys the Cold War as an external context against which to interpret the development of rational-choice theory. Interestingly, Amadae here employs the same external context that Gilman relies on in his account of modernisation theory. Both books share a tendency to narrate the intellectual agenda they study as if it were *the* main or obvious response of American social scientists to this context. Yet a juxtaposition of the two books makes clear that there was little overlap between the two projects they narrate. To the contrary, their basic assumptions were in conflict at key points. This conflict suggests to us that each author might have paid more attention to contingency and contention in the ways that American social scientists interpreted and responded to the Cold War. When read as a pair, Amadae and Gilman's books, like those of Gunnell and Oren, thus offer insights above and beyond those offered by either alone.

3

Scientific Study of Political Science

The question of "how do we know what we know" is, at its heart, a philosophical question. Scientists are lumped into different disciplines that develop standards for evaluating evidence. A core part of being a scientist and taking a scientific approach to studying the phenomena that interest you is always being willing to consider new evidence and, on the basis of that new evidence, change what you thought you knew to be true. This willingness to always consider new evidence is counterbalanced by a stern approach to the evaluation of new evidence that permeates the scientific approach. This is certainly true of the way that political scientists approach politics.

So what do political scientists do and what makes them scientists? A basic answer to this question is that, like other scientists, political scientists develop and test theories. A theory is a tentative conjecture about the causes of some phenomenon of interest. Once a theory has been developed, we can restate it into one or more testable hypotheses. A hypothesis is a theory-based statement about a relationship that we expect to observe. For every hypothesis there is a corresponding null hypothesis. A null hypothesis is also a theory-based statement but it is about what we would expect to observe if our theory was incorrect. Hypothesis testing is a process in which scientists evaluate systematically collected evidence to make a judgement of whether the evidence favours their hypothesis or favours the corresponding null hypothesis. If a hypothesis survives a series of rigorous tests, scientists start to gain confidence in that hypothesis rather than in the null hypothesis, and thus they also gain confidence in the theory from which they generated their hypothesis.

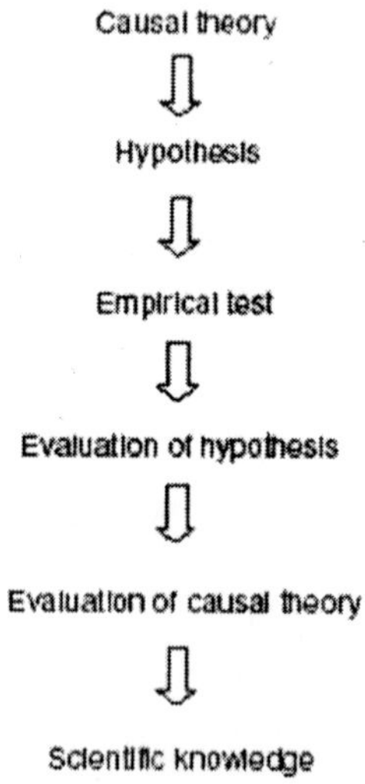

Figure 1. The road to scientific knowledge

Figure 1 presents a stylised schematic view of the path from theories to hypotheses to scientific knowledge. At the top of the figure, we begin with a causal theory to explain our phenomenon of interest. We then derive one or more hypotheses about what our theory leads us to expect when we measure our concepts of interest (which we call variables – as subsequently discussed) in the real world. In the third step, we conduct empirical tests of our hypotheses. From what we find, we evaluate our hypotheses relative to corresponding null hypotheses. Next, from the results of our hypothesis tests, we evaluate our causal theory. In light of our evaluation of our theory, we then think about how, if at all, we should revise what we consider to be scientific knowledge concerning our phenomenon of interest.

A core part of the scientific process is skepticism. On hearing of a new theory, other scientists will challenge this theory and devise further tests. Although this process can occasionally become quite combative, it is a necessary component in the development of scientific knowledge. Indeed, a core component of scientific knowledge is that, as confident as we are in a particular theory, we remain open to the possibility that there is still a test out there that will provide evidence that makes us lose confidence in that theory.

It is important to underscore here the nature of the testing that scientists carry out. One way of explaining this is to say that scientists are not like lawyers in the way that they approach evidence. Lawyers work for a particular client, advocate a particular point of view (like "guilt" or "innocence"), and then accumulate evidence with a goal of proving their case to a judge or jury. This goal of proving a desired result determines their approach to evidence. When faced with evidence that conflicts with their case, lawyers attempt to ignore or discredit such evidence. When faced with evidence that supports their case, lawyers try to emphasize the applicability of the supportive evidence. In many ways, the scientific and legal approaches to evidence couldn't be further apart. Scientific confidence in a theory is achieved only after hypotheses derived from that theory have run a gantlet of tough tests. At the beginning of a trial, lawyers develop a strategy to prove their case. In contrast, at the beginning of a research project, scientists will think long and hard about the most rigorous tests that they can conduct. A scientist's theory is never proven because scientists are always willing to consider new evidence.

The process of hypothesis testing reflects how hard scientists are on their own theories. As scientists evaluate systematically collected evidence to make a judgment of whether the evidence favours their hypothesis or favours the corresponding null hypothesis, they always favour the null hypothesis. Statistical techniques allow scientists to make probability-based statements about the empirical evidence that they have collected. You might think that, if the evidence was 50–50 between their hypothesis and the corresponding null hypothesis, the scientists would tend to give the nod to the hypothesis (from their theory) over the null hypothesis. In practice, though, this is not the case. Even when the hypothesis has an 80–20 edge over the null hypothesis, most scientists will still favour the null hypothesis. Why? Because scientists are very worried about the possibility of falsely rejecting the null hypothesis and therefore making claims that others ultimately will show to be wrong.

Once a theory has become established as a part of scientific knowledge in a field of study, researchers can build upon the foundation that this theory provides. Thomas Kuhn wrote about these processes in his famous book The Structure of Scientific Revolutions. According to Kuhn, scientific fields go through cycles of accumulating knowledge based on a set of shared assumptions and commonly accepted theories about the way that the world works. Together, these shared assumptions and accepted theories form what we call a paradigm. Once researchers in a scientific field have widely accepted a paradigm, they can pursue increasingly technical questions that make sense only because of the work that has come beforehand. This state of research under an accepted paradigm is referred to as normal science. When a major problem is found with the accepted theories and assumptions of a scientific field, that field will go through a revolutionary period during which new theories and assumptions replace the old paradigm to establish a new paradigm.

One of the more famous of these scientific revolutions occurred during the 16th century when the field of astronomy was forced to abandon its assumption that the Earth was the center of the known universe. This was an assumption that had informed theories about planetary movement for thousands of years. In the book On Revolutions of the Heavenly Bodies, Nicolai Copernicus presented his theory that the Sun was the center of the known universe. Although this radical theory met many challenges, an increasing body of evidence convinced astronomers that Coperinicus had it right. In the aftermath of this paradigm shift, researchers developed new assumptions and theories that established a new paradigm, and the affected fields of study entered into new periods of normal scientific research.

It may seem hard to imagine that the field of political science has gone through anything that can compare with the experiences of astronomers in the 16th century. Indeed, Kuhn and other scholars who study the evolution of scientific fields of research have a lively and ongoing debate about where the social sciences, like political science, are in terms of their development. The more skeptical participants in this debate argue that political science is not sufficiently mature to have a paradigm, much less a paradigm shift. If we put aside this somewhat esoteric debate about paradigms and paradigm shifts, we can see an important example of the evolution of scientific knowledge about politics from the study of public opinion in the United States.

In the 1940s the study of public opinion through mass surveys was in its infancy. Prior to that time, political scientists and sociologists assumed that U.S. voters were heavily influenced by presidential campaigns – and, in particular, by campaign advertising – as they made up their minds about the candidates. To better understand how these processes worked, a team of researchers from Columbia University set up an in-depth study of public opinion in Erie County, Ohio, during the 1944 presidential election. Their study involved interviewing the same individuals at multiple time periods across the course of the campaign. Much to the researchers' surprise, they found that voters were remarkably consistent from interview to interview in terms of their vote intentions. Instead of being influenced by particular events of the campaign, most of the voters surveyed had made up their minds about how they would cast their ballots long before the campaigning had even begun. The resulting book by Paul Lazarsfeld, Bernard Berelson, and Hazel Gaudet, titled The People's Choice, changed the way that scholars thought about public opinion and political behaviour in the United States. If political campaigns were not central to vote choice, scholars were forced to ask themselves what was critical to determining how people voted.

At first other scholars were skeptical of the findings of the 1944 Erie County study, but as the revised theories of politics of Lazarsfeld et al. were evaluated in other studies, the field of public opinion underwent a change that looks very much like what Thomas Kuhn calls a "paradigm shift." In the aftermath of this finding, new theories were developed to attempt to explain the origins of voters' long-lasting attachments to political parties in the United States. An example of an influential study that was carried out under this shifted paradigm is Richard Niemi and Kent Jenning's seminal book from 1974, The Political Character of Adolescence: The Influence of Families and Schools. As the title indicates, Niemi and Jennings studied the attachments of schoolchildren to political parties. Under the pre–Erie County paradigm of public opinion, this study would not have made much sense. But once researchers had found that voter's partisan attachments were quite stable over time, studying them at the early ages at which they form became a reasonable scientific enterprise.

Variables and Causal Explanations

So how do political scientists develop theories about politics? A key element of this is that they order their thoughts about the political world in terms of concepts that scientists call variables and causal relationships between variables. This type of mental exercise is just a more rigorous way of expressing ideas about politics that we hear on a daily basis. You should think of each variable in terms of its label and its values. The variable label is a description of what the variable is, and the variable values are the denominations in which the variable occurs. So, if we're talking about the variable that reflects an individual's age, we could simply label this variable "Age" and some of the denominations in which this variable occurs would be years, days, or even hours.

It is easier to understand the process of turning concepts into variables by using an example of an entire theory. For instance, if we're thinking about U.S. presidential elections, a commonly expressed idea is that the incumbent president will fare better when the economy is relatively healthy. If we restate this in terms of a political science theory, the state of the economy becomes the independent variable, and the outcome of presidential elections becomes the dependent variable. One way of keeping the lingo of theories straight is to remember that the value of the "dependent" variable "depends" on the value of the "independent" variable. Recall that a theory is a tentative conjecture about the causes of some phenomenon of interest.

In other words, a theory is a conjecture that the independent variable is causally related to the dependent variable; according to our theory, change in the value of the independent variable causes change in the value of the dependent variable. This is a good opportunity to pause and try to come up with your own causal statement in terms of an independent and dependent variable; try filling in the following blanks with some political variables:

_______________ causes _______________

Sometimes it's easier to phrase causal propositions more specifically in terms of the values of the variables that you have in mind. For instance,

higher _______________ causes lower _______________

or

higher _______________ causes higher _______________

Once you learn to think about the world in terms of variables you will be able to produce an almost endless slew of causal theories.

Let's return now to our working example in which the state of the economy is the independent variable and the outcome of presidential elections is our dependent variable. The causal explanation for this theory is that we believe that the state of the economy is causally related to the outcome of presidential elections because voters hold the president responsible for management of the national economy. As a result, when the economy has been performing well, more voters will vote for the incumbent. When the economy is performing poorly, fewer voters will support the incumbent candidate. If we put this in terms of the preceding fill-in-the-blank exercise, we could write

<u>economic performance</u> causes <u>presidential election outcomes,</u>

or, more specifically, we could write

higher economic performance causes higher incumbent vote.

For now we'll refer to this theory, which has been widely advanced and tested by political scientists, as "the theory of economic voting."

To test the theory of economic voting in U.S. presidential elections, we need to derive from it one or more testable hypotheses. Figure 2 provides a schematic diagram of the relationship between a theory and one of its hypotheses. At the top of this diagram are the components of the causal theory. As we move from the top part of this diagram (Causal theory) to the bottom part (Hypothesis), we are moving from a general statement about how we think the world works to a more specific statement about a relationship that we expect to find when we go out in the real world and measure (or operationalise) our variables.

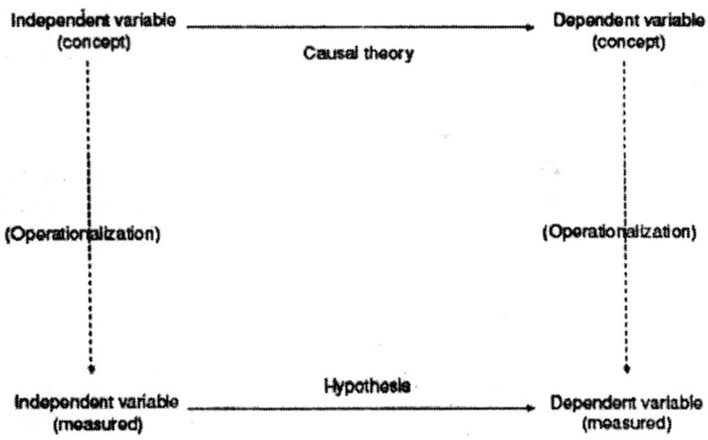

Figure 2. From theory to hypothesis

At the theory level at the top of Figure 2, our variables do not need to be explicitly defined. With the economic voting example, the independent variable, "Economic Performance," can be thought of as a concept that ranges from very strong to very poor. The dependent variable, "Incumbent Vote," can be thought of as a concept that ranges from very high to very low. Our causal theory is that a stronger economic performance causes the incumbent vote to be higher.

Because there are many ways in which we can measure each of our two variables, there are many different hypotheses that we can test to find out how well our theory holds up to real-world data. We can measure economic performance in a variety of ways. These measures include inflation, unemployment, real economic growth, and many others. "Incumbent Vote" may seem pretty straightforward to measure, but here there are also a number of choices that we need to make. For instance, what do we do in the cases in which the incumbent president is not running again? Or what about elections in which a third-party candidate runs? Measurement (or operationalisation) of concepts is an important part of the scientific process.

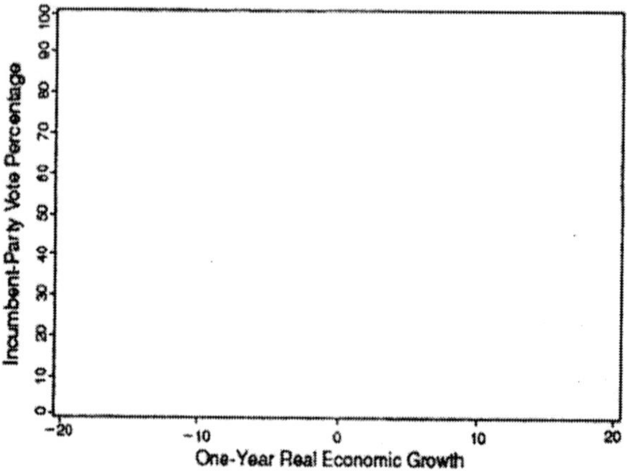

Figure 3.

Figure 3 shows the axes of the graph that we could produce if we collected the measures of these two variables. We could place each U.S. presidential election on the graph in Figure 3 by identifying the point that corresponds to the value of both "One-Year Real Economic Growth" (the horizontal, or x, axis) and "Incumbent-Party Vote Percentage" (the vertical, or y, axis). For instance, if these values were (respectively) 0 and 50, the position for that election year would be exactly in the center of the graph. Based on our theory, what would you expect to see if we collected these measures for all elections? Remember that our theory is that a stronger economic performance causes the incumbent vote to be higher.

Scientification of the Study of Politics

We call our discipline "political science." The term "science" implies use of the scientific method. "Science" has had different meanings at different times. In the archaic sense, science is just "knowledge", or knowledge gained by study. In modern usage (since the 18th century), science is a method of learning based on systematic observation using the scientific method. It is a method of learning different from the arts. The "scientification of the study of politics" refers to the process through which political science as an academic discipline has come to use the scientific method for the production and dissemination of knowledge about politics. The notion of scientification suggests a two-way relationship between science and politics. As Weingart says, it "can be described as a recursive coupling of two interdependent developments—the scientification of politics and the politicisation of science."

From the genesis of the discipline around the turn of the 20th century through every stage of development, there has been conflict and debate over the linkages between politics and science:

1. Is politics art or science?
2. If politics is a science, can political science be a "real" science and discover underlying laws of politics?
3. Even if political science is (or can be) a real science, is this a good thing?

KEY ELEMENTS OF THE SCIENTIFIC METHOD

The key elements of the scientific method are well known, so this will be a brief sketch of what we consider the most important. The beginning of scientific inquiry is the fact/value dichotomy. The scientist is concerned with the study of how and why things work as they do rather than with how they should work. Some philosophers object to this distinction—facts are values and values are facts. The choice of a puzzle to study, of which "facts" to collect, indeed, the very act of scientific study itself, involve value judgments. The objection is valid, but it does not negate the need for and worth of science.

Another feature of the scientific method is the systematic observation of empirical facts. Good art and good literature surely require the systematic observation of the empirical world. Great art and literature are produced by the most gifted observers. But scientific observation is done with an eye toward reliability and replication. Since science is based on the distinction between fact and opinion, scientists must provide information about how observations were made and analysed so that someone else can check our work. An independent check on our work involves more than catching errors, although that is part of it. John Ferejohn was surely right when he said, "The thing that keeps most empirical political scientists honest is that somewhere out there is [a] graduate student with your name on it". But replication is indispensable to the development of scientific theory. If another researcher cannot follow our procedures and reproduce the same results, then the measures constructed from our observations are meaningless—or at best the meaning is unknown. Measures, of course, must also be valid indicators of the concepts we are studying. But an unreliable measure cannot be valid. Any relationships found between unreliable, invalid measures cannot fit together with other discoveries to build theory.

A closely related element of the scientific method is quantification. Quantification is useful for systematically recording observations and for checking reliability. Quantification is indispensable for testing hypotheses and finding relationships in studies with a large number of cases.

Theory building involves testing hypotheses through empirical observation. Empirical testing implies falsifiability. An empirical theory or hypothesis cannot be scientific unless there is at least the possibility of proving it wrong. In science, being wrong is far from the worst that can happen. Disproving a false hypothesis is useful because it eliminates a dead end and allows us to look for more promising explanations. A theory that can't be falsified offers no such benefit. As theoretical physicist Wolfgang Pauli once said of a particularly weak student paper, "It is not even wrong". Thus, the scientific method proceeds not by proving what is true, but rather by eliminating what is false. It is much like Sherlock Holmes' description of how he solved mysteries: "when you have eliminated all which is impossible, then whatever remains, however improbable, must be the truth".

The scientific method also seeks theories that are generalisable beyond a particular case. Case studies have—and deserve—an important place in scientific research. We should recognise that case studies are empirical—they can explain how and why something happened through systematic observation of all the details of a particular event. Even extreme, atypical cases often reveal critical insights and suggest new variables and hypotheses. Indeed, finding a single nonconforming case will falsify a theory claiming that no such case exists.

Unlike case studies that seek to describe and explain reality by identifying all of the details in play for some event, however, the scientific method seeks to build a theory that is an abstraction of reality. That is, a scientific theory is not an accurate reflection of reality. Instead, it is a model that ignores facts and details that are not essential to explain some general process or a class of events. As Jim Rogers explains, "the unrealism of... any model... is not a vice, it is a virtue." He observes that a street map is a model of the earth's surface that distorts reality. Yet it contains the essential details necessary to achieve its purpose—to show motorists the streets and where they go. A more realistic depiction of a city would not be useful for navigation because the essential feature—the streets—would be obscured in a host of irrelevant details.

These are the essential elements of the scientific method. Each is necessary, but no one by itself is sufficient. The scientific method requires (at least) all of these features.

Landmarks

It is common to note that the empirical study of politics, including a systematic research agenda that involved sending students out to collect data, dates back at least to Aristotle.

The Early Decades

Although the empirical research published during the first two decades of the discipline was mainly descriptive, the prevailing vision was that political science is the objective study of government based on the fact/value dichotomy. In the first issue of the Political Science Quarterly, Munroe Smith outlined "The Domain of Political Science" using language that contains features of the scientific method. He says, "Science is the discovery of truth", and political science is the "science of the state" including "the organisation and functions of the state".

The method of political science is "comparison" of empirical data, and the goal sounds remarkably similar to model building: "The single fact means nothing to us; we accumulate facts that seem akin; we classify and reclassify them, discarding superficial and accidental similarities....". The American Political Science Association emerged from the American Economic and American Historical Associations in 1903. Reading the notes published by the political scientists who formed the initial organising committee, our Founders understood that they were engaged in a political process as they tactfully praised the parent organisations for the institutional support. They appear to use term "science" in the sense of objective study. Presidential addresses of early APSA presidents echoed the notion that political science is the study of politics that separates facts from values. In 1910, A. Lawrence Lowell drew an explicit parallel between science and politics in his presidential address "The Physiology of Politics." He urged political scientists to study the functions that the organs of government "actually do perform" rather than those that are intended. In addition, Lowell observed that "every action is the resultant of many forces which cannot be isolated, and hence is capable of being explained in different ways." Consequently, political scientists need knowledge of a wide range of conditions in order to "feel the motives" and "appreciate the reasons" why political actors do what they do. He even calls for the use of statistics.

Any review of the scientification of political science in the U.S. must begin with Arthur Bentley's The Process of Government. Bentley may be inordinately wordy, taking numerous discursive detours before getting to a point, but this work deserves its status as a classic study in political science, with the emphasis on science. Bentley analyses politics through systematic observation of behaviour. More importantly, the analysis is grounded in sociological theory that makes assumptions about what motivates political behaviour.

Another example of early research with elements of science is A. Lawrence Lowell's, *The Government of England*. This book is a remarkable example of scholarship. Its two volumes of more than 500 pages in each provide a comprehensive analysis of politics and government in England in the latter part of the 19th century. Although much of the specific details and processes have changed, the science in it continues to enlighten.

The basis of his argument is that what human beings see and remember about politics is not necessarily representative in general. In the case of political parties, for example, Lowell suggests that people are more likely to be conscious of "instances where party is abused for purposes that seem... improper," but to scarcely notice the cases where it is used for something deemed proper. Furthermore, he argues that it is "highly unsafe" to assume that something observed in one instance works the same in other cases. Therefore, "an observer... is likely to be misled in regard to the influence of party" unless the misperception is corrected by statistics.

Lowell's analysis of parties shows that party discipline is much stronger in the House of Commons than in the U.S. Congress and state legislatures. He defines a "party vote" as one on which more than 90 percent of the party vote together, and "true party votes" are those on which 90 percent of one party votes against 90 percent of the other party. Contemporary measures of party voting Congress are based on the logic of this century-old concept. And although there are no statistical hypothesis tests, Lowell explains the high level of party discipline in England as "a natural result" of the parliamentary system in which the loss of a key vote results in the fall of the government. The American Political Science Association adopted the goal of improving education in American government early in its development.

The much maligned American government textbook occupied a higher status in the scholarship of the day than is the case now. American government textbooks, even those intended for use in high schools, were routinely reviewed in the APSR. And the authors of this genre of scholarship included the most productive and most influential political scientists of the day.

There are elements of political behaviour. The chapter on political parties, for example, relies extensively on Bentley, and poses a version of the Why Parties? question:

> "inasmuch as a government is... a human institution, with a policy to execute and duties to perform, parties are inevitable...". Professor Beard's answers to why parties are essential to democratic governance are:

1. Parties reduce information costs, enabling voters to make "wise choice[s]" on the large number of elective offices in Americ; and
2. Parties are necessary to coordinate policy in a governmental structure fragmented by federalism and separation of powers "if the will of the voters is to be realised". The significance of this observation for the scientification of political science is that it presages V.O. Key's essentially functionalist theory that parties are necessary to the operation of popular government. And while it is not presented as such, this can be interpreted as a theory that political parties develop to overcome what we would now call collective action problems.

The 1920s

In the 1920s we see increasing evidence that the study of politics is becoming more scientific, with more emphasis on theory and quantification. The leader of this transition was Charles Merriam, though others contributed. Merriam's review of the state of the discipline in 1921 is an early recognition that the study of politics was becoming more theoretical in the way that we use the term today. Two years later. Merriam was able to review a considerable amount of research demonstrating significant progress toward the scientific study of politics. He notes several examples of studies that use the method of "comparison of various types of institutions, with the view of classifying, analysing, discovering similarities and dissimilarities in them, citing Lowell among others as examples. He also points to a "form of investigation which came to be called the survey" in which researchers attempt to "standardise some system of measurement" to objectively observe and explain political behaviour. He notes difficulties of developing accurate measures of political phenomena, and he observes that controlled experiments "seemed to be beyond the reach of the student of political or social science." Yet Merriam expresses optimism that this difficulty can be overcome because political processes are ongoing and that it "is possible to draw inferences and to verify these inferences by repeated observation". He followed this up with an analysis of "The Significance of Psychology for the Study of Politics" in which he advocated research testing hypothesized relationships derived from psychological theory, conducted in a way that the research could be repeated and replicated.

Arnold Bennett Hall organised conferences on the "science of politics" in the mid-1920s with the goal of advancing scientific theories and methods to study political behaviour. It is particularly noteworthy that several of those who attended reported using reports from the conferences as a basis for seminars, indicating that training in science was becoming part of graduate instruction. Extending scientific, behavioural analysis to the introductory political science course was the theme of conferences later in the 1920s. And increasingly technical articles begin to appear in the APSR. But the APSR was not the exclusive outlet for scientific analysis of political behavior in the 1920s. Notable examples of behavioural research appeared in books such as Merriam and Gosnell's, Non-Voting: Causes and Methods of Control and Gosnell's, Getting Out the Vote. Furthermore, judging from the literature cited in these studies, quantitative, theoretically based studies of political behavior were common in other social science journals (e.g., American Journal of Sociology, Social Forces, and Political Science Quarterly, among others). Political scientists who wanted a political science grounded in the scientific method had numerous examples and outlets by the 1920s.

The 1930s and 1940s

By the 1930s and 1940s, articles reporting quantitative research of political behavior grounded in theory were appearing with greater regularity in the APSR and the Journal of Politics. Articles by Gabriel Almond and Harold Lasswell and Harold Gosnell and Norman Gill report research containing the elements of the scientific method outlined earlier. Gosnell and Gill's analysis of the 1932 presidential election in Chicago, for example, used correlation, partial correlation, and factor analysis, and related the findings to theory. Although the analysis is not based on a representative national sample, the results of this study are remarkably consistent relationships found in later research. V.O. Key published a quantitative analysis of interest group (i.e., Veterans) influence and how support or opposition to that interest on roll call votes in Congress affected members' reelection. And his Southern Politics appeared in 1949. We see additional evidence of the scientification of the discipline in textbooks. V.O. Key published the first edition of his undergraduate textbook, Politics, Parties and Pressure Groups in 1942. The book is well grounded in the basic research available at that time. Although it is not explicit in this edition, we can see the beginnings of Key's tripartite definition of political party—party in the electorate, party in government, and party organisation—that appeared in later editions. Moreover, Key reports the results of numerous studies of voting behavior. For example, Key's book taught undergraduates about party voting and party discipline in Congress. They learned that informal groups of "radicals" and "progressives" were more cohesive than either party group because members' reelection goal causes them to support constituency over party if there is conflict. The chapter on Electoral Behavior reports dozens of quantitative studies explaining vote choice as a function of economic status, change in economic status, cultural background characteristics, and business cycles. He explains to undergraduates how to interpret a study by William F. Ogburn and Nell Snow Talbot published in Social Forces that uses partial correlation analysis to sort out the relative influence of several variables—foreign born, urban, Catholics, Democratic voters, and "wet voters"—on support for Al Smith in 1928. How many contemporary undergraduate textbooks attempt to educate students in techniques of the scientific method?

Key's presentation of this research is grounded in theory. The discussion of "Characteristics Associated with Voting" poses two questions: (1) are cleavages between parties in a particular election explained by wealth, economic interest, race, or something else; and (2) what accounts for changes in party affiliation from election to election? He tells undergraduates that "many hypotheses have been formulated", but that most of them "assume a rational political man who votes in accordance with his estimate of how his 'interests' may be defended or promoted". Although much of the early research focused on political parties, elections and voting behavior, scientific analysis of political behavior extended to other institutions. C. Herman Pritichett's analysis of the voting behavior of Supreme Court justices is a particularly important milestone in the behavioral evolution. At the same time that V. O. Key's parties textbook first appeared, Pritchett published studies of the voting behavior of Supreme Court justices in the American Political Science Review and in the Journal of Politics. In these articles, Pritchett laid the groundwork for his book The Roosevelt Court and launched what would evolve into the "attitudinal model" of judicial decision making.

The theoretical underpinning of this research is the stimulus-organism-response framework. Coming out of the realist theory of judicial decision making, Pritchett argues that "it is the private attitudes of the majority of the Court which become public law" and the justices' attitudes are revealed by their votes. He does not deny the importance of legal values in judicial decision making. Most decisions during the court term Pritchett studied were unanimous, and he assumes that in these cases "the facts and the law are so clear that no opportunity is allowed for the autobiographies of the justices to lead them to opposing conclusions." But the justices' votes in non-unanimous cases reveal their attitudes. Since the justices are exposed to the same stimulus—"an identical set of facts, and... roughly comparable training in the law"—when they come different conclusions, the "divisions of opinion grow out of the conscious or unconscious preferences and prejudices of the justices." The analysis allowed Pritchett to array the Justices along a left-right, liberal-conservative continuum with Black and Douglas anchoring the liberal bloc McReynolds and

Roberts on the right. And he defined ideology much as we do currently in terms of the use of governmental power—liberals favour the use governmental power in economic regulation cases and conservatives oppose, but in civil liberties cases the positions are reversed with liberals seeking to limit government authority and conservatives supporting government. Pritchett replicated the basic theory and findings with data from subsequent Court terms in articles published in the Journal of Politics and in a book.Thus, the use of the scientific method to study political behavior and the development of theory was advancing briskly through the 1930s and 1940s.

Current Status

The use of the scientific method to study political behavior was evident during the formative years, and became increasingly common during the 1920s. By the 1930s, the commitment to the scientific study of political behavior was firmly established, several decades before we began that raging debate over the so-called "behavioral revolution."

Despite having travelled a significant distance down the road to becoming a "real" science, however, we are still in an earlier stage of development than the natural and material sciences. Part of the reason for the lag in our development as a science is that political science is the truly "hard" science. The challenges to observation and measurement of our key concepts seem greater than those facing other sciences. Learning increasingly complex and sophisticated statistical methods will do much to advance our scientific development. The kind of revolution necessary to propel political science to the next level of development is a revolution in theory. Sir Isaac Newton's contribution to the science of physics was not the basic research he did, but rather it was his recognition of how put what physicists already knew together into a new overarching theory.

A review of the scientific research on politics published in the top political science journals over the past couple of decades indicates that economic theory is currently the dominant theoretical perspective in political science. Ronald Reagan defined economists as "people who see something that works in practice and wonder if it would work in theory." Or more precisely, they wonder if it would work in rational choice theory. The answer it seems is always "yes"—any political activity can be analysed and explained as rational actors making rational choices.

The scientist who corrects errors or reveals the limitations of even the greatest scientific discovery deserves a share of greatness, but the greatness of the original contribution remains undiminished. Greatness expands as new evidence and new ideas add to the storehouse of knowledge. The scientific method is a journey in search of truth. The first step is to ask important questions. An indication that you know enough to ask the important questions is the recognition of how much you don't know—that is, you have to know enough to be wrong. The mark of a scholar is a thirst to know more—to correct the errors and discover even more questions. The truths that we find along the way are always incomplete, transitory, and really quite secondary to the questions. This is the nature of education in greatness. The greatness of education is in the journey.

4

Study of Democratic Theory

The term *democracy* first appeared in ancient Greek political and philosophical thought. The philosopher Plato contrasted democracy, the system of "rule by the governed", with the alternative systems of monarchy (rule by one individual), oligarchy (rule by a small élite class) and timocracy (ruling class of property owners). Although Athenian democracy is today considered by many to have been a form of direct democracy, originally it had two distinguishing features: firstly the allotment (selection by lot) of ordinary citizens to government offices and courts, and secondarily the assembly of all the citizens.

All citizens were eligible to speak and vote in the Assembly, which set the laws of the city-state. However, the Athenian citizenship was only for males born from a father who was citizen and who had been doing their "military service" between 18 and 20 years old; this excluded women, slaves, foreigners and males under 20 years old. Of the 250,000 inhabitants only some 30,000 on average were citizens. Of those 30,000 perhaps 5,000 might regularly attend one or more meetings of the popular Assembly. Most of the officers and magistrates of Athenian government were allotted; only the generals (strategoi) and a few other officers were elected.

A possible example of primitive democracy may have been the early Sumerian city-states. A similar proto-democracy or oligarchy existed temporarily among the Medes (ancient Iranian people) in the 6th century BC, but which came to an end after the Achaemenid (Persian) Emperor Darius the Great declared that the best monarchy was better than the best oligarchy or best democracy.

A serious claim for early democratic institutions comes from the independent "republics" of India, *sanghas* and *ganas*, which existed as early as the sixth century BC and persisted in some areas until the fourth century AD. The evidence is scattered and no pure historical source exists for that period. In addition, Diodorus (a Greek historian at the time of Alexander the Great's excursion of India), without offering any detail, mentions that independent and democratic states existed in India. However, modern scholars note that the word *democracy* at the third century BC and later had been degraded and could mean any autonomous state no matter how oligarchic it was. The lack of the concept of citizen equality across caste system boundaries lead many scholars to believe that the true nature of *ganas* and *sanghas* would not be comparable to that of truly democratic institutions.

Even though the Roman Republic contributed significantly into certain aspects of democracy, only a minority of Romans were citizens. As such, having votes in elections for choosing representatives and then the votes of the powerful were given more weight through a system of Gerrymandering. For that reason, almost all high officials, including members of the Senate, came from a few wealthy and noble families. However, many notable exceptions did occur.

Sharp boundaries currently separate normative political theory from empirical political science. Rogers Smith notes that the major works in political theory from the 1960s through the 1980s composed by Strauss, Rawls, Nozick, Derrida, Dworkin, Foucault, Ackerman, Riker and Habermas "display only limited direct engagement either with contemporary political issues or with empirical social science." Ian Shapiro laments that "Normative and explanatory theories of democracy grow out of literatures that proceed, for the most part, along separate tracks, largely uninformed by one another." This division of labour has become a segregation of thought that now poses a fundamental obstacle to progress in democratic theory. Debates among the major contending conceptions of democracy—direct, representative, participatory, minimal, deliberative, and aggregative—proceed largely without the benefit of empirical evidence about whether the arrangements and practices they recommend are feasible, could be stable, or whether they would produce desirable outcomes. Democratic theorists frequently help themselves to so-called "stylised facts" to construct arguments that are valid but not necessarily true. Ascertaining truth requires replacing those stylised facts with real ones. That, in turn, entails bridging normative and empirical research. But how, precisely, should democratic theorists engage with empirical political science?

At least two research strategies have combined normative and empirical inquiry. Some scholars, often seeking to identify more desirable forms of political life, have sought to understand particular institutions that exhibit attractive democratic characteristics. Carole Pateman and Jane Mansbridge—two of the most important theorists of participatory democracy—studied actual worker-managed organisations to develop their ideals of democracy. Similarly, scholars have pursued inductive research on institutions such as the New England Town meeting, urban bureaucracies, and experimental deliberative arenas. This research strategy has revealed democratically promising institutional possibilities. But the difficulty of generalisation is its fundamental limitation. The successes of these practices often depend upon the rarified circumstances of their construction. It is therefore difficult to connect these inductive projects to broader conceptions of democracy that are intended to apply across a wide range of problems, circumstances, scales, and times.

William Galston, among others, notes that "grand political theories are rich sources of empirical conjectures." Political scientists have extracted falsifiable hypotheses from democratic theories or used empirical findings to qualify and criticise conceptions of democracy. Studies of juries, for example, reveal that their deliberations often reflect gender and social biases. Cass Sunstein has found that deliberation can cause participants to polarise rather than to moderate their views or reach consensus. In a recent book, Diana Mutz uses survey evidence to argue that there is a trade-off between the social heterogeneity that democratic theorists favour and the extent of political engagement. Decades of research in political participation has established that well off individuals participate more than those who are disadvantaged, and that this tendency is exacerbated in more intensive forms of participation. Thus it may be difficult to reconcile participatory and egalitarian commitments. In principle, democratic theories should be tested and developed in just this way. However, the tension between the empirical, scientific desire to establish general explanations and the normative goal of imagining more attractive forms of political life has complicated the dialog. Specifically, such general empirical findings may not apply to theorists' heavily qualified and conditioned arguments. In their own studies of deliberative polling, for example, James Fishkin and his colleagues find no strong tendency toward group polarisation or domination perhaps because those deliberations are moderated and because participants receive balanced briefing materials.

Similarly, scholars of participatory democracy have identified institutional designs in which socially and economically disadvantaged individuals are actually overrepresented and so reverse the predominant positive correlation between status and political engagement. Empirical investigators might respond by conditioning their investigations to examine political participation or deliberation under the circumscribed, favourable conditions that political theorists stipulate. The price of this normative relevance, however, would be that their findings would lack generality; they would no longer be studying deliberation or participation as such, or even as it typically occurs.

There is no reason to suppose that democratic theorists of different casts will converge on a unique pragmatic equilibrium point; there may be many pragmatic equilibria. A theorist who begins from Schumpeterian values and institutions may reach a very different pragmatic equilibrium point than one who begins from a deliberative conception; consequences acceptable to one will be rejected by the other. Furthermore, a conception of democracy that is consequentially consistent in this way may nevertheless be deeply flawed, perhaps because its values are morally objectionable. The standard of pragmatic equilibrium is not the only measure of a democratic theory, though it is one that has been hitherto neglected.

The pragmatic equilibrium standard and the method of practical reasoning respond to calls of critics such as Shapiro and Smith for political theorists to engage contemporary social problems more explicitly and empirical research more directly. Perhaps following the inclinations of Dewey himself, Smith has suggested that reconnecting normative work to practical concerns and empirical research entails a turn away from the "grand theories" of the 1960s and 1970s. But the pragmatic equilibrium approach—itself inspired by that grand theorist John Rawls—begins with ambitious models of democracy and seeks to improve them through encounters with contemporary problems and empirical realities. The synthesis of political theory with empirical research should aim to produce conceptions of democracy that are more, not less, grand in the sense that they combine an attractive and complete account of the values of democratic order together with demonstrations of empirical and institutional plausibility that available conceptions of democracy now lack.

Pragmatic Equilibrium

A conception of democracy articulates the central values that regulate collective decisions and actions in a democratic society, provides a benchmark against which to judge existing institutions, and guides efforts to improve those institutions. Much of the debate in democratic theory concerns whether elite, pluralist, deliberative, participatory, or other conceptions are attractive and feasible. Every conception of democracy must possess at least three components to be complete. First, it must offer an articulation of the values that relate collective decisions and actions to the interests and views of the individuals who compose a collectivity. All democrats adhere to the value of *nontyranny*—that no individual or group should decide collective issues regardless of others' interests and preferences. Beyond that, different kinds of democrats variously endorse other values, such as public accountability, self-government, reasoned rule, common good, political equality, private liberty, self-actualisation, and competent government. Second, every democratic conception must recommend institutions—for example, political liberties, competitive elections, universal suffrage, civic associations, referenda, town meetings, and peak bargaining arrangements—that advance its underlying values. Third, values and institutional prescriptions are typically connected deductively by presuming empirical facts—often quite stylised—about the political psychology and capabilities of individuals and about sociopolitical dynamics. The conceptions of democracy that normative theory produces can thus be conceived as packages of values, facts, and institutions in which institutional prescriptions are deduced from core values and presumed facts.

A conception of democracy is in pragmatic equilibrium just in case:

PE1. The consequences of

PE2. the institutions that it prescribes

PE3. realise its values

PE4. well and better than any other feasible institutional arrangements

PE5. over a wide range of problems and contexts.

Pragmatic equilibrium thus specifies a relationship among underlying values and goals, institutional prescriptions, and the empirical consequences of those prescriptions. This formulation of pragmatic equilibrium articulates a consequentialist standard that is at one level unobjectionable. Conceptions of democracy offer institutional prescriptions to realise certain values.

Applying the standard of pragmatic equilibrium is straightforward in principle but complicated in practice. The first step begins with a well-specified conception of democracy—one with clearly articulated values and institutional prescriptions such as those in the main streams of democratic theory. The second step is to delineate a set of problems that require collective decision and action (PE5). Because there are infinitely many social and political problems, it is sensible to begin with the large categories of public problems that are important to citizens and to democratic governance. These might include not only national decisions relating to social, economic, regulatory, and foreign policy but also local concerns such as education and community safety. The third step is to test that conception by noting the consequences—through direct observation when possible and informed reflection otherwise—of making collective decisions through the institutions prescribed by the democratic conception under review (PE1, PE3). Fourth, the theorist then specifies the alternative ways in which collective decisions might be made for the problem in question and assesses the consequences of those alternatives (PE4). Again, it is impossible in practice to assess all feasible alternatives, so one reasonable way to proceed is by analysing the most common ways of making the kinds of decisions in question together with uncommon methods that seem likely to have normatively desirable properties. If the originally prescribed institutions yield superior consequences, then that conception of democracy is in pragmatic equilibrium.

This standard creates a close link between normative theory and empirical research that is related to classical pragmatism, and especially to the political thought of John Dewey, in five distinct ways.

First, classical pragmatism takes problems as the source of reflective intelligence and it takes interpersonal problems, or externalities, that arise from social and political interactions as the source of political institutions. Pragmatic equilibrium takes problems and the contexts in which they occur as the domain of democratic theories. Just as theories of justice formulate judgments and principles to resolve disagreements between competing interests, democratic theories describe the values and principles that should guide collective decisions about social problems. The same underlying values and principles may well require different decision-making arrangements for different problems and contexts. A democrat for whom deliberation and public reason are cardinal values need not prescribe citizen deliberation, or even deliberation, for every problem. This focus on variations in problems and contexts is analogous to the rejection of universalism and the problem-driven approach to empirical investigation urged by Donald Green and Ian Shapiro. *Ceteris paribus*, a conception of democracy that encompasses a wider range of problems and contexts is better—because it is more complete—than one that addresses fewer problems and contexts. For example, a conception of democracy that successfully accounts for collective decision-making at the local, national, and international levels is better than one that covers only the national level.

Second, as classical pragmatism holds that the meaning of an idea or belief is given by its practical consequences, pragmatic equilibrium focuses attention on the consequences of institutional designs (PE3). Third, pragmatists are fallibilists; they "recognise that even those beliefs about which [they] are most convinced may turn out to be false". The pragmatic equilibrium standard focuses theoretical attention on the mistakes of democratic conceptions. In particular, a democratic conception is false when the facts of the world depart from its stylised facts; its institutions are likely then to generate consequences that fail to realise its values.

Fourth, pragmatic equilibrium focuses on institutional variation and choice. There are many ways to organise collective decision-making in democracies and Dewey writes that the task of political analysis is to understand them: "All intelligent political criticism is comparative. It deals not with all-or-none situations, but with practical alternatives." The menu of institutional alternatives is far richer than the dichotomy between representative and participatory democracy supposes, and most of the items on that menu remain empirically and normatively unexplored. PE2 and

PE4 of the above formulation stress this diversity and the importance of exploring institutional designs.

Fifth, the approach offers one way to make sense of the pragmatic rejection of the dichotomy between facts and values. In particular, pragmatic equilibrium and the method for reaching it reciprocally determine the democratic values and institutional consequences that constitute a democratic conception.

Much of the recent scholarship on pragmatism in political theory has addressed its substantive political and institutional implications. Richard Posner, for example, contends that contemporary pragmatists ought to endorse minimal, Schumpeterian institutions. Knight and Johnson respond that pragmatism entails radical democratic commitments. Though they disagree fundamentally with each other, both Posner and Knight and Johnson maintain a pragmatic orientation toward evidence that is shared by the approach laid out here. They seek to support their democratic conceptions with empirical materials and positive political theories. In contrast to these views, the idea of pragmatic equilibrium and its associated method of practical reasoning is initially neutral with respect to substantive conceptions of democracy. It is constructed as a tool for democratic theorising rather than as a way to justify a particular model, position, or set of values. Prior to applying the test, there are no special reasons to think that minimal conceptions will fare any better (or worse) than radical democratic ones.

Practical Reasoning about Institutions and Values

When a conception of democracy fails the test of pragmatic equilibrium, it may be modified in ways that bring it closer to fulfilling that standard. One straightforward procedure is to treat institutions instrumentally, as means to realise ends that are given by the values of a democratic conception. A procedure of revision would then search the space of feasible institutional alternatives for the combination that maximises the accomplishment of the values of a democratic conception over the relevant range of problems. But the difficulty with this instrumental approach is that institutions are deeply connected to the democratic values they advance. Imagine a Schumpeterian who begins with a commitment to a certain kind of official accountability and to citizens' private liberty as basic values, but then realises the facts of the world favour quite participatory arrangements to achieve these ends. Such outcomes can create pressures on a conception of democracy to revise not only its institutional prescriptions but also its underlying values.

The approach to pragmatic equilibrium favoured here subjects both the values and the institutions of a democratic conception to revision through reflection. This procedure extends Henry Richardson's account of practical reasoning for individual agents. According to Richardson, individual deliberation is not just instrumental; individuals' interests and goals can change when they act in concrete situations as a result of reflection, interaction, and discussion. *Pace homo economus*, it is a completely ordinary experience for individuals to use their practical reason not only to select the means that best satisfy their preferences and accomplish their goals but also to deliberate about ends themselves. When faced with new information, experiences, or situations, individuals may come to see the vagueness in their goals, recognise contradictions among them, and even adopt new ends. Imagine a rational politician whose overriding purpose is reelection. Surveying the field of possible wedge issues, he seizes on the scourge of homelessness as a means to political victory. But after meeting homeless men and women and their children during the campaign, he takes a genuine interest in their welfare. He becomes unable to stomach the cynicism that treating homeless people only as a means to electoral victory requires. Indeed, after his successful reelection, he occasionally supports policies that benefit the homeless in his city but that cost him votes. Homelessness begins for him as a means to the end of political success but it becomes an end in itself.

Analogously, a democratic theorist may adjust the institutional and ethical commitments of his conception of democracy by reasoning practically about which institutions will work best and then about what is democratically valuable. To illustrate, consider the stages through which practical reason about a problem in context can work to internally transform a conception of democracy. Suppose that some city actually adopts a participatory democratic system of neighbourhood assemblies to govern important local concerns such as the provision of city services, urban infrastructure, and land use. That city, furthermore, makes substantial investments that create favourable conditions for the success of this participatory endeavour—it funds community organisers to mobilise participants and training workshops to equip them to take on the work of sublocal governance. If these arrangements generate effective and just public decisions through a deliberative process that transforms individuals into more public regarding citizens, then a participatory conception of democracy is vindicated for at least this context.

Unintended consequences, however, may trigger the second step of the practical reasoning process. In many contexts, real facts do not conform to the stylised facts of a conception of democracy. Reality thus intrudes on theory by invalidating its institutional deduction. Suppose, for example, that in some neighbourhoods where participation is high, so many people show up to meetings that decision processes become unwieldy and many can only listen and observe rather than express and engage. In others, too few participate to make decisions competently. The system ends up working best where a handful of residents take a deep and ongoing interest in these affairs. The individuals in that small group gain the expertise necessary to comprehend the complexity of urban governance choices. They serve as a focal point for other neighbours who lack participatory inclinations to communicate their needs and interests. And they are generous and representative, so they produce public goods and perform genuine service.

The third step of this reasoning process involves revision of the conception of democracy in light of such new facts and experiences. The participatory democrat might respond by searching for other institutional forms that better vindicate his prior value commitments (to political equality, self-government, reasoned rule, and participation). In light of this experience, he may come to think that the best institutions for realising participatory democracy involve small groups of relative amateurs focusing on public problems in a sustained way, rather than on larger groups (in principle everyone) that deliberate less intensively. So long as there are enough small groups and issues so that everyone participates in some decisions (but not everyone in any particular decisions or anyone in every decision), he may regard his values as well served. More deeply, the participatory democrat might also revise the values that ground his conception. This experience might show, for example, that making wise infrastructure or land use decisions is difficult work and he might come to appreciate more deeply the consequences of bad decisions. This realisation might promote a previously subordinate value—that of governmental competence. He may also soften his objection to representation and thus respecify his notion of participation when he recognises that what the small groups of volunteers in the neighbourhood association are doing is in part representing the interests and views of those who do not participate directly.

In this third step, then, incommodious facts trigger the revision of a conception of democracy in two possible ways. When facts may make it clear that a received institutional prescription (everyone should participate in direct deliberation) fails to advance the values (self-government, participation, political equality) that justify it, the first response is to cast about for alternative institutional arrangements that better realise those values. A second response is to revise the democratic values themselves in ways that respond to the possibilities and constraints revealed by empirical analysis or reduce vagueness or inconsistency in a conception's values.

This process of practical reasoning occurs within a single conception of democracy. But if facts of contexts break the tight connection between configurations of democratic values and their institutional implications, then there is at least a possibility of agreement—in particular contexts—between previously antithetical conceptions of democracy. It may be, for example, that a Schumpeterian comes to acknowledge all of the failures of governance through a corrupt representative machinery in some city and to support the same institutions as a participatory democrat there. They may agree upon the same set of institutions based upon their very different unreconstructed value commitments. Or, more deeply, they may rearticulate the values that ground their respective conceptions of democracy in ways that are more compatible with one another. In the urban governance example, the Schumpeterian may come to think that the ordinary citizens need not "fall to a lower level of mental performance" at least when considering local issues and thus that some stronger notion of self-government is possible and desirable. He may also come to think that in particular hostile contexts, extensive citizen participation is necessary for effective public accountability. This method shows only that it is possible for proponents of particular conceptions of democracy to revise them rationally by reflecting upon the consequences of political practices, not that they will necessarily do so. For many problems, compelling evidence regarding the comparative effects of alternative institutions may be unavailable. In such cases, conceptions of democracy should make their empirical and institutional speculations explicit to facilitate further investigation. Even when faced with substantial disconfirming evidence, however, commonplace cognitive and social biases may lead theorists to ignore or reject it. The recent history and sociology of science has demonstrated that physicists and chemists often resist new facts that would require them to revise their settled theories. Political theorists are not immune from these same tendencies. But it is possible to mitigate their effects. Theorists who engage in practical reasoning should seek the stance of inquiry of Rawls's "competent judges." A competent judge "exhibits a desire to consider questions with an open mind, and consequently... is... always willing to reconsider it in light of further evidence and reasons" and "knows, or tries to know, his own emotional, intellectual, and moral predilections and makes a conscious effort to take them into account in weighing the merits of any question." This formulation is highly congenial to the emphasis that American pragmatists such as Pierce, James, and Dewey placed on actively seeking experiences and evidence that falsify beliefs and their hostility to dogma. The standard of pragmatic equilibrium vastly enlarges the range of potentially disconfirming data, and so the sources of reflection and refinement, by demanding that democratic theories account for the results of empirical research.

A related concern stems from the inevitable sensitivity of assessments to the specific problems and alternatives subjected to analysis through the pragmatic equilibrium standard. Suppose that we have reached what appears to be a pragmatic equilibrium for some conception of democracy by working through many contemporary problems and institutional prescriptions. It may be that considering additional problems or other institutions would reveal that this point is not a pragmatic equilibrium at all. Since the argument for any particular pragmatic equilibrium depends on the cases that have been selected to reach it, the method is vulnerable to selection bias. In this regard, however, it does not differ from most empirical methods and the general remedies apply. Those defending a conception—and their critics—should seek to test it with ever more problems and alternatives. Though the illustrations of practical reasoning below utilise brief case study materials, this method should in principle incorporate quantitative empirical studies as well. Even so, such a process can never be exhaustive. But in the course of progressively developing a conception of democracy, its values and institutions become more adequate, relevant, feasible, and actionable as it incorporates additional problems and contexts.

Four Conceptions of Democracy

To understand how the pragmatic equilibrium standard and the practical reasoning procedure operate in practice, consider four major conceptions of democracy—minimal, aggregative, deliberative, and participatory—as value-deduced institutional packages. 2 Each of these conceptions occupies a large place in political theory because it captures widespread intuitions about democracy. Each offers an attractive account of the values and institutions that ought to organise contemporary societies. Each has partisans who regard their conception as coherent and valid as well as critics who regard it as inconsistent, implausible, or otherwise unattractive. Perhaps for these reasons, there has not been much progress in resolving disputes between these dramatically different views. These are not the only conceptions of democracy. Indeed, other conceptions such as Theodore Lowi's juridical democracy or Bruce Ackerman's dualist democracy, might already be closer to pragmatic equilibrium. It would be desirable to test those and many others as well.

Minimal Democracy

Of the four conceptions, minimal democracy has the least ambitious expectations. On this account, democracy is more desirable than are other systems of government because it renders political leaders accountable to its citizens and because it protects private liberties. The minimal democrat rejects more demanding norms of decision making such as self-government, reasoned rule, and pursuit of a common good because he thinks that straightforward facts about political psychology and individual political capacities make them impossible. He agrees with public-opinion scholars who find that most citizens are remarkably uninformed about public affairs and that they have no coherent views, or quite stupid ones, on most issues. Even if citizens miraculously became more intelligent and well informed, the impossibility theorems of social choice theory—which show that under quite general conditions and constraints there is no unique way to combine the preferences of many individuals into a single aggregated choice—render terms like "self-government," "reasoned rule," and "common good" nonsensical.

In light of these chastening political realities, the minimal democrat favours regular competitive elections as the central political institution. He does not think that elections enable citizens to rule themselves by selecting the leaders or policies that they want. Instead, elections confer the right to rule on the victorious party or candidate until the next election. Elections thus realise the value of public accountability by providing regular occasions for leaders to explain themselves to citizens and for citizens to sanction leaders. Elections manifest the value of political equality when every adult has an equal right to stand for office and to vote. Competitive elections protect private liberty by enabling citizens to eject leaders who violate them. Furthermore, elections advance these values of public accountability, political equality, and protection of private liberty without requiring too much time, energy, or commitment from citizens or asking more of them than is psychologically or sociologically plausible.

Aggregative Democracy

In contrast to the minimal view aggregative democrats hold that citizens can and do have rational political preferences and views and that these can be sensibly combined. In this ideal, the opinions and judgments of citizens determine the content of laws, policies, and public actions. Aggregative democrats are well aware of the research in political science and social theory that leads minimal democrats to be skeptical about more demanding notions of democracy, but they reject their conclusions. In many contexts, for example, it is perfectly sensible to map citizens' preferences along a single dimension—say left to right—and then ask whether the actions of government respond to the preferences of the majority. Aggregative democrats thus think it reasonable to say that government is more democratic when laws and policies lie closer to the position of the median voter. Implicitly or explicitly, most empirical political scientists hold the aggregative norm of democracy.

Aggregative democracy begins with the value of self-government. If self-government is possible, there are many reasons to favour it as a central democratic value. One Millian starting point is that individuals are generally the best judges of their own interests and welfare. Therefore, laws and policies should flow from the views of citizens.

Political equality has two important dimensions in the aggregative conception. First, if every individual is the best judge of his own interest and each person's interest should count equally in determining law and public policy, then citizens should have equal opportunities to participate effectively and influence political decisions. But developing coherent and consistent political views and opinions that accurately reflect one's interests is not easy to do in complex contemporary societies. The second dimension of political equality thus requires that citizens enjoy equal opportunities to develop "enlightened understandings" about their political choices and preferences.

Aggregative democracy places less emphasis on three other values—reasoned rule, private liberty, and the common good—though these are not absent. Reason, or perhaps rationality, figures into the cognitive processes of reaching enlightened understanding. There are many issues on which individuals are uncertain or confused. Illumination requires information, discussion, and argument. Basic liberties such as freedom of association, conscience, person, and personal property are thus important to facilitate the development of political understanding, effective political participation, and autonomy. Aggregative democrats lack any thick sense of a common good beyond the good of a democratic process that generates laws and policies that flow from, and advance the welfare of, diverse citizens. Because the aggregative conception focuses on how decisions ought to be made rather than questions of policy and implementation, it places no particular priority on the value competence in government.

What kinds of institutions advance this notion of democracy as self-government and political equality? Aggregative democrats favour many of the same mechanisms that minimalists desire, but hold them to more demanding normative standards. Free and fair competitive elections, equal rights to hold political office, and universal suffrage help to ensure that the interests and views of each citizen will be counted equally in the process of making collective decisions. Beyond these devices, aggregative democrats typically also support freedom for and provision of resources to secondary associations, freedom of expression, and a robust press. through legislative deliberation, decisions produced there need not correspond to the position of the median voter. But because legislative decisions are necessarily general, laws cannot be passed on to administrative agencies as unambiguous orders. Instead, administrative agencies should themselves deliberate about the means to implement laws. In the course of their deliberations, tensions within ends arise and practical reason should be deployed to make ends more specific, actionable, and coherent. Because the process of agency rule-making and "execution" is deliberative, not technical, interested citizens should be invited to contribute.

Participatory Democracy

Though the value of participation is independent from deliberation, contemporary participatory conceptions of democracy also emphasize the importance of deliberation. As with the deliberative conception, participatory democrats such as Benjamin Barber agree that democracy is best conceived in terms of the values of self-government, political equality, and reasoned rule. Against the distributed and delegated institutions just described, however, Barber holds that citizens must take part directly—"not necessarily at every level and in every instance, but frequently enough and in particular when basic policies are being decided and when significant power is being deployed" in deliberative rule by themselves making arguments, hearing them, inventing new policies, and choosing among alternative laws. Many participatory democrats understand democracy as a community in which citizens resolve disputes and common dilemmas through a process of deliberative self-legislation that transforms "private individuals into free citizens and... private interests into public goods".

In the participatory conception, citizens engage directly with one another to fashion laws and policies that solve problems that they face together. Direct participation is important in this view for at least three general reasons. First, such laws and policies are democratically valuable. When they secure the active agreement of citizens, laws yield superior outcomes from the perspective of each party. Because cooperation is rooted in measures that are genuinely endorsed by each party, it achieves much more than liberal toleration or accommodation. Second, the solution is valuable because the parties created it themselves.

The participatory production process confers value upon the resulting product; citizens take pride in their work. Finally, parties transform themselves and each other in democratically valuable ways through participation. In deliberating about alternatives and their own values, each party gains an appreciation for the needs of others and reorganises his own values accordingly. Writ large, this transformation of individual desires and dispositions makes the ideal of a self-governing community possible through the creation of common goals, public ends, and provisional, flexible consensus.

The transformation of private individuals into citizens thus has two moments. Both require direct participation. There is an active moment in which individuals assert creative solutions to public problems. There is also a reciprocal moment in which citizens are themselves transformed when they recognise the partiality of their perspectives and consequently enlarge their own interests and values in ways that generate consensus around common ends. In this way, participation produces a politics that works not only to citizens' "mutual advantage, but also to the advantage of their mutuality".

This participatory conception of democracy implies far more extensive changes to the structures of representative government than the aggregative and deliberative views. Wide ranging institutional reforms are needed to enable citizens to directly discuss and decide issues of public concern.

Participatory democracy in a large and complex nation requires at least three novel political structures. First, following a strand of thought that runs through Jefferson and Dewey to the community control movement of the 1960s, there should be a comprehensive national system of local assemblies in every rural, suburban, and urban place. Such assemblies would enable individuals to consider local and national issues in face-to-face interaction with one another. This political intimacy is essential for citizens to appreciate the interests and perspectives of those who disagree with them and to transform their own views in light of those differences. Like the New England town meetings that inspire them, local assemblies should be vested with public power over local policies. Second, to curb the parochial tendencies of these assemblies, citizens should engage one another across great geographic distances. Though they have not yet been used effectively to this end, information and communication technologies could create national town meetings in which citizens from across a large nation discuss with one another national issues such as health care, social security, and foreign policy. But political participation is radically incomplete without decision and action. Unless they actually make decisions together, they do not create the public policies that organise their collective life and they take political discussions much less seriously. Therefore, a third important reform is a national initiative and referendum process.

This directly democratic mechanism would avoid the plebiscitary evils of many state level referendums by fostering citizen deliberation through institutional design. In particular, the issues decided by referendum would be deliberated in local assemblies and national town meetings. Many other measures might foster competent and informed political participation, but these three create empowered forums that are essential for a participatory democracy that deliberates and decides matters of nationalscale.

The next two sections show how these four conceptions of democracy are out of equilibrium with respect to two major problems: making political rules and minority tyranny.

Rules of the Game

From time to time, every democratic system must revise the arrangements through which political leaders are selected. These changes include adjusting the boundaries of electoral districts as well as altering voting rules, for example, by shifting from majority rule to proportional representation. Such procedural revisions are less common but more fundamental than the formulation of routine laws and policies. They also reveal substantial difficulties in the four conceptions of democracy. Consider three alternatives for deciding such questions:

I1. Elected representatives, authorised to make other laws and policies, also make decisions about political rules.

I2. Politically insulated and/or neutral experts—such as jurists, mathematicians, or civil servants—resolve such matters. In 20 American states and Canada, redistricting decisions are made at least in part through independent or bipartisan commissions.

I3. A body of ordinary citizens, as in a criminal jury, decides the issue. In 2004, the Canadian province of British Columbia created a Citizens' Assembly composed of 160 randomly selected individuals from across the province to deliberate about whether B.C. should replace its majoritarian electoral system with some form of proportional representation.

Empirical evidence regarding the consequences of the first alternative poses problems for the first three conceptions of democracy. Even if legislators are properly authorised to make many kinds of laws and policies, it may not be appropriate for them to fashion the rules according to which they gain and lose those powers. In such decisions, many elected officials may be principally interested in crafting rules that protect their incumbent individual or partisan advantages, whereas their electors desire nearly the opposite: extensive political competition or wide choice among representatives. In U.S. states, redistricting decisions occur primarily through the ordinary legislative process. Thirty-eight states make their Congressional redistricting plans and 26 compose the electoral boundaries of their state legislatures in this way. Two outcomes tend to result. If one or other party controls the legislature, they produce partisan gerrymanders that favour the controlling majority. If control of government is divided between the houses of a state's legislature, or between the legislature and the executive, lawmakers tend to ratify a compromise incumbent protection plan in which each party makes its own seats safe. A rule-making process whose central result is to protect the prerogatives of those who make the rules has little democratic value.

Commissions of experts are the principal alternative to ordinary legislative processes in fashioning the rules of politics. Compared to legislative redistricting, such commissions seem attractive for two reasons. First, they may be politically insulated from the corrosive calculus of incumbent advantage. Second, these commissions may be composed of individuals who possess legal, mathematical, ethical, or political expertise that enables them to make wise decisions. But autonomy is difficult to achieve when the stakes are so high. Most redistricting commissions in the United States do not even pretend to possess such independence. Members are frequently appointed because of their political affiliation and reliability. As a result, U.S. redistricting commissions often make decisions that resemble the incumbent-protecting outcomes of ordinary legislative processes.

But a degree of political insulation is possible. In Arizona, for example, a popular referendum in 2000 created a distinctive redistricting commission that operates with evident independence. State legislators appoint four members, two from each major party, from a pool created by the judicial appointments panel. Those four members then appoint a fifth, politically unaffiliated, member to serve as chair. The commission's charge is to develop a redistricting map that is attentive to compactness, existing boundaries, and competitiveness. The law prohibits the commission from considering party registration and voting history data in the initial phase of the mapping process, and from identifying the locations of incumbents' or candidates' residences altogether. The commission approves maps by majority vote and their plans are not subject to legislative review or gubernatorial veto. Though it is widely acknowledged as an exemplar of independent commission redistricting, the Arizona process is not without difficulties. Hispanic democrats have sued Arizona on the grounds that the map fails to produce sufficiently compact districts and the city of Flagstaff has sued on the ground that the commission failed to respect traditional communities of interest. Since 1992, more than 90% of incumbents seeking reelection in Arizona have won.

The important criterion of independence, however, does not substantially differentiate well-constituted commissions from citizens' assemblies. Indeed, a group of randomly selected citizens may be more politically autonomous than notables who have been vetted by legislators. But an assembly of experts may be more competent than one composed of ordinary citizens. Conversely, the enduring popularity of juries in criminal and civil trials suggests that the lay character of citizen assemblies confers a certain democratic legitimacy and virtue. They may introduce popular values and perspectives without the freight of partisan selfinterest. If there is a sharp and inevitable trade-off between the competence of expert commissions and the popular sentiments and legitimacy of citizens' assemblies, then different conceptions of democracy will balance these reasons differently. If, on the other hand, ordinary citizens generally possess or can with reasonable effort acquire the knowledge and skills necessary to make wise decisions in this area, then considered judgment favours assemblies of citizens over experts deploying their technical prowess.

A recent experience from Canada suggests that ordinary citizens can acquire the competence necessary to design political institutions. The Liberal Party government of British Columbia recently created a participatory mechanism to recommend whether the province should keep its system of single-member, plurality winner elections or replace it with some other voting system. The Citizens' Assembly was composed of 160 citizens who had been randomly selected from provincial voting lists. To assure a degree of descriptive representativeness, selection was stratified by region and gender. The Assembly convened every other weekend for day-and-a-half-long meetings over the course of a year. Over this time, members learned about various electoral designs, attended open meetings to solicit public opinions, and deliberated about the merits of various voting systems. Attendance was very high—around 94%.

Members decided that B.C.'s electoral system ought to serve three fundamental values: fairness, understood as proportionality in the allocation of legislative seats; local representation, understood as the connection between an elected representative and her geographic constituency; and voter choice, understood as the number of candidates and parties. To analyse the merits of alternatives, members simulated the operation of various voting systems. Eventually, Assembly members settled on two alternatives—a mixed member proportional (MMP) system and a version of the single transferable vote (STV). The STV option defeated MMP by a 123 to 31 in a vote of Assembly members. Bypassing the legislature, the citizens of British Columbia considered this recommendation in a provincial referendum in May 2005. The threshold for passage consisted of "double-majority" of (i) more than 60% of the total ballots cast and (ii) more than 50% of the ballots cast in 48 of the 79 constituencies (i.e., a simple majority in more than 60% of the ridings). The measure won majority in all but two of the constituencies, but it garnered only 57.4% of the total vote. Though the result fell just short of the required super-majority threshold, it appears that many voters did consider the Assembly process legitimate. As of this writing, the Liberal Party government has announced that it will hold a second referendum on the Citizens' Assembly proposal in 2008 to allow time for greater public debate. The situation also creates a certain awkwardness; the Liberal Party holds power by virtue of an electoral system that a majority has voted against.

Experience and analysis does not yet provide definitive conclusions regarding the consequences of these different institutional arrangements. Suppose, however, that the following propositions—backed by the compressed descriptions cited earlier—are true. First, elected officials will act to advance their own electoral prospects rather than other important values such as competitiveness or the coherence of districts when given the opportunity to make rules of the game. Second, citizens' assemblies are more easily insulated from undue political influence than expert commissions. Third, it is possible and feasible to structure a citizens' assembly in such a way that the participants gain sufficient mastery of the subject. That is, suppose that the alleged success of the British Columbia Citizens' Assembly can be repeated for other voting rules decisions and for electoral redistricting. These consequences compel revision to the four conceptions of democracy.

Prior to confronting these realities, the minimal democrat favours the prevalent method of redistricting in the United States: let the legislature work it out. After that, he supports the expert commission due to its presumed expertise, and his last choice (again for reasons of competence) is the citizens' assembly.

Letting a team of politicians make the rules of the game at one point in time undermines the competitiveness of the institution later, and competition is the lynchpin of public accountability for him. For similar reasons, he cannot support commissions that have difficulty maintaining their independence He is quite surprised that participants in the Citizens' Assembly managed to gain the topical mastery that they evidently did and that they were able to endorse a common solution.

The Citizens' Assembly experience also opens for him a limited sense of possibility regarding the values of common good and self-government. All citizens do have in common the good of an electoral system that preserves competition among elites. A kind of democratic self-government does seem possible in determining the content of that system, though he remains skeptical that these values are relevant for other issues. The Citizens' Assembly is a peculiar institution for the aggregative democrat because it successfully combines the interests of British Columbians but does so by privileging a handful of citizens. The aggregative democrat has little difficulty accepting the facts about institutional alternatives stipulated earlier. Given the incentives that institutions create, there is ample reason to think that the conclusions of a Citizens' Assembly would match more closely the interests of citizens at large than a legislative committee or commission of experts.

The institution thus offers the aggregative democrat a better way to establish rules that make good on his commitments to political equality and self-government. But the Assembly's experience is also troubling and may cause him to rethink the values of his conception in at least two ways. First, Assembly participants did not calculate their positions based on their own advantage. Instead, they developed a consensus around values that an electoral system should serve and then deliberated about which system best advances those values. This evidence presses the aggregative democrat to incorporate the possibility of deeper, deliberative agreement on fundamental questions such as design of the political structure. Second, he may be pressed to weaken his commitment to self-rule through universal participation, at least on complex and obscure issues such as electoral design. Most citizens of British Columbia—and most members of the Assembly when they began—had no command of alternatives such as MMP and STV systems.

Over the course of their deliberations, many of the Assembly's members became expert on these issues and so quite unlike the electorate at large. If their decision has democratic value, it is in part because Assembly members came to have views that were more informed and wiser than the general electorate and because they exercised more authority over that decision than other citizens. The Citizens' Assembly experience triggers relatively minor instrumental revisions for the deliberative democrat. It helps settle what was for him an open question: whether a legislative committee, independent commission, or popular assembly is more likely to produce electoral policies backed by reasons that are acceptable to all. In revising his view in this minor way, he moves closer to deliberative democrats who favour direct citizen participation than those who view representative bodies as the main sites of political deliberation. But his central commitment to self-government understood as reasoned rule survives unscathed.

Tyranny of Minorities

Decisions about political structure are by definition extraordinary and perhaps a democratic conception should not be much faulted for failing to account for them. A far more common problem in the governance of all contemporary democracies is the tyranny of powerful minority factions. Though democratic theorists have focused on majority tyranny and its remedies, minority tyranny remains a large and daunting challenge in every society. There are many kinds of minority tyranny and many have been rejected by pluralist critics—such as the notion that governments of capitalist societies operate as executive committees of the bourgeoisie—as either too vague to verify or plainly incorrect. Nevertheless, political science has established at least four major sources of unequal influence: material resources that can be translated into political influence, knowledge, strategic position, and institutional advantage.

In the urban areas of many developing countries and some developed ones, these sources of minority tyranny conspire to create a politics of patronage whose consequences are rejected by the four conceptions of democracy. When governance is infected with patronage, politicians make decisions about public investments in clinics, schools, houses, roads, and other basic infrastructure by selecting contractors and employers who advance their political fortunes rather than selecting projects to improve public welfare. Those who benefit from using public infrastructure are typically much more numerous, and so more difficult to organise, than the producers who gain by reaping public funds to build that infrastructure. Producers can therefore exert undue influence on decisions about what gets built by whom. In classic clientelist arrangements, they exert greater influence still by using their resources to organise popular support for politicians who direct favours to them. These arrangements are frequently protected from scrutiny and reform by the shield of expertise. Politicians, line departments, and contractors all benefit from claiming that such decisions are the province of analysts and technicians.

Participatory Budgeting (Orcamento Participativo ((or OP)) is a method of allocating public investments that has addressed the challenge of patronage. It was developed first in the southern Brazilian city of Porto Alegre and has spread in recent years to dozens of other cities in South America. Prior to 1989, control over municipal funds in Porto Alegre lay principally in the hands of city councilors. They made these investments according to a logic of patronage in which benefits were doled out in exchange for the support of well-organised groups of contractors and well-off residents. In 1989, the left-wing Workers' Party was elected to the city executive based in part on its promises to empower the city's civic organisations. Over the next 2 years, they developed the OP.

The mechanism shifts decisions over the capital portion of the budget from the city council to a system of neighbourhoods and citywide popular assemblies. Through a complex annual cycle of open meetings, citizens and civic associations meet to determine investment priorities. The infrastructure portion of the city's budget results from aggregating these priorities. Though it is a procedural reform, the Participatory Budget was born of a substantive motive to "invert" public spending priorities by shifting them away from the wealthy areas of the city to poor neighborhoods. It has achieved that goal remarkably well, and Porto Alegre's poor residents enjoy better public goods and services as a result. The percentage of neighborhoods with running water has increased from 75% to 98%, sewer coverage has grown from 45% to 98%, and the number of families offered housing assistance grew 16-fold since the initiation of the OP. Furthermore, the reforms seem to have suppressed patron–client relationships. In surveys, 18% of long-time neighbourhoods association leaders admit to engaging in client–patron exchanges of benefits for political support, whereas only 2% of leaders who became active after the initiation of theOP did so. Another study found that 41% of associations secured benefits by directly contacting politicians prior to the OP, whereas none relied on such unmediated channels after its establishment.

Suppose that there is a set of sociopolitical urban conditions under which allocating power over public infrastructure decisions to elected officials (I1) or public agencies (I2) will result in patronage. But adopting a system of participatory budgeting (I3) reduces patronage. These empirical assertions may be a fair characterisation of the recent history of Porto Alegre and other cities in developing countries. These consequences press the minimal, deliberative, and participatory conceptions closer to the aggregative one. Nothing about the consequences of I1 or I2 is inconsistent with the minimal democrat's emphasis on competitive elections or with its underlying commitments to public accountability and nontyranny. If patronage problems rise above some threshold—say under investing in public health to the extent that an epidemic strikes—the party in power would presumably suffer electoral consequences. Instead, pressure on the minimal conception comes not from the ills of patronage but from the possibility of a coherent and more demanding conception of self-governance revealed by the Participatory Budgeting experience. Minimal democracy favours comparatively low standards of public accountability in part because it supposes that citizens' preferences are unclear or unwise. The Participatory Budget shows that there are conditions under which citizens can have clear and reasonable preferences over issues concerning basic urban infrastructure and that feasible political institutions can make government responsive to those preferences. In these circumstances at least, the minimal democrat's skepticism regarding the existence and rationality of citizens' desires is unwarranted.

In light of these possibilities, the minimal democrat is compelled to revise the values of his conception. In particular, the very same reasons that justify the threshold of public accountability provided by competitive elections also favour increased governmental responsiveness when that notion is sensible, as it is in the case of Porto Alegre. Institutionally, competitive elections are for the minimal democrat an instrument of public accountability. If the invention of the Participatory Budget is more efficacious in that regard, it calls for revision of his institutional prescription. The Participatory Budget is more congenial to the aggregative conception. It constitutes the discovery of a form of direct participation for a relatively large city that seems to allow greater opportunities for participation and more responsive government than the aggregative democrat had previously supposed possible. Adoption of participatory budgeting is a relatively minor instrumental revision to the institutions of the aggregative conception that requires no adjustment of its underlying democratic values.

Residents may deliberate to an extent when they discuss the merits of various projects for the quality of neighbourhoods life. Even then, decisions in the Participatory Budget may revolve centrally around (aggregative) bargaining to satisfy individuals' needs and wants. Insofar as participants assert their interests and preferences without offering reasons to one another and pay little attention to any good that they have in common, the Participatory Budget falls short of deliberative expectations. But the gains from a more deliberative OP are unclear. Unlike deep moral disputes or conflicts over the rules of a common political system, the best reasons to support one public infrastructure choice—a clinic versus a school or paved street—over another may well hinge on the extent to which those choices satisfy preferences fairly. If so, then infrastructure investment decisions constitute an area in which deliberation reduces to aggregation; cases in which preference aggregation is the most reasonable procedure are degenerate instances of deliberation. It isn't that the participatory budget isn't deliberative, but rather that deliberative accounts add little, in this case, to the aggregative one.

The empirical assertions that drive these revisions depend on circumstances of institutional and political development. The extravagant participation that Participatory Budgeting requires can be regarded as a cost, but one worth paying to reduce corruption. If some fortunate cities possess professional bureaucracies, competitive elections, and vigorous media that are sufficient to generate honest and competent infrastructure investment decisions, then many of the reasons to favour participation fall away. The various conceptions of democracy would then diverge on institutional prescriptions. Minimal and perhaps aggregative democrats would favour representative arrangements whereas participatory democrats would still value the opportunities for direct citizen engagement created by the Participatory Budget.

These empirically informed thought experiments show how challenges such as minority tyranny can create occasions for rationally revising conceptions of democracy. Clear pressure for revision comes from the unintended and undesirable consequences of institutions recommended by various conceptions of democracy. But these institutional mismatches arise in turn because various problems and contexts make different democratic values salient and urgent. With making fair political rules, deliberation and constrained forms of citizen participation can be instrumentally valuable even to a minimal democrat due to the difficulties of political insulation faced by the other alternatives. With minority tyranny in urban clientelism, by contrast, fairness is secured primarily by institutions that accurately aggregate preferences over public goods and services, and public deliberation seems to be less relevant to the problem.

At minimum, these reflections suggest that each of the pure conceptions of democracy is institutionally incomplete. Each will be compelled to adopt ethical commitments and practices from the other views in the course of justifying particular democratic institutions in context. That is, the deliberative democrat will likely be compelled to make room for elements interest aggregation, and the minimal democrat may incorporate occasional deliberation and even direct participation. But this analysis does not produce a substantive judgment about the relative promise of the four conceptions of democracy. That would require considering many more problems and institutions. Other issues and contexts—perhaps political stability in transition societies or issues in which technical expertise is indispensable but difficult to acquire—might well highlight the comparative advantage of minimal democracy as a starting point.

Nevertheless, these applications illustrate how practical reasoning presses existing conceptions of democracy to develop institutional prescriptions and underlying values that are more differentiated and conditional in order to respect the complex texture of contemporary problems and conditions.

Pragmatic and Reflective Equilibrium

Pragmatic equilibrium as a standard for conceptions of democracy is a species of John Rawls' general idea of reflective equilibrium. Several differences between democratic theories and theories of justice make the version of reflective equilibrium developed here—a variant that focuses upon empirical consequences—more useful for the assessment and development of democratic conceptions than Rawls' formulation.

Rawls offers reflective equilibrium as a test for, and method of developing, principles of justice. Reflective equilibrium seeks fit between considered moral judgments in a limited set of settled cases on one hand and, on the other, a conception of justice composed of general principles that yield judgments in those and other cases. Rawls writes that "A conception of justice characterizes our moral sensibility when the everyday judgments we do make are in accordance with its principles". Reaching reflective equilibrium is not simply a matter of inducing principles of justice that best fit the data of considered judgments; rather it is a dialogic process that works back and forth between principles and judgments. That is, an appealing set of principles that generates a verdict contrary to strong moral intuition may cause one to revise one's judgment in that case in order to achieve greater coherence across many cases.

Pragmatic equilibrium shares this dialectical structure. The major difference is that its "data" consist of empirical evidence about the consequences of institutions rather than considered moral judgments. Three considerations necessitate this shift. First, democratic theory lacks the sort of relevant reliable judgments that Rawls contends are available for theories of justice. Even an intuition as basic as "one person, one vote" is contradicted by common and well-justified practices such as reserved legislative seats for women or minorities and the representation of political units without regard to population as in the U.S. Senate and the United Nations. Second, insofar as we possess them, untheorised beliefs about how collective political decisions should be organised likely grow out of acculturated background notions of government and democracy already in society—for example, participatory, representative, or elite convictions. If these judgments stem from more systematic conceptions of democracy, then a reflective equilibrium that relies on them would be circular. Third, Rawls correctly supposed that substantial advances could be made in determining correct principles of social justice based on already known empirical facts and that the hard work—or at least his part of it—lay in normative judgment.

The disputes among them are often inextricably empirical. Nevertheless, the pragmatic variant of reflective equilibrium maintains the insight that general conceptions, principles, and values must be disciplined by the everyday results of the phenomena they regulate. With conceptions of democracy, those results relate principally to the consequences of institutions. Such assessments require the help of political science and sociology; they are inaccessible through the sort of tranquil and educated introspection that reveals the content of considered moral judgments. For that reason, the method for testing and improving conceptions of democracy described here requires a working relationship—an intellectual synthesis—between political theory and political science in a way that is more immediate than for theories of justice.

After his discussion in *A Theory of Justice*, Rawls and subsequent theorists distinguished between narrow and wide reflective equilibrium. Pragmatic equilibrium is in one sense narrow but in another sense wide. In narrow reflective equilibrium, one works between a particular conception of justice (say, utilitarianism, libertarianism, or a Kantian view) and considered judgments about cases. This procedure may allow for "the smoothing out of certain irregularities" without subjecting the initial conception to fundamentally different and challenging alternatives. To attain wide reflective equilibrium, by contrast, one compares all of the possible conceptions of justice against one another to find the conception that best coheres with one's considered judgments. Rawls argues for his device of the Original Position and its veil of ignorance as justified by reflective equilibrium considerations. His pairwise comparison of the two principles with competing conceptions of justice is an argument that his two principles are those that survive the test of wide reflective equilibrium.

The concept of pragmatic equilibrium is clearly a kind of narrow reflective equilibrium. Each conception of democracy evolves to more coherent and consistent points through the practical reasoning process beginning from its initial values and institutional prescriptions. Pragmatic equilibrium as stated earlier offers no analog to the Original Position, no Archimedean point from which to compare minimal, aggregative, deliberative, participatory, and other conceptions of democracy. It may be that democratic theorists will develop such a device in the future. Or, it may be that a widely compelling justification for one pragmatic equilibrium democratic conception over the others will never be available because differences of fundamental values are too deep or, asDewey thought, because the interplay among changing problems, appropriate institutions, and related values renders all such equilibria temporary. These important questions lie beyond the current enterprise.

But the current level of development of conceptions of democracy, deliberative theory notwithstanding, is such that attaining the coherence among values, institutions, and consequences that pragmatic equilibrium requires—even temporarily—would be a breakthrough. Despite decades of work on both participatory and deliberative democracy, there is little in the way of suggestions at all, much less agreement, regarding the sorts of institutions that those conceptions require. Furthermore, working toward narrowly reflective, pragmatic equilibria for various conceptions of democracy may well eliminate some conceptions as unfeasible or undesirable. The process of conceptual development through practical reasoning may also reduce the extent of the differences among the conceptions.

Another way to distinguish narrow from wide reflective equilibrium, orthogonal to the first, refers to the sources of information used in making considered judgments that discipline more systematic and principled conceptions. On this dimension, narrow reflective equilibrium draws only on firm judgments that stand independently of most contingent and empirical considerations. Reflection that is wide on this dimension draws on the full range of knowledge about contexts, institutional alternatives, consequences, and other "all things considered" concerns. One can interpret Rawls moving from narrow to wide reflective equilibrium in this sense when he describes the "four-stage sequence" in which the veil of ignorance is gradually lifted to allow increasing amounts of information in the selection of principles of justice, constitutional design, legislation, and finally administration, adjudication, and citizen action.

5

Scientific Research on Bureaucracy

The study of bureaucracy within political science has an intellectual history that harkens back over a century. German sociologist Max Weber's notion that maintaining a "rational-legal authority" was the appropriate way to conduct the business of governance was both a normative and an empirical theory. He advocated the basis for *general* explanations regarding how bureaucratic institutions should be designed, including the need for a division of labour, career personnel with specialised training and expertise, hierarchical formal organisational structures that do not duplicate other administrative units, and explicit rules and procedures to ensure clear lines of authority and accountability within the organisation. This work has had a profound impact on our theoretical understanding of how superior-subordinate relationships within such organisations actually play out.

Similarly, Woodrow Wilson's argument for an administrative apparatus that is devoid of politics and meddling arose from a normative concern of the era that American bureaucracy served as a bastion for political patronage. Wilson's call for an independent administrative state not beholden to the particularistic interests of elected officials reflects issues of theoretical interest in understanding the role and functioning of bureaucracy within our American democracy that range from whether the bureaucracy responds to political control from electoral institutions to the importance of professional expertise in policy administration.

The early American study of bureaucracy finds its roots in the work of Goodnow, Gulick, and Taylor rather than that of Weber and Wilson. The influence of both Weber and Wilson, substantial as it was, came late to scholars of administration. Weber was not translated into English until 1946 and therefore his work was relatively inaccessible. Similarly, Wilson's original essay disappeared from the literature until it was republished in 1941. Goodnow also proposed a politics-administration dichotomy; he considered these to be two different functions but recognised that in practice politics was rarely separate from administration. This distinction became part of the progressive philosophy in public service training and was incorporated in the field's first textbook. The functional division allowed progress on two dimensions. On the administrative side, efforts were made to study implementation and the processes of bureaucracy in a scientific manner.

On the political side, the focus was on designing governmental institutions, that is, creating the institutions that would formulate, adopt, and implement policy. The latter was inherently prescriptive. This effort continued to occupy the time of public administration scholars until the 1950s. On the administrative side, efforts were made to discover the principles of administration, the one best way to design a work process or structure an organisation. Work process design is most closely associated with the work of Fredrick W. Taylor, who used experiments to determine how jobs should be structured. Taylor advocated a division of tasks with management charged with designing the optimal work processes and individual workers charged with responding based on the incentives offered for production.

Taylor's controversial motivation theory, the reliance on piecework and pure economic incentives, drew attention away from his scientific, albeit atheoretical, approach and generated skepticism (including a congressional investigation) about the contribution of Taylor.

Taylor's experimental approach also generated the first empirical challenge to this type of inquiry with Western Electric's Hawthorne experiments. Those experiments demonstrated how human factors and relationships subverted material incentives. Although scholars of public administration paid little attention to this work after the Hawthorne experiments, the fields of industrial engineering and operations research continue within the tradition of Taylor and the Hawthorne experiments.

A second stream of work went beyond production processes to examine how to structure organisations such as specialisation, span of control, unity of command, and similar factors. The method of analysis was observation rather than systematic data collection and analysis. Despite an impressive set of principles, Gulick himself lamented the lack of research supporting the principles and sketched out a research design to determine how one of them, span of control, could be systematically verified. That research agenda remained untouched, however. Simon's devastating critique of the "proverbs of administration" effectively ended this approach to the science of administration within public administration. The work of Progressive Era scholars arguing for a scientific approach to administration gave way to the behavioral revolution in the study of organisations.

The intellectual roots of this revolution can be traced to Barnard's *The Functions of the Executive,* in which issues of authority relating to superior-subordinate relationships were analysed. Central to Barnard's argument are joint issues: (1) what motivates bureaucrats to behave as they do? and (2) why are they willing to sacrifice their individual goals and belong to an organisation? This line of inquiry sought to develop generalisable theoretical principles to facilitate our understanding of how administrative agencies make decisions rather than emphasising normative descriptions as to how administrative agencies should function as entities in their own right and within a larger governmental system.

Simon's classic *Administrative Behavior* focused on individuals as the key unit of analysis in order to understand how organisations perform. The two major cornerstones of this work were an emphasis on (1) providing a theory of administration centered on efficiency and (2) analysing the nature of information processing by bureaucratic organisations by asserting that individuals' cognitive limitations did not allow for rational-comprehensive decision making. The latter subject is developed in March and Simon's *Organisations,* in which the rational comprehensive method is shown to be empirically unrealistic and theoretically ungrounded. This stream of work also emphasized how routines (standard operating procedures [SOPs]) could be employed to overcome uncertainty and individual cognitive limitations and allow individuals in organisations to behave in a more efficient manner. Within this intellectual stream, Cyert and March attack the foundations of the neoclassical theory of the firm by maintaining that organisations are not optimisers in the traditional sense of maximising profits. Instead, organisations behave inefficiently in a strict microeconomic sense since they will accrue slack resources.

Constitutional Perspectives

As the administrative science side of public administration focused on management and organisational questions, a parallel movement grappled with the issue of how to fit bureaucracy into the Constitution. The key challenge was reconciling the policy-making discretion of nonelected bureaucrats with the imperatives of democracy. Scholars were well aware of bureaucracy's potential to subvert democratic ends; Herring's work on bureaucratic power documented the ability of bureaucracy to engage in politics and shape the direction of public policy.

This debate was effectively framed by an exchange between Carl Friedrich and Herman Finer. Friedrich challenged the notion that elected officials could control the bureaucracy. Foreshadowing future principal-agent concerns about information asymmetry, Friedrich focused on the influx of scientists in government and how the possession of technical knowledge made political control difficult. In such a situation, the potential for a bureaucrat to dress his or her policy preferences in the guise of expertise was high. Friedrich's solution was a fellowship of science whereby competing sets of scientists would serve as a check on each other and thus provide multiple viewpoints for politicians.

Finer responded critically to this proposal, arguing that democracy was the preeminent value, not one on a par with technical competence. Finer contended that democratic institutions had sufficient methods with which to control bureaucracy and therefore abrogating their political responsibility was not necessary. The Friedrich-Finer debate established two competing camps on the question of bureaucracy and democracy—the proponents of overhead democracy or control by political institutions—and the proponents of the inner check or competition, ethics, participation, and so on. Significant for the development of public administration was the publication of Waldo's *Administrative State*. Waldo considered himself a normative theorist and generally eschewed empirical questions for normative ones. His approach provided a place for scholars not interested in the behavioral revolution but still concerned about the relationship between bureaucracy and democratic institutions.

Research questions in this area were not only concerned with how the bureaucracy fit into constitutional governance but also with alternative views of the constitutional chain of command. The separation of powers in the United States made the establishment of clear lines of bureaucratic authority difficult, a topic later known as the multiple principals problem. Although most scholars accepted the notion of presidential hierarchy in terms of the bureaucracy, a sizable group of scholars defended the constitutional pre-eminence of Congress. Accepting a Congress-centered view of the Constitution with regard to bureaucracy has clear implications for how the bureaucracy should relate to other political institutions.

Of the inner check proposals, one, representative bureaucracy, is of particular interest because it developed and tested a systematic body of midrange empirical theory of public bureaucracy. Representative bureaucracy in a nutshell contends that a bureaucracy representative of the general public in demographic terms is likely to produce policies generally in accord with public preferences. The logic of the theory was first set forth by Long, although he made no effort to test it. Critical tests and theoretical reformations came later. A consistent body of empirical literature now indicates when and under what conditions passive representative might lead to active representation (policy congruence) in terms of race, ethnicity, and gender.

Public Choice Approaches to Study Bureaucracy

Public choice approaches to the study of organisations focus on problems of control and responsiveness. Using economic tools of analysis, this brand of research analyses the pathologies of the administrative state and their implications for organisational performance. Tullock's work on hierarchical distortion posited the pernicious effects of misinformation that can be channelled both horizontally and, even more critically, vertically through administrative organisations. According to Tullock, agency efforts to combat information flow problems within organisations are essentially futile since "authority leakages" are both inevitable and cumulative.

In his classic treatise *The Bureaucratic Phenomenon,* Crozier arrived at conclusions similar to Tullock's. Rather than focusing on information flows, Crozier viewed the crux of the problem confronting administrative agencies as being centered on the question, How is power allocated within bureaucratic organisations? Crozier argued that organisations reflect imperfect social compromises that arise in bargaining among individuals and groups. Specifically, the organisational design, structure, and operation are not randomly determined but reflect an equilibrium agreement among actors and stakeholders behaving in a purposeful manner. Both Tullock and Crozier separately conclude that bureaucratic agencies are sufficiently ossified that they require abolishment. This lack of responsiveness to constituency demands, whether it be from elected officials, citizens, or pressure groups, is attributable to bureaucratic inertia that occurs within the organisational setting. Subsequent work by Niskanen extended this work on the limitations of administrative governance. Niskanen's central claim is that bureaucracy is preoccupied with resource (budget) maximisation and that its monopoly power over the distribution (administration) of the supply of public goods and services made it inefficient and unresponsive to both citizen and politician preferences. One notable departure from this malignant view of bureaucratic pathologies is Downs's *Inside Bureaucracy*. He argues that individual bureaucrats have different preference structures, thus making effective coordination and policy-making difficult. He extends the behavioral tradition, describing different behaviours exhibited by zealots, advocates, statesmen, conservers, and climbers.

The implication of these bureaucratic personality types is that communication channels in bureaucratic organisations will be muddled and will lead to performance distortions. Downs contends that bureaucratic pathologies can be corrected by finding the proper mix of agency personnel types, adopting extraorganisational means such as reorganisation, obtaining feedback on its performance from outside sources, or creating overlapping administrative responsibilities to encourage competition and discourage subordinate collusion.

Study of Bureaucracy Principal-Agent Theory

At the heart of much of the modern "scholarship" on administrative organisations is the application of the principal-agent model. According to Terry M. Moe,

> The principal-agent model is an analytic expression of the agency relationship, in which one party, the principal, considers entering into a contractual agreement with another, the agent, in the expectations that the agent will subsequently choose actions that produce outcomes desired by the principal.... [T]he principal's decision problem is far more involved than simply locating a qualified person—for there is no guarantee that the agent, once hired, will in effect choose to pursue the principal's best interests or to do so efficiently. The agent has his own interests at heart, and is induced to pursue the principal's objective only to the extent that the incentive structure imposed in the contract renders such behavior advantageous.

Implicit in the notion of a principal-agent relationship for studying the bureaucracy is not only the issue of task delegation by a superordinate (principal) to a subordinate (agent) but also the existence of inherent goal conflict between the principal and agent. This began as a means of investigating issues pertaining to incomplete information and uncertainty in microeconomic decision making. Incomplete information means that principals, who wish to delegate authority to perform tasks on their behalf, have neither full nor accurate information regarding agents' actions. Typically, agents possess specialised knowledge about the particular problem that the principal does not. Hidden information and actions are therefore embedded within these relations. Even in those rare instances in which the principal has specialised knowledge equivalent to that of the agent, he or she still experiences informational problems since the responsibility for task execution lies with the agent.

How do principals attempt to rein in the behavior of agents whose preference profiles are not in sync with their own? The dual cornerstones of the principal-agent model are its emphasis on the nature of incentives and the monitoring of behavior employed by the principal (superordinate) to ensure faithful action by an agent (subordinate). The principal, in theory, can structure incentives to get the agent to comply with the principal's wishes. For example, an elected official may provide greater slack resources to an agency that is faithfully executing the former's policy preferences (ex post incentive). He or she may also provide an agency possessing a credible organisational reputation with greater discretion vis-à-vis the rules and procedures issued through enactment legislation. Monitoring of agent behavior is a more intricate task than creating incentive structures, thus making the former more daunting for purposes of ensuring agent compliance. Intensive monitoring of bureaucratic performance initiated by congressional oversight committees akin to "police patrols" is a costly endeavour

Similarly, presidents who invest heavily in "activist" monitoring devices, such as detailed budgetary and performance auditing via the Office of Management and Budget (OMB), also incur transaction costs (i.e., costs incurred in carrying out such oversight activity) as well as opportunity costs (i.e., time and resources that could be spent on policy activities that would yield greater marginal net benefits to the administration's policy agenda). The use of active monitoring, therefore, contains the stigma of punishment and generates displeasure among agents who receive close and frequent scrutiny of their task performances.

The use of principal-agent theory in political science has generated conflicting models. Considerable work within this paradigm by scholars suggests that agencies' information asymmetries are sufficiently large to make it difficult for elected officials (principals) to monitor the behavior of administrative agencies (agents). Conversely, a larger body of work adopting the principal-agent perspective views incentive structures and monitoring activity employed by elected officials as being effective in reining in the behavior of administrative agencies. Specifically, these works are termed principal-agent models of political control over the bureaucracy since political institutions have various policy and administrative tools at their disposal to ensure bureaucratic compliance to their policy wishes. A voluminous body of empirical literature testing this theory in various manifestations over the past two decades has demonstrated strong support for the principal agent model of political control over the bureaucracy.

Principal-agent theory has both strengths and weaknesses as an analytic device for understanding public bureaucracies in a democratic system. One advantage of principal-agent theory is that it makes relationships between superordinates and subordinates tractable, which in turn can cull generalisable theoretical and empirical insights about how public bureaucracies function in a democracy. Also, while this paradigm at its elemental level is a static theoretical conceptualisation, it has the flexibility to allow for the dynamic elements of principal-agent relationships. Finally, not only can principal-agent theories be applied to study relationships external to the administrative organisation that are commonplace, but this paradigm can also be adapted to investigate intraorganisational relations within bureaucratic agencies.

Inherent limitations associated with principal-agent theory do exist. The theory assumes goal conflict from the onset. In numerous instances, however, agency-political relationships may typically reveal goal congruence. Second, the application of principal-agent relationships in numerous studies of public bureaucracy falsely views administrative agencies as being subservient agents of the principal(s). In such studies, hierarchy is imposed, which assumes that principals serve as superordinates to the agent's subordinate relational position. This alternative view, however, is problematic since a contract is an agreement between equals; introducing hierarchy negates the ability to use standard economic principles that do not assume an ability to coerce agents into compliance. Moreover, classical organisational theorists have long noted that agency-political as well as supervisor-subordinate relationships are predicated on a "zone of acceptance" where both parties have a stake and a voice in the agent's actions. Finally, principal agent models of bureaucracy are generally not flexible in how they handle the inherent complexity of structural relationships among relevant actors. For instance, the multiple levels containing multiple principals and agents that are common in bureaucratic organisations, and more broadly the administrative state, are difficult to fit into this framework. Relatedly, principal-agent models do not allow one to assess potentially vital relationships that fail to fit neatly within the confines of this theoretical paradigm. A principal, for example, can possess noncontractual authority over an agent whereby the former is not responsible for appointing or selecting individuals to represent his or her interests yet the latter perform this role anyway given both the positions that they hold within an organisation and the resulting policymaking authority that it possesses.

Transaction Cost Theory

Running parallel to the evolution of the principal-agent approach has been the increasing use of transaction cost economics. Transaction costs are distinguishable from production costs in that the former term refers to the costs incurred by operating in a complex environment where information and coordination problems exist while the latter pertains to the "nuts and bolts" of the production process found in neoclassical theory of the firm. Simply, the transaction is the unit of analysis for investigating institutions. What matters according to this theory is not simply the production of outputs by the firm or administrative agency but rather the costs incurred in the contractual arrangements and production processes that go beyond conventional factors such as labour, capital, and land. Transaction cost theory places an emphasis on how interactions among individuals or institutions will invariably incur costs of information acquisition and task performance concerning either ex post or ex ante activities. Examples of the former include drafting, negotiating, and safeguarding an agreement, and cases of the latter are disequilibrium costs when transactions drift out of alignment, corrections to ex post misalignments, the start-up and operating costs corresponding to government institutions where disputes are typically handled, and those costs incurred in the process of obtaining commitments from other parties.

Information costs among institutions and actors are nonzero (or at least nontrivial). Knowledge about other actors' preferences and actions is costly because the value of items is not known with certainty and monitoring the behavior of others is expensive. Transaction costs will result in decisions that are allocatively inefficient. While monitoring costs are considered in principal-agent models in matters of delegation, measurement costs usually are not. Transaction costs are thus simply the costs associated with planning, adapting, and monitoring task completion under alternative governance structures. In this light, the underpinnings of this theory serve as a means of gauging the flow of information and subsequent behavior of relevant actors. Since human, organisational, and institutional relations are not frictionless, positive transaction costs will be incurred by these entities.

The transaction cost perspective of public organisations complements the research on public organisations that views public bureaucracies as experiencing information deficiencies, failing to operate in a neatly ordered, authoritative hierarchical fashion, and having structures and jurisdictions that play a notable role in defining the parameters of performance. While this theory has been applied to studying how chief executives and legislatures bargain to determine whether or not the former wish to delegate administrative authority to the latter, it has yet to be explored by political scientists with regard to specific questions of how public bureaucracies make decisions or how they behave in either a political setting or as organisations in macro- or microlevel terms. The analysis of public bureaucracies through a transaction cost lens makes sense since these types of costs can be viewed as the operating costs of a system. As a result, the application of transaction cost theory to the study of public bureaucracy could be quite useful for understanding how these entities operate in a larger political environment as well as within their organisational subunits and subfunctions.

Transaction cost approaches can also illustrate some advantages of organisations. If, for instance, one views public institutions, including bureaucracies, as having the potential to generate increasing returns to scale in the production of public goods and services, this can result in greatly reduced transaction costs. Government, for example, has the ability to coerce, and thus it can eliminate some transaction costs by at (declaring standards for products [e.g., high-definition television] or processes [pollution control]). The ability to apply a uniform pattern of policy to all situations nationwide dramatically reduces the overall transaction costs of implementing a government policy.

Organisational Theory Perspectives

Although political scientists rarely contribute to organisational theory, they frequently use it to guide their research. Four strains of work in organisational theory are relevant to our discussion here—the open systems approach of Thompson, the organisational behavior approach of Argyris and others, the empirical work on public versus private organisations, and the contributions of Herbert Kaufman. Each will be discussed in turn.

Interest in organisational structure per se (rather than in how external political institutions use structure) has roots in the work of Gulick but was brought back to respectability by Thompson and Perrow. Thompson presented the classic theory of organisations as open systems; within this presentation, he provides a series of testable hypotheses about how organisations respond to environmental pressures and how structures influence what the organisation does. Although Thompson's hypotheses have not been of interest to political scientists, his open systems approach can be found in the work of several scholarly works in political science. Perrow's work, in turn, is a vigorous defense of organisational sociology and the importance of structure in studying organisations. It interprets the literature, stressing structural rather than "people" questions. Within sociology, the work of Perrow and Thompson is most fully developed in Mintzberg's research agenda on structural influences in organisations.

The organisational behavior approach traces its roots to the Hawthorne experiments, but the key work was McGregor's distinction between theory X and theory Y management. The influence of McGregor meant that devotees of organisational behavior was interested in internal management questions (rather than political ones) and how to generate greater performance in the organisation. Management theories based on the organisational behavior literature proliferated, including those of Likert and Argyris. The applied nature of the theory (e.g., in management) means that it has not spawned a significant body of empirical research among scholars of public administration. On a more theoretical level, Mosher linked many organisational behavior questions to the political side of bureaucracy and in the process presented a strong argument for the inner check on bureaucratic autonomy.

One active area of empirical scholarship is that of public versus private sector differences. This literature starts with March and Simon's notion of a generic theory of organisations. Subsequent work has found that the public sector attracts individuals with different values than does the private sector; public organisations are also likely to have more and conflicting goals, more restrictive procedures, lower levels of turnover except at top levels of the organisation, and different incentive structures. These differences provide a fertile ground for hypotheses for scholars interested in external control over the bureaucracy and how public bureaucracy is likely to respond to efforts aimed at control.

The other notable stream of research is Herbert Kaufman's series of studies on public organisations. In *The Forest Ranger*, Kaufman documented the ability of an organisation to socialise its members by structuring personnel policies. In *Administrative Feedback*, he found evidence that agency heads had sufficient tools to monitor subordinate behavior but did not necessarily use them. In *Red Tape*, Kaufman analysed both the functional and the dysfunctional aspects of procedural controls. In *Are Government Organisations Immortal?*, he found empirical evidence that government organisations, once created, are difficult but not impossible to eliminate. Finally, in *Time, Chance, and Organisations,* Kaufman provocatively argues that government organisations survive not because they perform well but because they are blessed with favourable environments. Although Kaufman generally used case studies and qualitative methods, his systematic approach to key organisational questions and his willingness to probe inside the black box of organisations make his work a key forerunner of contemporary scientific studies of bureaucracy.

Modern Approaches to Study Bureaucracy

The preceding approaches have one ingredient in common—they have each assisted our systematic thinking on how bureaucratic organisations operate. For instance, the principal-agent approach has helped make the relationship within bureaucratic agencies, and in relation to their political superordinates, a tractable one in which one can deal with the moral hazard and adverse selection problems inherent in the delegation of authority.

The traditional public administration literature has demonstrated the importance of the values held by bureaucrats and the impact that these values have on both political control and public policy outputs. Additional research has demonstrated Downs's concerns about external control; specifically, attempts to impose rational budgeting systems have been altered and even subverted by bureaucrats in the implementation process. Open systems theories of bureaucracy have demonstrated their value in focusing research on how organisations cope with the political environment and as a general framework for assessing political control.

These approaches also have one common ingredient lacking for continued rapid progress—they apply theories of behavior from economics, sociology, or psychology to understand bureaucratic organisations. As a result, many key issues have been neither addressed nor resolved. Uniquely political science theories of the administrative state are uncommon, even given the notable advances made in this field of inquiry over the past two decades by political scientists. This is not to imply that interdisciplinary approaches to the study of bureaucracy should be eschewed; instead it is meant to encourage the development of theories and methods that are appropriate for understanding administrative organisations as governmental institutions, not just externally but internally as well. For instance, how do conflicting policy preferences within an agency come about? How does this, in turn, affect its ability to execute its policy mission?

More recent research over the past twenty years has typically (though not always) been more preoccupied with external political forces than with what goes on inside the agency. As a result, our knowledge of how politicians structure rules, procedures, and incentives; the tools that apply to elicit responsiveness from public bureaucracies; and the bargaining among electoral institutions that takes place in determining the fate of administrative agencies is well developed.

Unfortunately, the systematic, generalisable body of knowledge concerning what makes administrative agencies tick is still largely uncharted territory in need of theoretical and empirical investigation. We know little about how bureaucratic agencies make decisions in a political environment or how bureaucratic structures affect responsiveness and performance in a variety of settings. While we know that all public organisations deal with multiple and conflicting goals, we have little information about how they resolve goal conflict on a day-to-day basis. Similarly, we are just beginning to ask how external performance criteria affect bureaucracies and how they can shape responses in unexpected ways. Finally, we only have general ideas about how well organisations socialise their members and have little empirical knowledge about how effective such methods are and whether or not they can be overcome by external political actors.

This volume intends to shed light on several issues of considerable importance to understanding public bureaucracies as both governmental institutions and administrative organisations. One basic theme underlying these works is an emphasis on theory-ladeness, whether it involves mathematical/ symbolic logic, statistical analysis, or verbal conceptualisation. Another is a bureaucentric focus that places administrative agencies front and center in understanding how the administrative state functions. We feel that the original scholarly essays contained in this volume will stimulate ideas and research on topics that either have not been addressed or need to be reexamined in a distinct, fresh manner that will challenge our current way of thinking. While the vast majority of research on public administration within political science has focused on top-down accountability issues involving political control over the bureaucracy by democratic institutions, this volume is intended to redirect some of those energies toward administrative decision making and behavior. The dual emphasis on systematic social scientific inquiry and a bureaucentric focus contained in this volume reflects a neoorganisational approach to studying administrative institutions. This general thematic approach parallels that of new institutionalism, which has risen to prominence within political science over the past two decades. Daniel P. Carpenter's essay, "Why Do Bureaucrats Delay? Lessons from a Stochastic Optimal Stopping Model of Agency, Timing, with Applications to the FDA," advances a theoretical model of bureaucratic decision-making processes that allows us to gain insight into the *timing* of decisions. With theoretical roots linked to March and Simon, Carpenter's approach can be refined and applied to other bureaucratic settings in which we wish to understand *when* agencies make policy decisions such as the timing of prosecution cases.

George A. Krause's essay, "Agency Risk Propensities Involving the Demand for Bureaucratic Discretion," focuses attention on the demand side of this commodity, as opposed to the supply side commonly analysed within political science. Krause derives comparative-static results concerning the risk-bearing nature of an administrative organisation based on a simple model of agency demand for discretion under uncertainty derived from the separate impact of discretion and policy outcome (implementation) uncertainty. Thomas H. Hammond's essay, "Veto Points, Policy Preferences, and Bureaucratic Autonomy in Democratic Systems," provides us with an important theoretical window into the amount of bureaucratic autonomy agencies enjoy based on the preference configuration of elected officials in relation to potential veto points across different institutional designs. Hammond entices us to grapple with important cross-national differences in the design of electoral institutions and administrative governance that often get overlooked in the study of political control over the bureaucracy.

6

Approaches to Study Public Policy

The absence of system dynamics methods in political science would surprise no one. System dynamics is not taught in political science graduate programs, but has thrived on business applications as a result of the continuing commitment of the Massachusetts Institute of Technology's Sloan School of Management. On the other hand, however, systems thinking, of a sort, and systems analysis began in political science and the social sciences more generally in the 1950s. Theory building and systems analysis generated substantial interest in academic political science through the 1960s, stimulated primarily by David Easton's final volume *A Systems Analysis of Political Life*. Easton's work was so influential that systems analysis is still presented, thirty-five years later, as one of a handful of primary approaches to the study of political science and public policy.

Despite the development of this systems approach in politics and its continuing mention in texts, systems thinking is largely dormant in academic political science while system dynamics appears to be thriving. Some of the explanation is obvious to practitioners of system dynamics. Though appearing at the same time, system dynamics originated in engineering and was then applied by Jay Forrester in the business setting and later to social systems. It now seems likely that disciplinary boundaries kept political systems theorists from communicating with those working in system dynamics. A comparison of the literature in both fields reveals no interaction whatsoever. True, political scientists took note of the publication of *The Limits to Growth*, but they had the skills neither to critique the work nor develop models of their own adopting the same method. Developments since 1972 have done little to change the situation. The absence of system dynamics in political studies is even more noteworthy because of it its appearance (admittedly by another name) in two works that gained substantial attention in traditional political science circles. Lave and March in *An Introduction to Models in the Social Sciences*, for example, discusses diffusion models and Stokey and Zechauser in their widely cited *A Primer for Policy Analysis*, begin with a chapter on difference equations including a discussion of models using stocks and flows.

Despite these examples of what appears to be system dynamic method in the politics and policy literature, and despite the appearance of mathematical modelling political science, the absence of true systems modelling in the political science literature may have even deeper origins. Political scientists, frankly, associate all academic discussion of system methods with the work of Easton. Since Easton is seen ultimately as a failure, someone who basically spent his life time translating what we all knew about politics into different terms, political scientists seem to believe that system analysis failed to reveal either anything new or a research agenda that could be developed after Easton's death. After Easton, researchers became enamored of the related field of structural functionalism and then the more powerful game theory and rational choice approaches. Efforts to build a science of politics turned from the study of behaviours broadly defined, to the study of decisions made by rational actors and modelled after research in microeconomics.

Now instead of an active systems research agenda in politics, we have a situation in which a small number of policy analysts use difference equations or true system dynamic models in their work and academically trained political scientists are largely unaware of the developments in system dynamics methods. This is unfortunate because it appears that system dynamics is an approach can that provide virtually unlimited avenues for political research. Political systems are dynamic, do contain feedback mechanisms and delays, as Easton explained, and political and policy problems can be understood in terms of stocks and flows. Furthermore, like all social scientists, political scientists continue to see the quality of their research questioned when they find their work confined to the measurement of objectively verifiable data. The ability of system dynamics models to use non-quantitative variables is, therefore, a distinct advantage in social system modelling.

For example, there are, in the politics literature, interesting models of policy change. These are models that attempt to illustrate how changes in a political environment may alter the outputs of legislatures or agencies. The work is significant, among other reasons, because democratic theory suggests that public decision makers should be both representative of public opinion and needs, and accountable to the public. Plainly these decision makers operate in a complex political environment that includes many forces besides public opinion. Models of these processes can help to identify these forces and their relative influence. Unfortunately, these models though sometimes informed by systems analysis, are not informed by systems thinking.

A brief literature review of theory in public policy research is sufficient to illustrate the substantial difficulties in this field. Some problems might be attributed to the youth of the discipline. Public policy as a recognised sub-field is barely thirty years old. Many problems, however, do not result from naive or undeveloped theory. Instead they arise either from complex theory with limited empirical value or theory limited to variables that allow traditional social science hypothesis testing. In both cases, there is a poor match between theory and method. Authors of complex theories tend to be disregarded by empiricists for obvious reasons and those writing empirical studies are thought, by traditionalists, to work with limited causal understandings artificially constrained by measurable variables. In sum, the existing theory of policy change tends to be either 1.) very general in scope or very narrow and specific to a particular agency's decision processes, 2.) reliant on a single or several case studies that are often of limited utility, and/or 3.) derived from multiple regression analysis that usually disregards dynamic change and any element of feedback despite a foundation in an otherwise complex causal theory.

One approach to the study of public policy is the "stages heuristic" as described by Paul Sabatier. Derived from David Easton and others, this approach is evident in widely used public policy texts. The stages, roughly agenda setting, policy formulation, policy adoption, implementation and evaluation, are process oriented and conceptually useful, but are not developed in the form of a causal model. Worse, from a testing standpoint, the authors who use such models take great pains to explain to readers that policy making is messy. It does not happen in stages. The stages are used, nonetheless, both for teaching about public policy and, more importantly, for setting research boundaries. The famous studies of agenda setting by Kingdon and implementation by Pressman and Wildavsky are obvious examples. The problem with the stages approach for public policy theory is that, like Easton's systems theory before it, it is both too general and does not explicitly and adequately specify the causal forces that might move a policy through the stages toward adoption. Easton's systems theory fills a three volume work but is generally represented in policy texts like Anderson and Dye by the diagram below. This is a gross simplification of such a lengthy work, but serves the purpose because Easton's longer work merely adds substantial detail to the basic concepts of a system located in an environment turning inputs into outputs.

The obvious value of this view is that the political system is correctly portrayed as a dynamic feedback system. Though feedback in politics is apparent, for example, the success of politicians depends on public support and this support depends on the success of politicians, Easton was perhaps the first to use the term and explicitly provide for feedback effects in his general systems theory approach. Still, as the diagram makes obvious and as his more complex and rich exposition of his theory makes plain, Easton did not develop a model that could be formally specified or empirically tested. Contemporary political theorists have set it aside as unlikely to lead to further theoretical developments.

On the other end of the spectrum are studies which are overly narrow. These studies tend to focus on one act or one agency. Examples of non-formal, historical studies include Waldman's recitation of the origin and adoption of the national service program Americore and Garvey's "insider's" look at decision making in the Federal Energy Regulatory Commission. Despite limitations, these studies are of obvious value as they establish the rich contextual detail of political decision making and, in doing so, provide the foundation upon which more formal and general causal theory can be built. The authors, however, generally fail to take this next step and often fail to specify the more general hypotheses or lessons that might be revealed by their work.

A case study approach, especially when used as a method of testing hypotheses, can be advantageous for several reasons. The use of multiple case studies will place a work in the middle ground between overly general and narrow studies, and some authors take that important methodological step towards theory specification. Interesting examples include Mazmanian and Sabatier's implementation studies, Sabatier and Hunter's study of the mental models of the causes of pollution among environmental policy elites and Sabatier and Jenkins-Smith's study of policy change based on interest groups or "advocacy coalitions." This last work is of particular interest as the authors map out a policy system, use case studies to test hypotheses derived from their understanding of the system and then revise their understanding based on the data developed. The case studies are both qualitative and quantitative and cover a range of policy issues from education and environment to airline deregulation and telecommunications.

Though on the cutting edge of policy theory and more formal than many approaches, Sabatier and Jenkins-Smith's model is not designed to support simulation.

As evident from the diagram above, the authors envision a simplified model in which two opposing coalitions attempt to influence decisions with the assistance of policy brokers who manage conflict with an interest in resolving disputes. Decisions result in policy outputs and impacts that influence external events and feedback to the resources and strategies of the subsystem actors. The model thus includes both feedback effects and dynamic changes over time. Both are elements often partially or completely missing from studies of policy change.

The weakness of this approach, especially from a system dynamicist point of view, is that the authors fail to specify variables that can be modelled even though the authors are clearly interested in the performance of a dynamic feedback system. By way of illustration, the following are two of many hypotheses examined by Sabatier and Jenkins-Smith:

> *Hypothesis 4:* The core (basic attributes) of a governmental program is unlikely to be significantly revised as long as the subsystem advocacy coalition that instituted the program remains in power.
>
> *Hypothesis 5:* The core (basic attributes) of a governmental action program is unlikely to be changed in the absence of significant perturbations external to the subsystem, that is, changes in socio-economic conditions, system-wide governing coalitions, or policy outputs from other subsystems.

The authors tested their hypotheses by asking independent coders to review the case studies to determine whether each hypothesis held true for each of the six case studies presented. In general, the hypotheses are supported, although, in conclusion, the authors revise several hypotheses in response to their data. Such case studies, therefore, represent an interesting, but plainly limited approach to empirically and qualitatively validating the causal theory presented.

One could recast much of this model using the concepts of system dynamics. For example, using the hypotheses presented above, one could specify the core attributes of a program in several ways. This variable might be defined in terms of changing (increasing or decreasing) agency staff, delegated powers, program operations, budget, grants funded, population served, enforcement actions taken or regulations promulgated or repealed. Without trying to construct a definition of "core attributes" that matches the authors' usage, it is evident that it is possible to define government functions using variables that represent changes in these functions over time. One might represent the growing (or declining) power or influence of an advocacy coalition in similar terms. Hypothesis 5 refers to "external perturbations" in the system such as changes in economic conditions. Such conditions are often elements in system dynamics models. Changes in governing coalitions could be represented by changes in party representation (strength in a legislature), in the resources of opposing interest groups, or in public opinion on questions regarding the role of government or more specific questions like support for public assistance programs or tax cuts.

Most models used in political science are constructed using regression equations. Coleman is a recent example. He uses a number of variables representative of party control of governmental institutions to determine whether unified or divided government is more productive. The analysis is repeated several times using different measures of legislative productivity. Although Coleman uses a number of other variables, such as the size of budget deficits and the "activist mood" of the public, the result is still a model in which all the variables are assumed to be independent and there is no provision for feedback effects among the variables despite the use of time-series data.

A few mathematical models of policy adaptation are more sophisticated in approach. For example, Bender and Moe use an adaptive and dynamic model to determine whether and how agencies, legislatures and business or interest groups interact to adjust agency enforcement budgets and enforcement activity in response to previous agency actions and public pressure. They developed the model further to apply it to agenda setting. The problem with this approach is that the model includes limited feedback assuming that, for example, agencies only influence legislatures by means of the public and not directly. The model also assumes that the public is incapable of influencing the agency directly.

The approach was severely criticised by Krause for these very reasons. Krause's study of bureaucratic politics is, perhaps, the most sophisticated to date as it uses vector auto-regression to examine the same questions of institutional outputs employing a dynamic model with multiple feedback loops. The weakness in this study is that, after developing a relatively complex mathematical model, Krause is limited to using that model to study the forces that affect the number of agency enforcement actions in two agencies. Although this is one approach to understanding the relationship between the Congress and agencies, it omits many other aspects of this relationship, for example, programmatic activity which might be more important in many agencies than enforcement actions. He also fails to acknowledge that the number of violations or violators present in the environment or estimates of illegal activity might by an influential factor in agency enforcement activity. Nonetheless, Krause's effort is perhaps the most sophisticated and complete study of change in administrative and legislative policy to date. It is interesting to note that though he is apparently not trained in system dynamics, Krause's main criticisms of the literature relevant to his book is that prior research did not accomplish what the system dynamics method was designed to accomplish: develop testable causal models of complex, dynamic systems with multiple feedback loops.

Throughout this discussion of theory and research in policy outputs and policy change, we have suggested that a system dynamics approach to these questions might solve many of the conceptual and methodological problems apparent in the literature. There are reasons, however, to think that system dynamics is not appropriate for research questions of this nature.

Frohock, for example, raises the more general question of whether politics is an appropriate subject for systems methods. He suggests both advantages and disadvantages. In reference, again, to Easton, Frohock writes: The advantages of a systems model are these: (a) the *process* character of policy is easily caught, thus avoiding the mistake of seeing policy as a static, random, or totally disjointed collection of activities; and (b) a high level of generality is maintained, persuading us to see a more total picture of policy than partial models or simple case studies permit.

But Frohock also suggests that the systems approach can lead to two important mistakes. The first is to suggest that politics is "a smooth continuum of *actual* policy activities," and the second, related mistake is to substitute the generalities of a theory for the "particulars of real-life experiences". Frohock suggests that we need to develop secondary theories to "connect systems models to realworld politics". The problem for Frohock is that politics must be understood as consisting of both patterned and recurring activity, *and* other events or perhaps dominant personalities that are difficult to place in a causal model of patterned activity. He offers assassination as an example of the these other events. The argument here is, of course, not the simplistic "politics does not contain systems" or "politics can completely be understood in terms of systems." Rather it is the more complex idea that 1.) systems approaches are appropriate tools if their limitations are recognised and 2.) there may be times or circumstances in which the apparently messy, random or arbitrary nature of political outcomes may justifiably overwhelm attempts to identify general causal theory.

With this caution in mind, however, it appears that system dynamics might still be the best approach for moving beyond a journalistic diary of political personality and history toward a social science of politics. There are two reasons this is true. To the extent that modellers are working with historic data and events, system dynamic models can be built to accommodate changes in the environment or the system itself over time. The method allows the introduction of new causal factors or decision rules part-way through a simulation.

Secondly, in a similar manner, it is possible to introduce shocks into a system that might radically alter the system's performance. In a political setting that might be, for example, a declaration of war that radically and fundamentally alters public opinion on a key variable for an extended period of time. To the extent that one is using a model to forecast outcomes, more substantial problems remain. The modeller can propose scenarios in which, to follow the example above, public opinion shifts dramatically due to some external event. But one would obviously make grave errors if such a scenario were to be understood as a prediction of events that will happen.

With those cautionary words in mind, system dynamics has much to offer the study of politics and policy. Political scientists might do well to recognise the important contribution system dynamics has made in business management where "politics" is also evident in apparently random events, seemingly arbitrary decisions, the interplay of committee members in reaching a result, and the interaction of multiple actors with different powers and abilities in a company or industry. Despite the messiness of politics in public or private life, there are still important institutional structures; traditional, habitual or legislated processes; consistent or changing, but identifiable decision rules and patterns of behavior that are worthy of study. System dynamics can be a powerful tool for this work.

Political Psychology and Study of Politics

Fields of scientific inquiry follow a common pattern. At the outset, excitement and enthusiasm prevail as a small group of founders offers a new conceptual framework and, usually, a new, related methodology. Sometimes the specific topics of inquiry are also new, at other times only the ways to think about them. Other, often young, scholars adopt the new perspective, and before long it becomes an active, visible part of the discipline. Typically, this very growth in prominence portends the beginning of a levelling off, if not decline, in research activity. Continuing scholarship takes the form of adding small increments of knowledge to the key central questions that the founders had posed much earlier.

Often missing from this sequence is a self-evaluation by the practitioners themselves. Concerned, as they should be, with substantive questions, the researchers don't stop to scrutinise what they do and how it fits into the larger discipline of which they are part. The criticisms usually come from elsewhere and consequently tend to undercut rather than strengthen the field.

In this volume, political psychologists take a hard look at political psychology. They pose, and then address, the kinds of tough questions that those outside of the field would be inclined to ask and those inside should satisfactorily be able to answer. Not everyone will agree with the answers the authors provide, and, in some cases, the best an author can do is offer well-grounded speculations.

But, one might protest, the idea of political psychologists evaluating political psychology is equivalent to the idea of police officers monitoring their own department. In both cases, the conclusions are foreordained, such that the scientific field in one case and the department in the other will be evaluated more positively than it should be.

Fields of scientific inquiry should be definable. Sullivan, Rahn, and Rudolph offer a tour de force of political psychology, and in the process show how diverse and ill-defined the field is. Political psychologists, unlike, say, students of rational choice, do not share a single set of assumptions or even a general perspective. As Sullivan, Rahn, and Rudolph state in their opening paragraph, the field "includes – has always included – a wide diversity of theories, approaches, quantitative and qualitative research methods, and verdicts." They identify three distinct eras – the first dominated by studies of personality, the second by attitude theory and change, and the third by human cognition and information processing – and note that today all three perspectives are a part of what is normally called political psychology.

The diversity in fact is even wider and deeper. Even within the currently dominant information-processing perspective, which is the focus of this volume, scholars examine a variety of cognitive processes ranging from attribution to cognitive heuristics to on-line processing. Researchers have also begun to ascertain how affect and emotions interact with cognition to shape political judgments.

So what, exactly, is political psychology? A simple answer is also a pretty good one: the study of mental processes that underlie political judgments and decision making. Because there are many mental processes, and to date no general framework that integrates them, a political psychologist can – must? – focus on those that seem most applicable to the political task people are facing. This freedom to pick and choose is both a plus and a minus. On the one hand, the wide range of perspectives on political decision making can be compared and contrasted within the academic marketplace. In time, presumably, the strongest and most beneficial will prevail. On the other hand, the accumulation of agreed-upon evidence is slow and, at worst, could not occur at all.

Sullivan, Rahn, and Rudolph also note that political psychologists have overwhelmingly used psychoanalysis to study elites and information processing to study citizens. In principle, this dichotomy need not and should not exist. That it does reflects the extreme difficulty of gaining access to public officials for the purpose of conducting the kinds of surveys and experiments that are at the core of the information processing perspective. Unfortunately, the dichotomy precludes systematic comparisons of the two groups. One outstanding question, for example, is whether elected officials and other political activists make the same kinds of errors – anchoring, overconfidence, and so on – that ordinary citizens make. Or do the institutional settings in which they function reduce such errors? Lacking equivalent experiments across the two groups, we really cannot say. To assume that the latter make better political judgments is understandable, but it might not be right.

Similarly, political psychologists have not been inclined toward crossnational analysis. This is an opportunity lost. Differences in political structures – presidential versus parliamentary systems, two-party versus multiparty systems, and so on – are natural manipulations that facilitate examining how structures affect and interact with individual decision making.

Theory and Context

A typical psychological study entails formulating a hypothesis and then testing it experimentally (political psychologists often substitute experimental surveys for the laboratory). Both Lupia and Conover and Searing find problems with this venerable approach to research, although for very different reasons.

Lupia argues for a closer relationship between formal theory and political psychology. In his words, "interactions between political psychologists and rational choice theorists can generate substantial *gains from trade*" (italics in the original). Political psychologists tend to use experiments to test hypotheses and make inferences. By design, experiments simplify the world by holding constant everything except those factors that interest the researcher. This very strength, the isolation of a cause and-effect relationship, is also the experiment's primary vulnerability. It is a big inferential leap from an experiment to a much more complex political environment. Whether the experimental results hold in the real world is always open to question.

How, then, can researchers maintain the strength of experiments while at the same time increase confidence that the experimental results are externally valid? One answer might be to uncover similar relationships in the real world. As Lupia argues, however, the complexity of politics renders this a difficult if not impossible task; indeed, it is this complexity that motivates experimental work in the first place. Lupia proposes, instead, that experimentally oriented political psychologists look to formal models. Based on a deductive logic, these models begin with a set of assumptions from which the researcher then can derive precise and testable implications. However, models also simplify – they must be analytically tractable – and thus they are not especially good analogues of actual human behavior, either.

What Lupia recommends, therefore, is the joint use of axiomatic theory and experiments. On the one hand, rigorous theory leads to precise predictions about human behavior that not only shape the design of the experiment but also serve as the test criteria. On the other, experimental research directs theorists to a realistic set of assumptions about political decision makers and also provides the vehicle by which to test their models empirically. In Lupia's words, "an explanation that combines political psychology and rational choice theory trumps explanations that ignore either or both approaches." As he cautions, however, a formal model is no panacea for a badly designed experiment, nor is a poorly formulated model a panacea for experimental research. Lupia then presents an illustrative study, of political persuasion, that includes a formal model of the relationship between speakers (public officials) and listeners (citizens) and an experiment embedded in a national survey designed to test its implications.

Lupia's study builds on the idea that the typically uninformed citizen must use available cues that more informed others provide. Reviewing the major psychological studies of persuasion of the past fifty years, Lupia argues that past work has not satisfactorily explained what differentiates a persuasive from a nonpersuasive cue. Specifically, none of the extant models identifies the necessary or sufficient conditions for cue persuasion.

The formal theoretical framework that Lupia offers begins with the theorem that "perceived common interests and perceived speaker knowledge are each necessary for persuasion." Satisfaction of both necessary conditions, plus the condition that the listener be sufficiently uncertain about two (or more) alternatives so as to be open to influence, comprise the sufficient condition. But listeners often cannot directly observe a speaker's knowledge and common interest, and thus they will look to speaker attributes that help them decide whether or not the speaker is knowledgeable and shares their interests. As a matter of empirical research, the task for the researcher is to identify such attributes, for only they can have a nonspurious correlation with cue persuasiveness. Speaker attributes that people ignore might be statistically related to persuasiveness, but they cannot be a cause of it.

Elaboration of the basic model entails introducing a third actor, an observer. This leads to the revised theorem that if the observer believes his interests conflict with both the speaker's and the listener's, and if the speaker has an incentive to be truthful, then the speaker can persuade the observer. An Illinois liberal who hears Jesse Helms criticize a pending bill before his most devoted North Carolina constituents should be persuaded to favour it.

The call for increased formalisation in political psychology warrants serious consideration. Rational choice theorists have demonstrated its value, and there is no obvious reason why political psychologists should not benefit from it. This said, two comments are in order. First, it would be wrong to leave the impression that deduction belongs solely to the realm of rational choice and experimental testing of hypotheses to political psychology. Zaller's *The Nature and Origins of Mass Opinion* is a notable example of deductive reasoning in political psychology. Borrowing from extant psychological research on persuasion, Zaller systematically deduces a set of predictions that he then tests. Although most other research programs in political psychology admittedly are less axiomatic, they too build on assumptions about individual thought processes. The on-line processing model, for example, takes as its point of departure the importance of affect and the limitations of long-term memory. Given these features of human thinking, it follows that people will forget the specific events that occur during a political campaign but will incorporate their reactions toward the events via a "running tally" of affect toward the candidates.

The second observation is the more crucial. It is one thing to propose that political psychologists use formal theory, quite another to propose that they use rational choice theory. Lupia understandably recommends bringing political psychology into a rational choice framework. To be sure, he rejects the traditional assumption of omniscience found in rational choice models and adopts the psychology-sounding idea "that people do the best they can with the knowledge and skills they have." Nonetheless, he employs a signalling model that has its roots fully in economics and that assumes the ordinary citizen to be a rational, strategic actor. Whether political psychologists will readily adopt a rational choice framework that they themselves might modify further remains to be seen.

Some of the most influential psychological research on which political scientists draw portrays people as incapable of even approximating the canons of rationality in their decision making. For example, they consistently and unknowingly use rules of thumb that lead to biased errors in judgment. Emotions are not an element of rational choice models, and yet they apparently precede and are a necessary condition for rational thinking. More generally, the diversity of political psychology, noted earlier, would seem to preclude an easy incorporation of the one field into the other.

Conover and Searing use their study of citizenship in the United States and Great Britain to offer a fundamentally different set of recommendations for the.eld of political psychology. Not only do these recommendations eschew formalisation, they also challenge the very foundations of the kinds of empirical research that political psychologists conduct. The authors' recommendations draw heavily on interpretivist ideas.

The authors explicitly state their central presumption as follows: "there are no context-free thinking processes... and... political thinking... is therefore best studied in the cultural and political contexts of meaning in which it occurs." By implication, this means, first, that people cannot be studied in laboratories or via traditional surveys and, second, that the pursuit of universal laws is ill-directed. Conover and Searing readily acknowledge the radical nature of their premise, which departs markedly from the assumptions underlying their own past work.

The second implication, that social scientists should not strive for universal generalisations, is perhaps the more profound, for it runs counter to a widely accepted principle that motivates nearly all empirical research in political psychology and the study of public opinion more generally. What is it that Conover and Searing believe political psychologists should do? The single word that best captures their answer is "discover." Typically, researchers set forth hypotheses that they then verify. More importantly, in Conover and Searing's eyes, the researchers also select the concepts and language that motivate the hypotheses. Very much in the interpretivist tradition, the authors urge researchers to discover the categories that people use in their everyday lives rather than impose them. This entails, in turn, identifying the political culture within which people function and that shapes how they interpret and give meaning to the world around them. In short, political thinking is contextual, and the most directly relevant context is the political culture.

As an empirical matter, focus groups and in-depth interviews replace experiments and surveys. Conover and Searing discuss how they themselves are employing focus groups to identify the descriptive categories that people use when thinking about citizenship and their roles as citizens. Some of their focus groups consist of students and parents, others of eight adults plus a moderator who asks the participants a set of questions that are accompanied by specific probes. Other than that, the subjects simply talk with one another, using their own concepts, themes, and language. All of the sessions are recorded, and the researchers then use the transcripts to create a coding scheme. Thus the final coding scheme emerges from the participants' own words and the meanings they share.

Interestingly, the focus groups lend themselves to experimental manipulation that could define more precisely what the boundaries of a culture are. Suppose, for example, that one were to undertake some of the focus groups with uneducated rural residents and others with educated urban residents. Suppose, furthermore, that the two demographic groups use distinctly different concepts and language. To ascertain whether the different cultures are due to education or place of residence (or both), one would then conduct parallel focus groups in which one or the other demographic is held constant.

Comparative political psychology lends itself to connecting the psychology of individual thought to the institutions – family, school, media, voluntary associations – of a particular culture. Adopting the prescription for this case-oriented approach requires accepting the twin ideas that universal laws are not attainable and (thus) that social scientists should be engaged in discovery. Many political psychologists will reject this idea out of hand, pointing to its single case orientation as the very thing that is wrong with comparative politics. Why transport this weakness into one's own.eld? Nonetheless, the Conover and Searing prescriptions warrant a second thought. One of the principal criticisms of political psychology is that in reducing everything to mental processes it loses sight of politics and political institutions. The authors offer one way to help ensure that this does not happen. Moreover, theirs is simultaneously a call for comparative political psychology, which currently is notable for its absence.

One can be sure that many political psychologists will resist the argument that research findings are necessarily limited to a particular time and place. Nonetheless, Conover and Searing's chapter is intended to provoke debate about a goal of social science – generalisation – that most social scientists have long taken for granted. Such a discussion is particularly important to political psychology, where laboratory-based research has already raised questions about ecological validity. If laboratory findings cannot be generalised anyway – this is a point of debate, not a conclusion – then the call for a case-oriented political psychology at least warrants a hearing.

Krosnick raises some fundamental issues even for those who conduct more traditional modes of research, such as experiments and analysis of survey data. To make his case,

Krosnick focuses on attitude perception research, to which he has made substantial contributions. What he has to say, however, applies equally well to all topical areas within political psychology.

The first lesson to be learned, he argues, is that political psychologists rely far too heavily on cross-sectional data, even when those data are not appropriate for the task at hand. As he pointedly states, "nearly every causal hypothesis of significance in political psychology is tested initially using cross-sectional data." It is easy to understand why: cross-sectional data, either survey or experimental, are the most readily available. Using the projection hypothesis as his example, Krosnick thoroughly documents how researchers tried but failed to use cross-sectional data as a legitimate test of the hypothesis. Some, for example, employed models that extracted correlated measurement error. Others used instrumental variables to account for possible mutual causation between variables. Despite the creative and highly sophisticated statistical manoeuvres, however, no one fully succeeded in either eliminating alternative hypotheses or ascertaining causal direction. Krosnick's point is that no one could, since cross-sectional data simply are not appropriate for the kinds of tests the projection hypothesis calls for.

The second lesson goes hand in hand with the first not only do political psychologists typically begin with cross-sectional data, they also unthinkingly use linear measures of association. This characterisation, of course, applies to just about all areas of political science. Krosnick demonstrates, in a highly detailed and careful manner, precisely why linear measures do not always work in tests of the projection hypothesis. Specifically, he convincingly argues that "although measures of linear association are well suited to estimating the magnitude of positive projection onto liked candidates, assessing negative projection with a measure of linear association is wholly inappropriate." More generally, Krosnick shows how not using the right data or not using the right statistical analysis leads to contradictory and often wrong conclusions. His most important message is that researchers can avoid the problems of wasted time and wasted effort by carefully considering what it will take to test their hypothesis correctly. Linear statistical analysis of cross-sectional data might be the easiest route, but more often than not it is also the wrong one. Although Krosnick's discussion applies specifically to a single hypothesis, his discussion is required reading for everyone who conducts survey or experimental research. It sets a new standard for thinking through the relationship between theory and data analysis *before* the research begins.

Psychology–Politics Nexus

The single most consistent criticism of political psychology (and political behavior more generally) is its neglect of politics or, at best, its reduction of politics to a psychological phenomenon. For the most part, political psychologists have dismissed the criticism out of hand and pursued their research unabated.

Rahn, Sullivan, and Rudolph begin by documenting the dramatic growth in published research on political psychology during the last decade or so. Although publications on rational choice grew more rapidly, the increased influence of psychologically oriented research is undeniable, which renders questions about its value to the study of politics even more crucial.

Rahn, Sullivan, and Rudolph begin at the beginning: when critics deem political psychology to be insufficiently political, what do they mean by "insufficiently political?" They offer three plausible constructions of what the "naysayers" (their term) might have in mind and refute all three. The first possibility is that political psychologists do not pay enough attention to the role of elites in mass political behavior. This criticism, they argue, fails on the evidence. Numerous works have considered the connection between mass decision making, on the one hand, and elite discourse and behavior, on the other. To be sure, the authors continue, these studies typically incorporate elites as informational sources, not strictly as political actors, but the provision of political cues and messages is an integral part of the political process.

Second, perhaps the critics deem political psychology to be insufficiently political because it concentrates too heavily on the individual as the unit of analysis. After all, it is aggregate opinion, not individual choices and judgments, that elected officials see, hear, and pay attention to. True, admit Rahn, Sullivan, and Rudolph, but even students of macro politics draw on psychological models developed at the individual level, and "the question is not whether we will rely on psychological models to explain both individual and aggregate phenomena, but whether we will rely explicitly or implicitly, naively or with expertise, on such models." An even stronger assertion, which Rahn, Sullivan, and Rudolph do not make, is that the nature of collective opinion will never be fully understood without understanding the psychological processes underlying the individual decisions that get aggregated in democratic societies. Finally, Rahn, Sullivan, and Rudolph speculate that what critics really have in mind is a specific approach, best exemplified by the Stony Brook School.

This approach relies heavily on experimentation, some of it involving students, and delves deeply into psychic processes. Best known is the on-line processing model, which is described with nonpolitical sounding terms like "updating" and "judgment operators". Reductionism, Rahn, Sullivan, and Rudolph state, is an inherent feature of political psychology for which researchers need not apologise. Moreover, the study of the most extremely micro psychological processes might well have big payoffs for the more traditional concerns in political science. It just takes time and hard work to get there. Moving from the defensive to the offensive, Rahn, Sullivan, and Rudolph posit that just about everyone would identify the three most basic elements of politics as power, conflict, and governing. If political psychology is to be sufficiently political, therefore, it should have something to say about each. The authors then review literatures that, in toto, speak to all three elements of politics. In fact, they conclude, it is impossible to imagine how political scientists would study power, conflict, and governing without psychological concepts.

7

Theory Building in Political Research

Researchers adopting a case study design face a number of challenges in making their argument. If this warning applies to positivist researchers, then it applies even more so to interpretive researchers aiming at theory building through an inductive thinking process. Commonly, misunderstanding of the logic behind theoretical sampling as opposed to statistical sampling, and theoretical generalisation as opposed to statistical generalisation, can lead to unjustified criticisms of case study based papers. Simply adopting the criteria proposed to overcome the aforementioned criticisms of case study, construct validity, internal validity, external validity, and reliability may not be appropriate under an interpretive approach.

Interpretive researchers aiming at theory building need to adapt the case study guidelines. It is at this point that grounded theory, which over four decades has evolved from its positivist origins to an interpretive stance, intersects the case study design. An interpretive approach provides a deep insight into "the complex world of lived experience from the point of view of those who live it". Interpretive research assumes that reality is socially constructed and the researcher becomes the vehicle by which this reality is revealed. This approach is consistent with the construction of the social world characterised by interaction between the researcher and the participants. The researcher's interpretations play a key role in this kind of study bringing "such subjectivity to the fore, backed with quality arguments rather than statistical exactness".

Researchers' basic beliefs and worldviews lie behind their theoretical perspective. Guba and Lincoln talk about the need of researchers to make explicit both their ontological and epistemological assumptions before embarking on any research project. Answering the ontological question, "What is the form and nature of reality and, therefore, what is there that can be known about it" is the first step in the definition of how researchers can approach a research problem. The interpretive researcher's ontological assumption is that social reality is locally and specifically constructed "by humans through their action and interaction". Neuman affirms that "social reality is based on people's definition of it". From the previous assertions, it is apparent that interpretive researchers do not recognise the existence of an objective world. On the contrary, they see the world strongly bounded by particular time and specific context.

Therefore, the epistemological question, "What is the nature of the relationship between the knower or would-be knower and what can be known" must be answered in a consistent way with the ontological view. The interpretive researcher's epistemological assumption is that "findings are literally created as the investigation proceeds". Moreover, they explicitly recognise that "understanding social reality requires understanding how practices and meanings are formed and informed by the language and tacit norms shared by humans working towards some shared goal".

Case Study Design

The case study is "an empirical inquiry that investigates a contemporary phenomenon within its real-life context, especially when the boundaries between phenomenon and context are not clearly evident". Since the case study design is conducted in a natural setting with the intention to comprehend the nature of current processes in a previously little-studied area, it allows the researcher to grasp a holistic understanding of the phenomenon under investigation.

Instead of seeking answers to questions such as "how much" or "how many," case study design is useful for answering "how" and "why" questions. Orlikowski and Baroudi declare that, in the information systems research field, case study has demonstrated its appropriateness to generate a well-founded interpretive comprehension of human/technology interaction in the natural social setting. Consequently, from an interpretive perspective, the researcher can obtain sufficient material from the selected case(s) for subsequent analysis. Siggelkow's discussion on persuasiveness provides a compelling argument for the appropriateness of the case study design, even from a single case, to contribute to a deep understanding of the phenomenon being studied. After recounting the case of Phineas Gage, a nineteenth century American railroad construction foreman who survived and continued living for 12 years with a large hole in his head and major destruction to his brain's frontal lobes, after suffering an accident with an iron rod, Siggelkow argues that any criticism regarding the lack of representativeness and bias in choosing the sample should be rejected simply because of the value of such a rare incident to researchers, even for the most sceptical ones. Missing the opportunity to document, investigate, and explain this kind of phenomena might restrict our knowledge prospects.

Researchers, however, do not come across this kind of unique situation very often. Otherwise, we might be relieved of the burden of giving justification for conducting our research. However, it is not only a matter of justification.

Researchers using case studies have the extra burden of convincing their readers of the legitimacy of and drawing conceptual implications from their findings.

Interpretive Case Studies

It is recognised that case studies can follow either quantitative or qualitative approaches or any mix of both. Walsham goes one step further and highlights the value of interpretive case studies. In qualitative and interpretive case studies the researcher is directly involved in the process of data collection and analysis; however, in the latter, the researcher, through a close interaction with the actors, becomes a "passionate participant". Let's imagine a scenario at the beach in which a huge wave is approaching the shore. There is an excited surfer on top of the big wave and two scared children in a small inflatable boat right below the colossal wave. On the shore, a girl is admiring her boyfriend's dexterity and the petrified children's mother is watching the looming mass of water approaching the boat. On the adjacent cliff there is a relaxed monk meditating on the infiniteness of the universe, while enjoying the sea breeze and the sound of the sea. If we want to conduct research on what that wave means for beach-goers, our results will depend on who the respondent is. Interviewing one of the participants would give insights from that participant's perspective only, which may be insufficient, or even misleading, because their personal and intimate experiences with the wave are quite different from that of the others. If the interpretive researcher wants to create an integral and persuasive piece of research around this phenomenon, each participant's different perspectives should be included.

Case Study for Theory Building

So far, the conditions that make conducting an interpretive

case study a suitable option have been discussed. However, the issue of theory building has not been addressed yet. Eisenhardt and Eisenhardt and Graebner, from a positivistic perspective, affirm the usefulness of the case study approach for building theory, which is expected to be strongly attached to empirical reality. This claim is also applicable for interpretive researchers; the resultant theory should emerge from the data. This inductive thinking process is more than simply generating hypotheses, of which the alleged "goal is not to conclude a study but to develop ideas for further study". This assertion hints that theory building is subordinated to theory testing. It is not. Yet the case study design is suitable for assisting the researcher in the definition of the unit of analysis to be studied, the "bounded system... by time and place". This is the main contribution of case study design. However, interpretive researchers aiming at theory building may find case study guidelines insufficient, not only because of its reduced length (no more than three pages including a one-page exhibit), but also for the lack of a detailed procedure, cf. Yin's "explanation building".".

Grounded Theory

Grounded theory, "the discovery of theory from data", provides the opportunity for the researcher to theorise from evidence existing in the data. Through the correct application of this systemic process, the researcher can produce either substantive theory, which is generated from within a specific area of enquiryor formal theory, which is focused on conceptual entities. Although one can blend into the other, both substantive and formal theories are conclusive theories, they stand by themselves and are well grounded on the data.

The major advantage of grounded theory is its inductive, contextual, and processbased nature. These characteristics prove to be particularly useful for interpretive researchers. It does not mean that grounded theory is an approach exclusively appropriate for interpretive researchers. Indeed, it is a neutral analytical process that fits well within either the positivist or interpretive approach.

Theory Building Exercise

Researchers can take their previous knowledge into account, either from the existing literature or from their previous experience. It assists them in forming a theoretical basis for the approach to the issue to be studied. Although some researchers might erroneously assume that grounded theory implies going into the fieldwork without having reviewed the literature, it is a serious misunderstanding of the technique. Siggelkow explains that "our observations [are] guided and influenced by some initial hunches and frames of reference" and emphasizes that "an open mind is good; an empty mind is not." The literature review should not make the researchers simply impose previous theories when analysing the data instead of generating original categories; it informs the researchers' ideas and helps them to produce a preliminary theoretical framework that should be regarded as a "sensitising device", only which could be modified according to the actual findings; that might result in a serendipitous discovery. Interpretive researchers should not lose theoretical sensitivity.

Strauss and Corbin describe theoretical sensitivity as the "awareness of the subtleties of meaning of data" and elaborate that "one can come to a research situation with varying degrees of sensitivity depending upon previous reading and experience with or relevant to that area." Ultimately, the researcher has to evaluate the relevance of their preliminary theoretical framework vis-à-vis the actual findings. Urquhart and Fernández stress that the "preliminary literature review is conducted on the understanding that it is the generated theory that will determine the relevance of the literature,"", which must be revisited and contrasted to the emergent theory from the data.

Criteria for Interpretive Case Studies

The four criteria and their specific tactics suggested by Yin to establish the quality of case studies, and to address the criticisms cast on case studies, are insufficient for interpretive researchers aiming at theory building. Grounded theory provides better tools for this purpose.

Construct Validity

The case study design recognises the problematic nature of defining a correct "operational set of measures", but does not discard it at all. Instead, the case study design proposes using multiple sources of evidence in a triangulation fashion to contribute to addressing any potential problem: "data triangulation... essentially provide[s] multiple measures of the same phenomenon". As a replacement for the word triangulation, interpretive researchers should prefer, and feel more comfortable with, the term corroboration, which denotes "the act of strengthening [an argument] by additional evidence".

Eventually, participants reviewing the report (member checking) might disagree with the researcher's conclusions, but they ideally should not dispute the factual account presented by the researcher. Furthermore, considering on the previous argument of operational measures, we cannot assume that even in the situation where all the participants agree with the researcher's conclusions we have achieved construct validity. Participants' agreement is not an indicator of the appropriateness of the operational measures: Theoretical ; theoretical meaning is what confers construct validity. Instead of construct validity as is defined by the case study design, "theoretical sufficiency" should allow interpretive researchers to build up and work upon constructs which emerge from the problem under investigation.

Internal Validity

Pattern-matching, by which the researcher compares an observed pattern against a predicted one, is regarded as a valuable tactic for case study analysis, while explanation building is considered as a special type of pattern matching. However, as was explained earlier, in an attempt to achieve internal validity according to the precepts of the case study design, interpretive researchers may downgrade the essence of theory building. Once again, theory-building studies can produce conclusive theories and are useful not simply for the generation of hypotheses.

In addition, looking for rival explanations, other than the posed theoretical propositions, is a principle that is not exclusive for positivist researchers using the case study design. Searching alternative reasons for the occurrence of a phenomenon is a task that adds rigour to the piece of research. This is particularly true for interpretive researchers, who must keep an open mind when looking for any cause-effect relationship that can offer a plausible explanation of the phenomenon under study. This exercise adds to the credibility of the analysis and findings. The coding procedure assists interpretive researchers in establishing the causal relationships that ultimately produce theory. Notwithstanding the major divergence between Glaser and Strauss on the correct application of grounded theory, Glaser defends the emergent nature of selective coding, while Strauss proposes doing axial coding under the coding paradigm, they both concur on one point: coding is an essential step in grounded theory. During the coding procedure the researcher advances "creating and assigning categories, continue[s] by exploring connections between them, and conclude[s] by focusing on an integrating core". Indeed, interpretive researchers aiming at theory building strive to detect the existence of conceptual links among codes that generates theory, which in broad terms denotes "conjectures models, frameworks, or body of knowledge".

External Validity

External validity refers to the extent that the findings from a particular study are able to be generalised. However, the term should not be restricted to a statistical definition based on generalisations to the population from the sample. Lee and Baskerville convincingly argue that generalising implies going "from particular instances to general notions".". Interpretive researchers should include the temporal and spatial dimensions of the phenomenon under study in their analysis in order to produce theoretical generalisations. These dimensions can yield important explanations of past data in particular contexts that could be useful to other settings in the future.

Interpretive researchers may or may not agree with the suggestion to test the emergent theory from one case to a second one and so on under the "replication logic". This approach returns us to a hypothesis-testing exercise, and although a correct approach from a positivistic perspective, it diverts the interpretive researchers aiming at theory building away from their main objective. Either from one case or from multiple cases, they intend to produce theoretical generalisations instead of testing theory.

Reliability

Using a case study protocol and developing a case study database assists in organising data during the research process. However, from an interpretive approach, the purpose in doing so is not to guarantee that a second researcher will arrive at exactly the same conclusions as the first one might have; the second researcher can use the same data and give a different interpretation based on her/his own beliefs and abilities to grasp the essence of the emotional context; i.e., "empathetic or appreciative accuracy". Rather than presenting a completely different picture, the second researcher might discover a different angle to the problem at hand. Presenting the chain of evidence contributes to the trustworthiness of the analysis. Indeed, reliability for qualitative research "means producing results that can be trusted and establishing findings that are meaningful and interesting to the reader" instead of showing consistent results by repeated analyses.

8

Research Design Process

Before examining types of research designs it is important to be clear about the role and purpose of research design. We need to understand what research design is and what it is not. We need to know where design fits into the whole research process from framing a question to finally analysing and reporting data.

Descriptive Research

Although some people dismiss descriptive research as 'mere description', good description is fundamental to the research enterprise and it has added immeasurably to our knowledge of the shape and nature of our society. Descriptive research encompasses much government sponsored research including the population census, the collection of a wide range of social indicators and economic information such as household expenditure patterns, time use studies, employment and crime statistics and the like.

Descriptions can be concrete or abstract. A relatively concrete description might describe the ethnic mix of a community, the changing age profile of a population or the gender mix of a workplace. Alternatively the description might ask more abstract questions such as 'Is the level of social inequality increasing or declining?', 'How secular is society?' or 'How much poverty is there in this community?'

Accurate descriptions of the level of unemployment or poverty have historically played a key role in social policy reforms. By demonstrating the existence of social problems, competent description can challenge accepted assumptions about the way things are and can provoke action.

Good description provokes the 'why' questions of explanatory research. If we detect greater social polarisation over the last 20 years (i.e. the rich are getting richer and the poor are getting poorer) we are forced to ask 'Why is this happening?' But before asking 'why?' we must be sure about the fact and dimensions of the phenomenon of increasing polarisation. It is all very well to develop elaborate theories as to why society might be more polarised now than in the recent past, but if the basic premise is wrong (i.e. society is not becoming more polarised) then attempts to explain a non-existent phenomenon are silly. Of course description can degenerate to mindless fact gathering or what C.W. Mills called 'abstracted empiricism'. There are plenty of examples of unfocused surveys and case studies that report trivial information and fail to provoke any 'why' questions or provide any basis for generalisation. However, this is a function of inconsequential descriptions rather than an indictment of descriptive research itself.

Explanatory Research

Explanatory research focuses on why questions. For example, it is one thing to describe the crime rate in a country, to examine trends over time or to compare the rates in different countries. It is quite a different thing to develop explanations about why the crime rate is as high as it is, why some types of crime are increasing or why the rate is higher in some countries than in others.

The way in which researchers develop research designs is fundamentally affected by whether the research question is descriptive or explanatory. It affects what information is collected. For example, if we want to explain why some people are more likely to be apprehended and convicted of crimes we need to have hunches about why this is so. We may have many possibly incompatible hunches and will need to collect information that enables us to see which hunches work best empirically. Answering the 'why' questions involves developing causal explanations. Causal explanations argue that phenomenon Y (e.g. income level) is affected by factor X (e.g. gender). Some causal explanations will be simple while others will be more complex. For example, we might argue that there is a direct effect of gender on income (i.e. simple gender discrimination). We might argue for a causal chain, such as that gender affects choice of field of training which in turn affects occupational options, which are linked to opportunities for promotion, which in turn affect income level. Or we could posit a more complex model involving a number of interrelated causal chains.

Prediction, Correlation and Causation

People often confuse correlation with causation. Simply because one event follows another, or two factors co-vary, does not mean that one causes the other. The link between two events may be coincidental rather than causal.

There is a correlation between the number of fire engines at a fire and the amount of damage caused by the fire (the more fire engines the more damage). Is it therefore reasonable to conclude that the number of fire engines causes the amount of damage? Clearly the number of fire engines and the amount of damage will both be due to some third factor ± such as the seriousness of the fire.

Similarly, as the divorce rate changed over the twentieth century the crime rate increased a few years later. But this does not mean that divorce causes crime. Rather than divorce causing crime, divorce and crime rates might both be due to other social processes such as secularisation, greater individualism or poverty.

Students at fee paying private schools typically perform better in their final year of schooling than those at government funded schools. But this need not be because private schools produce better performance. It may be that attending a private school and better final-year performance are both the outcome of some other cause. Confusing causation with correlation also confuses prediction with causation and prediction with explanation. Where two events or characteristics are correlated we can predict one from the other. Knowing the type of school attended improves our capacity to predict academic achievement. But this does not mean that the school type affects academic achievement. Predicting performance on the basis of school type does not tell us why private school students do better. Good prediction does not depend on causal relationships. Nor does the ability to predict accurately demonstrate anything about causality.

Recognising that causation is more than correlation highlights a problem. While we can observe correlation we cannot observe cause. We have to infer cause. These inferences however are 'necessarily fallible... [they] are only indirectly linked to observables'. Because our inferences are fallible we must minimise the chances of incorrectly saying that a relationship is causal when in fact it is not. One of the fundamental purposes of research design in explanatory research is to avoid invalid inferences.

Deterministic and Probabilistic Concepts of Causation

There are two ways of thinking about causes:

deterministically and probabilistically. The smoker who denies that tobacco causes cancer because he smokes heavily but has not contracted cancer illustrates deterministic causation. Probabilistic causation is illustrated by health authorities who point to the increased chances of cancer among smokers. Deterministic causation is where variable X is said to cause Y if, and only if, X invariably produces Y. That is, when X is present then Y will 'necessarily, inevitably and infallibly' occur. This approach seeks to establish causal laws such as: whenever water is heated to 100 °C it always boils.

In reality laws are never this simple. They will always specify particular conditions under which that law operates. Indeed a great deal of scientific investigation involves specifying the conditions under which particular laws operate. Thus, we might say that at sea level heating pure water to 100 °C will always cause water to boil.

Alternatively, the law might be stated in the form of 'other things being equal' then X will always produce Y. A deterministic version of the relationship between race and income level would say that other things being equal (age, education, personality, experience etc.) then a white person will [always] earn a higher income than a black person. That is, race (X) causes income level (Y).

Stated like this the notion of deterministic causation in the social sciences sounds odd. It is hard to conceive of a characteristic or event that will invariably result in a given outcome even if a fairly tight set of conditions is specified. The complexity of human social behaviour and the subjective, meaningful and voluntaristic components of human behaviour mean that it will never be possible to arrive at causal statements of the type 'If X, and A and B, then Y will always follow.' Most causal thinking in the social sciences is probabilistic rather than deterministic. That is, we work at the level that a given factor increases (or decreases) the probability of a particular outcome, for example: being female increases the probability of working part time; race affects the probability of having a high status job.

We can improve probabilistic explanations by specifying conditions under which X is less likely and more likely to affect Y. But we will never achieve complete or deterministic explanations. Human behaviour is both willed and caused: there is a double-sided character to human social behaviour. People construct their social world and there are creative aspects to human action but this freedom and agency will always be constrained by the structures within which people live. Because behaviour is not simply determined we cannot achieve deterministic explanations. However, because behaviour is constrained we can achieve probabilistic explanations. We can say that a given factor will increase the likelihood of a given outcome but there will never be certainty about outcomes.

Despite the probabilistic nature of causal statements in the social sciences, much popular, ideological and political discourse translates these into deterministic statements. Findings about the causal effects of class, gender or ethnicity, for example, are often read as if these factors invariably and completely produce particular outcomes. One could be forgiven for thinking that social science has demonstrated that gender completely and invariably determines position in society, roles in families, values and ways of relating to other people.

Theory Testing and Theory Construction

Attempts to answer the 'why' questions in social science are theories. These theories vary in their complexity (how many variables and links), abstraction and scope. To understand the role of theory in empirical research it is useful to distinguish between two different styles of research: theory testing and theory building.

Theory building

Theory building is a process in which research begins with observations and uses inductive reasoning to derive a theory from these observations. These theories attempt to make sense of observations. Because the theory is produced after observations are made it is often called post factum theory or ex post facto theorising. This form of theory building entails asking whether the observation is a particular case of a more general factor, or how the observation fits into a pattern or a story. For example, Durkheim observed that the suicide rate was higher among Protestants than Catholics. But is religious affiliation a particular case of something more general? Of what more general phenomenon might it be an indicator? Are there other observations that shed light on this? He also observed that men were more suicidal than women, urban dwellers more than rural dwellers and the socially mobile more than the socially stable. He argued that the common factor behind all these observations was that those groups who were most suicidal were also less well socially integrated and experienced greater ambiguity about how to behave and what is right and wrong. He theorised that one of the explanations for suicidal behaviour was a sense of normlessness ± a disconnectedness of individuals from their social world. Of course, there may have been other ways of accounting for these observations but at least Durkheim's explanation was consistent with the facts.

Theory testing

In contrast, a theory testing approach begins with a theory and uses theory to guide which observations to make: it moves from the general to the particular. The observations should provide a test of the worth of the theory. Using deductive reasoning to derive a set of propositions from the theory does this. We need to develop these propositions so that if the theory is true then certain things should follow in the real world. We then assess whether these predictions are correct. If they are correct the theory is supported. If they do not hold up then the theory needs to be either rejected or modified.

For example, we may wish to test the theory that it is not divorce itself that affects the wellbeing of children but the level of conflict between parents. To test this idea we can make predictions about the wellbeing of children under different family conditions. For the simple theory that it is parental conflict rather than divorce that affects a child's wellbeing there are four basic 'conditions'. For each 'condition' the theory would make different predictions about the level of children's wellbeing that we can examine.

If the theory that it is parental conflict rather than parental divorce is correct the following propositions should be supported:

— *Proposition 1:* children in situations (a) and (b) would be equally well off That is, where parental conflict is low, children with divorced parents will do just as well as those whose parents are married.

— *Proposition 2:* children in situations (c) and (d) should be equally poorly off That is, children in conflictual couple families will do just as badly as children in post-divorce families where parents sustain high conflict.

— *Proposition 3*: children in situation (c) will do worse than those in situation (a) That is, those with married parents in high conflict will do worse than those who have married parents who are not in conflict.

— *Proposition 4:* children in situation (d) will do worse than those in situation (b) That is, those with divorced parents in high conflict will do worse than those who have divorced parents who are not in conflict.

— *Proposition 5:* children in situation (b) will do better than those in situation (c) That is, children with divorced parents who are not in conflict will do better than those with married parents who are in conflict.

— *Proposition 6:* children in situation (a) will do better than those in situation (d) That is, children with married parents who are not in conflict will do better than those with divorced parents who are in conflict.

No single proposition would provide a compelling test of the original theory. Indeed, taken on its own proposition 3, for example, would reveal nothing about the impact of divorce. However, taken as a package, the set of propositions provides a stronger test of the theory than any single proposition.

Although theory testing and theory building are often presented as alternative modes of research they should be part of one ongoing process. Typically, theory building will produce a plausible account or explanation of a set of observations. However, such explanations are frequently just one of a number of possible explanations that fit the data. While plausible they are not necessarily compelling. They require systematic testing where data are collected to specifically evaluate how well the explanation holds when subjected to a range of crucial tests.

What is Research Design

How is the term 'research design' to be used in this book? An analogy might help. When constructing a building there is no point ordering materials or setting critical dates for completion of project stages until we know what sort of building is being constructed. The first decision is whether we need a high rise office building, a factory for manufacturing machinery, a school, a residential home or an apartment block. Until this is done we cannot sketch a plan, obtain permits, work out a work schedule or order materials.

Similarly, social research needs a design or a structure before data collection or analysis can commence. A research design is not just a work plan. A work plan details what has to be done to complete the project but the work plan will flow from the project's research design. The function of a research design is to ensure that the evidence obtained enables us to answer the initial question as unambiguously as possible. Obtaining relevant evidence entails specifying the type of evidence needed to answer the research question, to test a theory, to evaluate a programme or to accurately describe some phenomenon. In other words, when designing research we need to ask: given this research question (or theory), what type of evidence is needed to answer the question (or test the theory) in a convincing way?

Research design 'deals with a logical problem and not a logistical problem'. Before a builder or architect can develop a work plan or order materials they must first establish the type of building required, its uses and the needs of the occupants. The work plan flows from this.

Too often researchers design questionnaires or begin interviewing far too early ± before thinking through what information they require to answer their research questions. Without attending to these research design matters at the beginning, the conclusions drawn will normally be weak and unconvincing and fail to answer the research question.

Design versus Method

Research design is different from the method by which data are collected. Many research methods texts confuse research designs with methods. It is not uncommon to see research design treated as a mode of data collection rather than as a logical structure of the inquiry. But there is nothing intrinsic about any research design that requires a particular method of data collection. Although cross-sectional surveys are frequently equated with questionnaires and case studies are often equated with participant observation, data for any design can be collected with any data collection method. How the data are collected is irrelevant to the logic of the design.

Failing to distinguish between design and method leads to poor evaluation of designs. Equating cross-sectional designs with questionnaires, or case studies with participant observation, means that the designs are often evaluated against the strengths and weaknesses of the method rather than their ability to draw relatively unambiguous conclusions or to select between rival plausible hypotheses.

Quantitative and Qualitative Research

Similarly, designs are often equated with qualitative and quantitative research methods. Social surveys and experiments are frequently viewed as prime examples of quantitative research and are evaluated against the strengths and weaknesses of statistical, quantitative research methods and analysis. Case studies, on the other hand, are often seen as prime examples of qualitative research ± which adopts an interpretive approach to data, studies 'things' within their context and considers the subjective meanings that people bring to their situation.

It is erroneous to equate a particular research design with either quantitative or qualitative methods. Yin, a respected authority on case study design, has stressed the irrelevance of the quantitative/ qualitative distinction for case studies. He points out that:

> a point of confusion... has been the unfortunate linking between the case study method and certain types of data collection ± for example those focusing on qualitative methods, ethnography, or participant observation. People have thought that the case study method required them to embrace these data collection methods... On the contrary,

> the method does not imply any particular form of data collection — which can be qualitative or quantitative.

Similarly, Marsh argues that quantitative surveys can provide information and explanations that are 'adequate at the level of meaning'. While recognising that survey research has not always been good at tapping the subjective dimension of behaviour, she argues that:

> Making sense of social action... is... hard and surveys have not traditionally been very good at it. The earliest survey researchers started a tradition... of bringing the meaning from outside, either by making use of the researcher's stock of plausible explanations... or by bringing it from subsidiary in-depth interviews sprinkling quotes... liberally on the raw correlations derived from the survey. Survey research became much more exciting... when it began including meaningful dimensions in the study design. [This has been done in] two ways, firstly [by] asking the actor either for her reasons directly, or to supply information about the central values in her life around which we may assume she is orienting her life. [This] involves collecting a sufficiently complete picture of the context in which an actor finds herself that a team of outsiders may read off the meaningful dimensions.

The need for research design stems from a sceptical approach to research and a view that scientific knowledge must always be provisional. The purpose of research design is to reduce the ambiguity of much research evidence.

We can always find some evidence consistent with almost any theory. However, we should be sceptical of the evidence, and rather than seeking evidence that is consistent with our theory we should seek evidence that provides a compelling test of the theory. There are two related strategies for doing this: eliminating rival explanations of the evidence and deliberately seeking evidence that could disprove the theory.

Plausible Rival Hypotheses

A fundamental strategy of social research involves evaluating 'plausible rival hypotheses'. We need to examine and evaluate alternative ways of explaining a particular phenomenon. This applies regardless of whether the data are quantitative or qualitative; regardless of the particular research design (experimental, cross-sectional, longitudinal or case study); and regardless of the method of data collection (e.g. observation, questionnaire). Our mindset needs to anticipate alternative ways of interpreting findings and to regard any interpretation of these findings as provisional ± subject to further testing.

The idea of evaluating plausible rival hypotheses can be illustrated using the example of the correlation between type of school attended and academic achievement. Many parents accept the causal proposition that attendance at fee paying private schools improves a child's academic performance. Schools themselves promote the same notion by prominently advertising their pass rates and comparing them with those of other schools or with national averages. By implication they propose a causal connection: 'Send your child to our school and they will pass (or get grades to gain entry into prestigious institutions, courses).' The data they provide are consistent with their proposition that these schools produce better results.

But these data are not compelling. There are at least three other ways of accounting for this correlation without accepting the causal link between school type and achievement.

There is the selectivity explanation: the more able students may be sent to fee paying private schools in the first place. There is the family resources explanation: parents who can afford to send their children to fee paying private schools can also afford other help (e.g. books, private tutoring, quiet study space, computers). It is this help rather than the type of school that produces the better performance of private school students. Finally, there is the family values explanation: parents who value education most are prepared to send their children to fee paying private schools and it is this family emphasis on education, not the schools themselves, that produces the better academic performance.

All these explanations are equally consistent with the observation that private school students do better than government school students. Without collecting further evidence we cannot choose between these explanations and therefore must remain open minded about which one makes most empirical sense. There might also be methodological explanations for the finding that private school students perform better academically. These methodological issues might undermine any argument that a causal connection exists. Are the results due to questionable ways of measuring achievement? From what range and number of schools were the data obtained? On how many cases are the conclusions based? Could the pattern simply be a function of chance? These are all possible alternative explanations for the finding that private school students perform better.

Good research design will anticipate competing explanations before collecting data so that relevant information for evaluating the relative merits of these competing explanations is obtained. In this example of schools and academic achievement, thinking about alternative plausible hypotheses beforehand would lead us to find out about the parents' financial resources, the study resources available in the home, the parents' and child's attitudes about education and the child's academic abilities before entering the school.

Fallacy of Affirming the Consequent

Although evidence may be consistent with an initial

proposition it might be equally consistent with a range of alternative propositions. Too often people do not even think of the alternative hypotheses and simply conclude that since the evidence is consistent with their theory then the theory is true. This form of reasoning commits the logical fallacy of affirming the consequent. This form of reasoning has the following logical structure:

— If A is true then B should follow.

— We observe B.

— Therefore A is true.

If we apply this logic to the type of school and achievement proposition, the logical structure of the school type and achievement argument becomes clearer.

Initial proposition

— Private schools produce better students than do government schools.

The test

— If A then B If private schools produce better students (A) then their students should get better final marks than those from government funded schools (B).

— B is true Private school students do achieve better final marks than government school students (observe B).

— Therefore A is true Therefore private schools do produce better students (A is true).

But, the better performance of private school students might also reflect the effect of other factors. The problem here is that any number of explanations may be correct and the evidence does not help rule out many of these. For the social scientist this level of indeterminacy is quite unsatisfactory. In effect we are only in a position to say:

— If A [or C, or D, or E, or F, or...] then B.
— We observe B.
— Therefore A [or C, or D, or E, or F, or...] is true.

Although explanation (A) is still in the running because it is consistent with the observations, we cannot say that it is the most plausible explanation. We need to test our proposition more thoroughly by evaluating the worth of the alternative propositions.

Falsification

Unfortunately some theories are closed systems in which any evidence can be interpreted as support for the theory. Such theories are said to be non-falsifiable. Many religions or belief systems can become closed systems whereby all evidence can be accommodated by the theory and nothing will change the mind of the true believer. Exchange theory is largely non-falsifiable. It assumes that we always maximise our gains and avoid costs. But we can see almost anything as a gain. Great sacrifices to care for a disabled relative can be interpreted as a gain (satisfaction of helping) rather than a loss (income, time for self etc.). We need to frame our propositions and define our terms in such a way that they are capable of being disproven.

Provisional Nature of Support for Theories

Even where the theory is corroborated and has survived attempts to disprove it, the theory remains provisional:

> falsificationism stresses the ambiguity of confirmation... corroboration gives only the comfort that the theory has been tested and survived the test, that even after the most impressive corroborations of predictions it has only achieved the status of 'not yet disconfirmed'. This... is far from the status of 'being true'.

There always may be an unthought-of explanation. We cannot anticipate or evaluate every possible explanation. The more alternative explanations that have been eliminated and the more we have tried to disprove our theory, the more confidence we will have in it, but we should avoid thinking that it is proven. However we can disprove a theory. The logic of this is:

— If theory A is true then B should follow.

— B does not follow.

— Therefore A is not true.

So long as B is a valid test of A the absence of B should make us reject or revise the theory. In reality, we would not reject a theory simply because a single fact or observation does not fit. Before rejecting a plausible theory we would require multiple disconfirmations using different measures, different samples and different methods of data collection and analysis.

9

Non-experimental Political Research

In contrast to experimental research, nonexperimental research involves variables that are not manipulated by the researcher and instead are studied as they exist. One reason for using nonexperimental research is that many variables of interest in social science cannot be manipulated because they are attribute variables, such as gender, socioeconomic status, learning style, or any other personal characteristic or trait. For example, a researcher cannot randomly place individuals into different groups based on gender or learning style because these are naturally existing attributes.

Another reason to use nonexperimental research is that, in some cases, it would be unethical to randomly assign individuals to different treatment conditions. A classic example of this is that one could not study the effects of smoking by randomly assigning individuals to either a smoking or a nonsmoking group for a given number of years. The only ethical way to investigate the potential effects of smoking would be to identify a group of smokers and a group of nonsmokers and compare them for differences in their current state of health. The researcher, however, would also need to take other variables into account, such as how long people had smoked, their gender, age, and general health level. To do so would be important because the researcher cannot take for granted that the groups are comparable in aspects other than smoking behavior. This is in contrast to experimental groups, which, due to the process of random assignment, start out equal in all respects except for the treatment condition in which they are placed. In nonexperimental research, groups based on different traits or on self-selection, such as being or not being a smoker, may differ for any number of reasons other than the variable under investigation. Therefore, in nonexperimental studies, one cannot be as certain as in experimental studies that outcome differences are due to the independent variable under investigation. The researcher needs to consider possible alternative explanations, to jointly analyse several variables, and to present conclusions without making definitive causal statements.

Variables and their Measurement

A variable is any characteristic or attribute that can differ across people or things; it can take on different values. Some variables are inherent traits, such as gender or height. Others may vary due to experimenter manipulation, such as treatment groups of drug versus placebo, or due to self-selection, such as attending a two- or a four-year college. In quantitative research, variables are measured in some way and those numerical values are then used in statistical analyses. The nature of variables is important because, to some extent, it dictates the way research questions are asked and which analysis is used.

One basic distinction is that variables can be either categorical or quantitative. Categorical variables are those that differ across two or more distinct categories. The researcher assigns arbitrary numbers to the categories, but the numbers have no interpretable numerical meaning. For example, for categories of the variable "employment status," we could assign the value "1" to employed full-time, "2" to employed part-time, and "3" to not employed. Additional examples of categorical variables that are individual traits are gender, ethnicity, and learning style; some that are self-selected are marital status, political party affiliation, and field of study.

Quantitative variables can be measured across a scale, their numeric values have meaning, and they can be subjected to arithmetic operations. The following are all examples of quantitative variables: age, height, weight, grade point average (GPA), job satisfaction, and motivation. There is an important distinction between the first three and the last three variables in this list. For such variables as age, height, and weight, zero is a meaningful value that indicates the absence of the characteristic being measured, as in something that is brand new or has no weight. The numbers have interpretable meaning. We know what five years or five feet means because there is no arbitrariness about these values or how to interpret them.

In contrast, zero is an arbitrary value for variables such as GPA, satisfaction, or motivation. A zero motivation score does not mean one has no motivation, but merely that one attained the lowest possible score for the particular instrument being used. GPA in most schools in the United States is given on a continuum from 0.0 to 4.0 but, for example, at the Massachusetts Institute of Technology (MIT), it goes from 0.0 to 5.0. The International Baccalaureate grades range from 1 to 7, based on a rubric developed from the standardised curriculum.

For another example, consider measurements for temperature. The freing point of water is represented as zero on a Celsius thermometer, but as 32 on a Fahrenheit thermometer. In neither case does a zero represent the absence of temperature. In each case, we understand what the numbers mean because specific interpretations have been assigned to them.

Interpretation of different grading schemes or thermometers is possible because of commonly understood unit descriptors. This is not so for such variables as job satisfaction or motivation, where scores are arbitrary and depend on the measurement instrument being used and how it has been designed. Typically, such scores are the sum or the average of responses to a set of items. The items may be statements, constructed so that all are related to the variable to be measured, and responses are often, but not always, on a Likert scale from 1 (strongly agree) to 5 (strongly disagree). The terms scale and index are often used to describe such sets of related items that, together, produce a score about some characteristic or phenomenon. For example, the Multidimensional Job Satisfaction Scale contains eleven different subscales, each a multi-item scale measure of a different dimension of job satisfaction. Another instrument, the Job Satisfaction Survey, consists of nine four-item subscales to assess employee attitudes about the job.

Exact interpretation of a scale score's value, or measure, for variables such as motivation or satisfaction is not important. What is important is to know that the higher the score, the more one has of the characteristic being measured and vice versa. One could, for example, examine whether males or females had higher levels of job satisfaction or if people with higher levels of job satisfaction also tended to have higher levels of motivation. To be confident of results, it is also important to know that the measures being used are reliable and have been validated.

Reliability relates to the consistency or dependability of a measure. Basically, if it is reliable, you can be confident that all the items that make up the measure are consistent with each other and that, if you were to use the measure again with the same individuals, they would be rated similarly to the first time. Validity relates to whether it is measuring what we intend it to measure, and represents the overarching quality of the measure. The purpose of using the measure is an important consideration in evaluating validity because it could be valid for one use but not for another. As a consumer of research, you should at least be aware of them and look for how research authors deal with these concepts. Do they describe their measures in detail and provide some indication of reliability and validity?

Defining Variables

Although some variables are inherently categorical or quantitative, others may be defined in either way. Imagine, for example, that you are interested in measuring the education level of a group of individuals. You could do this categorically, by defining education as "highest degree earned" and using five values representing none, high school, college, masters, or doctorate as different levels of education. Or, you could do this quantitatively by defining education as "number of years of schooling," where the resulting values would be meaningfully interpreted. This distinction is important if one is interested in studying the relationship between educational level and salary, a quantitative variable, because it relates to how the data might be analysed and how research questions would be phrased. Using the categorical definition, you could compare the median salary value across the five categories of "highest degree earned." The median represents the midpoint when all the salaries are listed from lowest to highest. One could then determine if there were any appreciable differences in salary across the five groups and whether more education (represented by having a higher degree) corresponded to higher salary.

Using the quantitative definition, you could graph the two variables in a scatter plot or compute a correlation coefficient (a measure of strength and direction of relationship for two variables) for the number of years of schooling and salary. The first would provide a visual representation of their relationship and the second a numerical one.

Classifying Nonexperimental Research

In the literature on experimental studies, there is agreement on the distinction between true- and quasi-experiments. Although both involve treatment manipulation, true-experiments use random assignment of subjects to groups and random assignment of groups to treatments. Quasi-experiments use preexisting intact groups, which are randomly assigned to treatment conditions.

For nonexperimental designs, there appears to be no consistent agreement on typology. In 1991, Elazar Pedhazur and Liora Schmelkin stated that "there is no consensus regarding the term used to refer to designs" which were presented in their chapter on nonexperimental designs. Two commonly used terms for nonexperimental studies are "correlational research" and "survey research." However, the term correlation relates more to an analysis strategy than to a research design and the term survey describes a method of gathering data that can be used in different types of research.

Ten years later, Burke Johnson came to the same conclusion. Based on a review of twenty-three leading methods textbooks in education and related fields (thirteen explicitly from education and the rest from anthropology, psychology, political science, and sociology), he found little consistency in how nonexperimental studies were classified. He discovered over two dozen different labels being used, sometimes with slight variations in the wording. The most frequently used labels in these texts were survey (twelve times), correlational (ten times), descriptive (eight times), and causal-comparative (five times).

Classification Based on Purpose

The categories of the first dimension for classifying nonexperimental studies, which are based on the main purpose of the study, are:

1. Descriptive nonexperimental research, in which the primary focus for the research is to describe some phenomenon or to document its characteristics. Such studies are needed in order to document the status quo or do a needs assessment in a given area of interest.
2. Predictive nonexperimental research, in which the primary focus for the research is to predict some variable of interest (typically called the criterion) using information from other variables (called predictors). The development of the proper set of predictors for a given variable is often the focus of such studies.
3. Explanatory nonexperimental research, in which the primary focus for the research is to explain how some phenomenon works or why it operates. The objective is often to test a theory about the phenomenon. Hypotheses derived from a given theoretical orientation are tested in attempts to validate the theory.

The three categories could be seen as answers to the question: Was the main purpose of the research to describe a phenomenon, to study how to predict some future event, or to understand how something operates or what drives it? To help explain these three categories, consider the use of exit interviews. Such interviews are often conducted by organisations with employees who leave or by school systems with departing teachers and graduating seniors. An exit interview study can be descriptive if the purpose is to collect data in order to get a comprehensive picture of reasons for employees leaving their organisation or school. These descriptions might be used to determine if people leave for reasons related to the organisation or for personal reasons. On the other hand, the study would be predictive if exit data were collected and then related to hiring data for the same individuals for the purpose of using the results to screen potential employees and hiring people who might be less likely to leave. Finally, the study would be explanatory if the data were analysed with the purpose of testing hypotheses about how personal characteristics might be related to employee or student feelings about their organisation or school.

A good example of a published descriptive study is the 39th Annual Phi Delta Kappa/Gallup Poll of the Public's Attitudes toward the Public Schools. Begun as an effort to inform educators, the annual survey now provides information that has policy implications. Although the accumulated database can be used to track changes in attitudes about Pre-K–12 schooling over a long period of time, the design for each yearly survey is purely descriptive in terms of its purpose. Results are a descriptive representation of how the general public feels about different aspects of public schools.

A study by Leslie Halpern and Thomas Dodson to develop a set of indicators that could identify women likely to report injuries related to intimate partner violence is an example of a predictive study. They tried to develop markers that could be used in hospital settings to make predictions about likelihood of intimate partner violence. They identified two variables as potential predictors: injury location and responses to a standard screening questionnaire. They included them, along with demographic variables, in developing a prediction model.

An explanatory study was done to examine the relationships among the variables of attachment, work satisfaction, marital satisfaction, parental satisfaction, and life satisfaction. This research was informed by attachment theory, which describes "parental attachment as a stable connection that provides a feeling of safety and security for the child". The researchers used five published instruments and present a very good description of reliability and validity for each one.

Classification Based on Time

The categories of the second dimension for classifying nonexperimental research, which refer to time, are:

1. Cross-sectional research, in which data are collected at one point in time, often in order to make comparisons across different types of respondents or participants.
2. Prospective or longitudinal research, in which data are collected on multiple occasions starting with the present and going into the future for comparisons across time. Data are sometimes collected on different groups over time in order to determine subsequent differences on some other variable.
3. Retrospective research, in which the researcher looks back in time using existing or available data to explain or explore an existing occurrence. This backwards examination may be an attempt to find potential explanations for current group differences.

These categories could be seen as answers to the question: Were the data collected at a single time point, across some time span into the future, or were already existing data explored? You could think of them as representing the past (retrospective), present (cross-sectional), and future (prospective) with respect to timing of data collection. As an example, suppose you were interested in assessing differences in college students' attitudes toward potential careers. In a cross-sectional study, you might take a random sample of first-year college students (freshmen) and fourth-year college students (seniors) and compare their attitudes. Your purpose might be to show that more mature students (seniors) view career options differently from less mature students (freshmen).

Now consider assessing career attitudes in a prospective study. There are actually three options: trend, cohort, or panel study. To distinguish among these three approaches, think of a four-year prospective study starting in 2008 with college freshmen. The population of interest is all college freshmen in the United States. In 2008, a random sample of college freshman is taken for all three approaches.

In the trend study, the same general population (college freshmen) is tracked. In the cohort study, the same specific population is tracked. In the panel study, the same individuals are tracked. One of the advantages of a panel study is that you can look for changes and not simply report on trends. A disadvantage is that you have to start with a fairly large sample due to attrition over time, particularly for a lengthy study.

An example of a retrospective study could be an examination of the educational background and experience of very successful teachers and less successful teachers. The idea is to look backward in time and examine what differences existed that might provide an explanation for the present differences in success. To the extent that such a study needed to depend on people's memories of relevant background information, it would be less accurate than if prior data were available for examination. For a published example, consider one question addressed by Michael Heise, which was whether key actors in a criminal court case view case complexity in the same way. The results of his cross-sectional comparison of three key actor groups (juries, attorneys, and judges) suggest that they do possess slightly different views on whether crimes are complex.

Examples of both prospective and retrospective research are based on the Nurses' Health Study, a large scale longitudinal study started in 1976 with a mailed survey of 121,700 female registered nurses between thirty and fifty-five years of age who lived in eleven states. Descriptive information about risk factors for major chronic diseases and related issues were gathered every two years. Although most of the information gathered was identical, new questions were added periodically. The Nurses' Health Study Web page contains a complete list of publications based on these data.

One such study was conducted by Francine Laden et al.. They examined the responses from the 87,497 women who answered newly included questions about lifetime use of electric blankets and heated waterbeds. Using data from the larger study, Laden and her colleagues focused their attention on the relationship between electric blanket use and breast cancer from both a prospective and retrospective view. This was done because electric blanket use is a source of electric and magnetic fields (EMFs) exposure, and EMF exposure had been hypothesized to increase the risk of breast cancer. The relevant year is 1992, when information about use of electric blankets and waterbeds was first documented. For the prospective part of their study, they considered women who had not been diagnosed with cancer as of 1992 and analysed the occurrence of breast cancer from 1992 to 1996 for groups according to electric blanket or waterbed usage. For the retrospective part, they used records from 1976 to 1992, considering only women who were cancer free in 1976. In the prospective part of the study "exposure to electric blankets and waterbed use was assessed prior to the occurrence of breast cancer," while in the retrospective analysis "exposure was ascertained after diagnosis".

Retrospective studies may be based on past records, as in the previous example, or on retrospective questions, that is, on questions about past behaviours or experiences.

Merely using already existing data, however, does not make it retrospective. The key distinction is the study's purpose. Are you looking backwards to discover some potential cause or explanation for a current situation, or are you using data from one point in time to predict data from a later time? Notice that Laden and her colleagues used preexisting data for both retrospective and prospective studies. For the prospective part, women who had not been diagnosed with cancer in 1992 were divided into groups based on whether they did or did not use electric blankets, and the groups were then compared with respect to breast cancer incidents by 1996. For the retrospective part, they divided the women into two groups based on whether they had or had not been diagnosed with cancer as of 1992 and then compared them in terms of reported prior use of electric blankets.

Combining Classification Dimensions

When used together, Johnson's two dimensions combine to form a 3 × 3 design for a total of nine distinct categories that may be used to describe nonexperimental research. Examples of all nine may be found in the National Education Longitudinal Study of 1988 (NELS:88), which was a large-scale data collection effort. A nationally representative sample of eighth graders were first surveyed in 1988, with subsequent follow-up surveys every two years until 1994, and then once again in 2000. The National Center for Education Statistics' Web page describes this study, and also provides an annotated bibliography of research done using the various data sets. Depending on which data were selected for each study and the study purpose, different NELS:88 studies might be classified using all nine of the purpose by time frame classifications.

Type 1—Descriptive retrospective. Using retrospective chart review, Anne Marie Higley and Karen Morin (2004) described the behavior of infants whose mothers had a drug history. Their findings supported the use of an assessment tool to guide parents in providing a supportive care environment to help infants recover.

Type 2—Descriptive cross-sectional. This study was discussed earlier as an example of a cross-sectional study. It is descriptive because the goal was to document the extent to which juries, attorneys, and judges held similar or different views about a case. The results have implications for legal reform efforts.

Type 3—Descriptive prospective. This was an investigation of the stability of test anxiety measures over time and testing formats, with data collected at three time points in an academic semester, therefore making it prospective. The purpose for the description was to determine if test anxiety was a stable condition or if it is necessary to include a test anxiety measure with every test in a longitudinal study. Results indicated that it is not necessary to measure anxiety with every test; it is only necessary to measure anxiety in one test-taking situation.

Type 4—Predictive retrospective and Type 6—Predictive prospective. The two parts of this study were described earlier as examples of retrospective and prospective studies. Both parts were predictive in nature, using a backward and a forward perspective to determine the extent to which electric blanket and waterbed use could be used to predict breast cancer. Although results did not exclude small risks, neither analysis supported an association between breast cancer risk and use of electric blankets and waterbeds.

Type 5—Predictive cross-sectional. In this study, discussed as an example of a predictive study, a one-time data collection was used. The authors' aim was to develop and validate a predictive model. They subdivided their sample, using one group to develop their model and the second group to validate, or test it. Their work produced a predictive and validated model of three components: risk of self-report of intimate partner violence related injury, age, and race. The researchers then hypothesized that these three variables could be used to develop a protocol to assist in the early diagnosis of intimate partner violence in an emergency department and outpatient clinical setting.

Type 7—Explanatory retrospective. This study was explanatory because a goal was to further previous work on giftedness and knowledge and understanding of several related variables. The data came from the High School and Beyond database, a longitudinal study with baseline information on 14,825 students who were high school sophomores in 1980. The data for this study included the base year and the third follow-up survey, four years later, after graduation. The data set "allowed for more comparisons than could reasonably be included in a single study. Variables were chosen that would either serve to replicate previous findings or expand psychological and behavioral profiles of gifted male and female students into more detail". A retrospective conclusion was that educational attain-ment differences of gifted males and females had their origins in the early high school years.

Type 8—Explanatory cross-sectional. Already discussed as an example of an explanatory study, this study was based on data from the fifteenth annual survey of a longitudinal study that started in 1988 with 1,724 participants. About 1,200 participants were lost in the first three years. Only 108 participants were left for this study, which shows the dramatic attrition that can happen in a longitudinal study. Although the data were from a longitudinal study, these authors only used the fifteenth year's data, thereby making it cross-sectional.

Type 9—Explanatory prospective. The authors suggested that "Assessing the predictive validity of an interest inventory is essentially answering the question, 'Do early interest scores match one's future occupation?'" (Rottinghaus et al., 2007, p. 7). To answer this question, they did a thirty-year follow-up of 107 former high school juniors and seniors whose interests were assessed in 1975. The first author had collected the initial data. Their results extend research on vocational interests, indicating that interests were fairly stable even after such a long time span.

Causal Explanations and Nonexperimental Studies

Using Johnson's classification system, many nonexperimental studies are either descriptive or predictive. For those, the notion of causation is not relevant. However, a goal for many explanatory nonexperimental research studies is to explore potentially causal relationships. A causal relationship is one in which a given action is likely to produce a particular result.

The terms independent and dependent refer to the different roles variables play in experimental studies. If a causal relationship exists, then the outcome depends on, or is a direct result of, the nature of the assigned independent treatment condition. Strictly speaking, these terms are not applicable in nonexperimental research, although they are often used. The more appropriate terms in nonexperimental studies are criterion and predictor variables, criterion being the presumed outcome of one or more predictor variables. When the intent is to use nonexperimental research to study potential cause-and-effect relationships where experimentation is not possible, the concept of IV and DV may still be of interest, but conclusions about causation that can be made from nonexperimental studies are weaker than those that can be made from true-experimental studies. Additionally, great care needs to be taken to assure that nothing essential has been overlooked.

As explained earlier, the distinction is often made between nonexperimental studies that involve both categorical and quantitative variables and those that involve only quantitative variables. Considering only two variables for the sake of simplicity, an example of the first type of study is a comparison of gender differences in mathematics achievement in high school. Gender, with male and female as the two categories, is considered the independent variable and some mathematics achievement score is the measured dependent variable. Examples where both variables are quantitative might be an examination of the relationship between test scores and time spent studying, or between scores on some measure of motivation and scores on an achievement test. Examples like these, of very simple cases involving only two variables, are neither very interesting nor very informative. Additional variables could be included in order to examine more complex relationships.

No matter which type of design or which type of variable is used, evidence of a relationships would not be convincing evidence of causality. Recall the example described earlier about investigating the relationship between education level and salary and the two ways that education level could be measured. Regardless of whether education level was construed as categorical (highest degree earned) or as quantitative (number of years of schooling), it should not be concluded that one's educational level caused or produced a different level of salary. If dramatic differences across the five groups with different degrees were found such that those with higher education had higher median salaries, all that can be concluded is that there was a relationship between educational level and salary. This same conclusion would be possible if results indicated a strong positive correlation between years of schooling and salary: that people with fewer years of school tended to have low salaries and people with more years of school tended to have high salaries. The scatter plot for a negative relationship would go from the upper left corner to the lower right corner, indicating that low scores on one variable tended to go with high scores on the other variable.

The differences in the wording of the research questions in the previous two cases reflect the nature of the variables used (categorical or quantitative). They would require different analysis strategies, either to test if the median values did differ more than you might expect by chance, or to determine the strength and direction of the relationship. Differences in wording or analysis do not, however, reflect any difference in the nature of the relationship between the variables. Explanatory nonexperimental research articles often have conclusions phrased in causal language.

Requirements for Causality

There are three conditions necessary in order to be able to argue that some variable X (the presumed independent) causes another variable Y (the presumed dependent).

1. The two variables X and Y must be related. If they are not related, it is impossible for one to cause the other. For nonexperimental research, that means that it must be demonstrated that differences in X are associated with differences in Y.
2. Changes in X must happen before observed changes in Y. This is always the case when X is a manipulated treatment variable in an experiment. But establishing that a cause happened before an effect needs to be documented in some way or logically explained in nonexperimental studies. This is impossible to do when the data are cross-sectional and collected simultaneously.
3. There is no possible alternative explanation for the relationship between X and Y. That is, there is no plausible third variable that might explain the observed

relationship between X and Y, possibly having caused both of them.

In nonexperimental studies, the first requirement can be established easily with correlational analyses. The second could also be established if longitudinal data are used so that predictor variables are measured before the criterion. The third requirement is more difficult to demonstrate. To do so requires a thorough knowledge of the literature and the underlying theory or theories governing the topic being investigated, logical arguments, plus testing and ruling out of alternative possibilities.

The fact that two variables are related does not inform us of which one influences the other. There are at least three reasons why two variables could be related and it is not possible to know from the correlation which one is the correct reality. Three potential explanations are: (1) that X causes or influences Y, (2) that Y causes or influences X, or (3) that Z, a third variable, causes both X and Y. Consider the following headline: "Migraines plague the poor more than the rich." It could be argued that the stresses of living in poverty and other poverty-related conditions could trigger migraine headaches. It could also be argued that migraines cause one to miss work and eventually lose employment, thereby inducing poverty for a subset of individuals prone to migraines. Which is the correct interpretation? It is impossible to tell.

Although there is no formal way to prove causation in nonexperimental research, it may be possible to suggest it. This is done through careful consideration, by referring to the three conditions for cause, by presenting logical arguments, and by testing likely alternatives in order to make a case for the likely conclusion of a causal relationship. One must be careful, however, not to phrase conclusions as proof of causation.

Ruling Out Alternative Hypotheses

To demonstrate the process for ruling out alternative hypotheses, we will use a medical example. Consider the process a doctor goes through in diagnosing a new patient's illness. First, the doctor considers the symptoms. The list of symptoms is used to select potential problems with similar symptoms and to rule out problems with different symptoms. Tests are ordered to confirm the most likely diagnosis and remedies are tried. If the test results are negative or the remedies do not work, then the original diagnosis is discarded, and other possible diagnoses are considered and tested. How does this process relate to research? The first step is matching observations (the reported symptoms) to theory (known symptoms for an illness). The second step is to test a hunch or tentative hypothesis (initial diagnosis) and rule out alternative hypotheses (other potential diagnoses). The process continues until a reasonable conclusion is reached. The analogy breaks down because, ideally, the correct diagnosis is made and the patient is cured, although results are never as conclusive in nonexperimental studies.

Given a theory that is driving the research, how does one rule out potential alternative hypotheses? One way is to consider all likely confounding or lurking variables. In an experimental study, two variables are confounded when their effects on a dependent variable cannot be distinguished. The following example, although purely correlational, should clarify the concept of confounding or lurking variables.

One would expect that grades and standardised tests, such as SAT scores, would be related more to each other than they would to socioeconomic status (SES). In many studies, however, SES and SAT appear to have a much stronger relationship than do grades and SAT. Rebecca Zwick and Jennifer Green explored reasons for such results with data from a random sample of 98,391 students from

7,330 high schools. They performed two different analyses. In the first analysis, they found the correlation for grades and SAT for the entire sample and, in the second analysis, they did so for each school individually and then averaged the school-level results to get one overall measure of relationship. The second analysis produced a much stronger relationship between grades and SAT scores than did the first analysis. This is because the first analysis ignored the fact that there are school-level differences in SES as well as other variables.

Analysis and Interpretation in Nonexperimental Studies

Data analyses in nonexperimental studies depend on both the goal for the study and the nature of the variables in the data set. Almost any analysis may be possible and a useful presentation is not reasonable here. There are ample books and sources for details about statistical methods and their use.

You need to be aware of the basic distinction between descriptive and inferential statistics. Descriptive statistics involve summarising and describing quantitative information in meaningful ways. For example, a mean, or arithmetic average, is a statistic used to describe a central value for a set of numbers. Inferential statistics are used to make conclusions beyond the data collected and to test hypotheses. Statistical tests are used to make conclusions about populations based on results from random samples or to determine the probability that results are not due to random chance.

Interpretation of results in nonexperimental studies should be consistent with the nature of the work, which is based on nonmanipulated variables. Therefore, conclusions about cause and effect are not appropriate in any nonexperimental study. As you read empirical articles, you should be attuned to how conclusions are discussed and be wary of causal language. Robinson, Levin, Thomas, Pituch, and Vaughn reviewed 274 empirical articles in five teaching-and-learning research journals in 1994 and 2004. They recorded causal and noncausal language use in abstracts and discussion sections. Their two main conclusions were: (1) experimental articles in teaching-and-learning declined in the ten-year span, and (2) on average, the use of causal conclusions made in nonexperimental and qualitative studies increased. They conclude by saying that "as journal readers, we have an obligation to search an article for information about how the data were collected so we are not unduly influenced by unwarranted conclusions".

10

The Research Process

Until the sixteenth century, human inquiry was primarily based on introspection. The way to know things was to turn inward and use logic to seek the truth. This paradigm had endured for a millennium and was a well-established conceptual framework for understanding the world. The seeker of knowledge was an integral part of the inquiry process.

A profound change occurred during the sixteenth and seventeenth centuries. Copernicus, Kepler, Galileo, Descartes, Bacon, Newton, and Locke presented new ways of examining nature. Our method of understanding the world came to rely on measurement and quantification. Mathematics replaced introspection as the key to supreme truths. The *Scientific Revolution* was born.

Objectivity became a critical component of the new scientific method. The investigator was an observer, rather than a participant in the inquiry process. A mechanistic view of the universe evolved. We believed that we could understand the whole by performing an examination of the individual parts. Experimentation and deduction became the tools of the scholar. For two hundred years, the new paradigm slowly evolved to become part of the reality framework of society. The *Age of Enlightenment* had arrived. Scientific research methodology was very successful at explaining natural phenomena. It provided a systematic way of knowing. Western philosophers embraced this new structure of inquiry. Eastern philosophy continued to stress the importance of the one seeking knowledge. By the beginning of the twentieth century, a complete schism had occurred. Western and Eastern philosophies were mutually exclusive and incompatible.

Then something remarkable happened. Einstein's proposed that the observer was not separate from the phenomena being studied. Indeed, his theory of relativity actually stressed the role of the observer. Quantum mechanics carried this a step further and stated that the act of observation could change the thing being observed. The researcher was not simply an observer, but in fact, was an integral part of the process. In physics, Western and Eastern philosophies have met. This idea has not been incorporated into the standard social science research model, and today's social science community see themselves as objective observers of the phenomena being studied. However, "it is an established principle of measurement that instruments react with the things they measure." The concept of *instrument reactivity* states that an instrument itself can disturb the thing being measured.

Problem Recognition & Definition

All research begins with a question. Intellectual curiosity is often the foundation for scholarly inquiry. Some questions are not testable. The classic philosophical example is to ask, "How many angels can dance on the head of a pin?" While the question might elicit profound and thoughtful revelations, it clearly cannot be tested with an empirical experiment. Prior to Descartes, this is precisely the kind of question that would engage the minds of learned men. Their answers came from within. The modern scientific method precludes asking questions that cannot be empirically tested. If the angels cannot be observed or detected, the question is considered inappropriate for scholarly research.

A paradigm is maintained as much by the process of formulating questions as it is by the answers to those questions. By excluding certain types of questions, we limit the scope of our thinking. It is interesting to note, however, that modern physicists have began to ask the same kinds of questions posed by the Eastern philosophers. "Does a tree falling in the forest make a sound if nobody is there to hear it?" This seemingly trivial question is at the heart of the observer/observed dichotomy. In fact, quantum mechanics predicts that this kind of question cannot be answered with complete certainty. It is the beginning of a new paradigm.

Defining the goals and objectives of a research project is one of the most important steps in the research process. Clearly stated goals keep a research project focused. The process of goal definition usually begins by writing down the broad and general goals of the study. As the process continues, the goals become more clearly defined and the research issues are narrowed.

Exploratory research (e.g., literature reviews, talking to people, and focus groups) goes hand-in-hand with the goal clarification process. The literature review is especially important because it obviates the need to *reinvent the wheel* for every new research question. More importantly, it gives researchers the opportunity to build on each others work.

The research question itself can be stated as a hypothesis. A hypothesis is simply the investigator's belief about a problem. Typically, a researcher formulates an opinion during the literature review process. The process of reviewing other scholar's work often clarifies the theoretical issues associated with the research question. It also can help to elucidate the significance of the issues to the research community.

The hypothesis is converted into a null hypothesis in order to make it testable. "The only way to test a hypothesis is to eliminate alternatives of the hypothesis." Statistical techniques will enable us to reject a null hypothesis, but they do not provide us with a way to accept a hypothesis. Therefore, all hypothesis testing is indirect.

CREATING THE RESEARCH DESIGN

Defining a research problem provides a format for further investigation. A well-defined problem points to a method of investigation. There is no one best method of research for all situations. Rather, there are a wide variety of techniques for the researcher to choose from. Often, the selection of a technique involves a series of trade-offs. For example, there is often a trade-off between cost and the quality of information obtained. Time constraints sometimes force a trade-off with the overall research design. Budget and time constraints must always be considered as part of the design process.

Many authors have categorised research design as either *descriptive* or *causal*. Descriptive studies are meant to answer the questions of who, what, where, when and how. Causal studies are undertaken to determine how one variable affects another. McDaniel and Gates state that the two characteristics that define causality are *temporal sequence* and *concomitant variation*.

The word *causal* may be a misnomer. The mere existence of a temporal relationship between two variables does not prove or even imply that A causes B. It is never possible to prove causality. At best, we can theorise about causality based on the relationship between two or more variables, however, this is prone to misinterpretation. Personal bias can lead to totally erroneous statements. For example, Blacks often score lower on I.Q. scores than their White counterparts. It would be irresponsible to conclude that ethnicity causes high or low I.Q. scores. In social science research, making false assumptions about causality can delude the researcher into ignoring other (more important) variables.

There are three basic methods of research: 1) survey, 2) observation, and 3) experiment. Each method has its advantages and disadvantages. The *survey* is the most common method of gathering information in the social sciences. It can be a face-to-face interview, telephone, or mail survey. A personal interview is one of the best methods obtaining personal, detailed, or in-depth information. It usually involves a lengthy questionnaire that the interviewer fills out while asking questions. It allows for extensive probing by the interviewer and gives respondents the ability to elaborate their answers. Telephone interviews are similar to face-to-face interviews. They are more efficient in terms of time and cost, however, they are limited in the amount of in-depth probing that can be accomplished, and the amount of time that can be allocated to the interview. A mail survey is generally the most cost effective interview method. The researcher can obtain opinions, but trying to meaningfully probe opinions is very difficult.

Observation research monitors respondents' actions without directly interacting with them. It has been used for many years by A.C. Nielsen to monitor television viewing habits. Psychologists often use one-way mirrors to study behavior. Social scientists often study societal and group behaviors by simply observing them. The fastest growing form of observation research has been made possible by the bar code scanners at cash registers, where purchasing habits of consumers can now be automatically monitored and summarised.

In an *experiment*, the investigator changes one or more variables over the course of the research. When all other variables are held constant (except the one being manipulated), changes in the dependent variable can be explained by the change in the independent variable. It is usually very difficult to control all the variables in the environment. Therefore, experiments are generally restricted to laboratory models where the investigator has more control over all the variables.

SAMPLING

It is incumbent on the researcher to clearly define the target population. There are no strict rules to follow, and the researcher must rely on logic and judgment. The population is defined in keeping with the objectives of the study.

Sometimes, the entire population will be sufficiently small, and the researcher can include the entire population in the study. This type of research is called a *census* study because data is gathered on every member of the population.

Usually, the population is too large for the researcher to attempt to survey all of its members. A small, but carefully chosen *sample* can be used to represent the population. The sample reflects the characteristics of the population from which it is drawn.

Sampling methods are classified as either *probability* or *nonprobability*. In probability samples, each member of the population has a known probability of being selected. Probability methods include random sampling, systematic sampling, and stratified sampling. In nonprobability sampling, members are selected from the population in some nonrandom manner. These include convenience sampling, judgment sampling, quota sampling, and snowball sampling. The other common form of nonprobability sampling occurs by accident when the researcher inadvertently introduces nonrandomness into the sample selection process. The advantage of probability sampling is that *sampling error* can be calculated. Sampling error is the degree to which a sample might differ from the population. When inferring to the population, results are reported plus or minus the sampling error. In nonprobability sampling, the degree to which the sample differs from the population remains unknown.

Random sampling is the purest form of probability sampling. Each member of the population has an equal chance of being selected. When there are very large populations, it is often difficult or impossible to identify every member of the population, so the pool of available subjects becomes biased. Random sampling is frequently used to select a specified number of records from a computer file.

Systematic sampling is often used instead of random sampling. It is also called an *Nth name selection* technique. After the required sample size has been calculated, every Nth record is selected from a list of population members. As long as the list does not contain any hidden order, this sampling method is as good as the random sampling method. Its only advantage over the random sampling technique is simplicity.

Stratified sampling is commonly used probability method that is superior to random sampling because it reduces sampling error. A stratum is a subset of the population that share at least one common characteristic. The researcher first identifies the relevant stratums and their actual representation in the population. Random sampling is then used to select subjects for each stratum until the number of subjects in that stratum is proportional to its frequency in the population.

Convenience sampling is used in exploratory research where the researcher is interested in getting an inexpensive approximation of the truth. As the name implies, the sample is selected because they are convenient. This nonprobability method is often used during preliminary research efforts to get a gross estimate of the results, without incurring the cost or time required to select a random sample.

Judgment sampling is a common nonprobability method. The researcher selects the sample based on judgment. This is usually and extension of convenience sampling. For example, a researcher may decide to draw the entire sample from one "representative" city, even though the population includes all cities. When using this method, the researcher must be confident that the chosen sample is truly representative of the entire population.

Quota sampling is the nonprobability equivalent of stratified sampling. Like stratified sampling, the researcher first identifies the stratums and their proportions as they are represented in the population. Then convenience or judgment sampling is used to select the required number of subjects from each stratum. This differs from stratified sampling, where the stratums are filled by random sampling.

Snowball sampling is a special nonprobability method used when the desired sample characteristic is rare. It may be extremely difficult or cost prohibitive to locate respondents in these situations. Snowball sampling relies on referrals from initial subjects to generate additional subjects. While this technique can dramatically lower search costs, it comes at the expense of introducing bias because the technique itself reduces the likelihood that the sample will represent a good cross section from the population.

Data Collection

There are very few hard and fast rules to define the task of data collection. Each research project uses a data collection technique appropriate to the particular research methodology. The two primary goals for both quantitative and qualitative studies are to maximise response and maximise accuracy. When using an outside data collection service, researchers often *validate* the data collection process by contacting a percentage of the respondents to verify that they were actually interviewed. Data *editing* and *cleaning* involves the process of checking for inadvertent errors in the data. This usually entails using a computer to check for out-of-bounds data.

Quantitative studies employ deductive logic, where the researcher starts with a hypothesis, and then collects data to confirm or refute the hypothesis. *Qualitative* studies use inductive logic, where the researcher first designs a study and then develops a hypothesis or theory to explain the results of the analysis.

Quantitative analysis is generally fast and inexpensive. A wide assortment of statistical techniques are available to the researcher. Computer software is readily available to provide both basic and advanced multivariate analysis. The researcher simply follows the preplanned analysis process, without making subjective decisions about the data. For this reason, quantitative studies are usually easier to execute than qualitative studies.

Qualitative studies nearly always involve in-person interviews, and are therefore very labor intensive and costly. They rely heavily on a researcher's ability to exclude personal biases. The interpretation of qualitative data is often highly subjective, and different researchers can reach different conclusions from the same data. However, the goal of qualitative research is to develop a hypothesis—not to test one. Qualitative studies have merit in that they provide broad, general theories that can be examined in future research.

Data Analysis

Modern computer software has made the analysis of quantitative data a very easy task. It is no longer incumbent on the researcher to know the formulas needed to calculate the desired statistics. However, this does not obviate the need for the researcher to understand the theoretical and conceptual foundations of the statistical techniques. Each statistical technique has its own assumptions and limitations. Considering the ease in which computers can calculate complex statistical problems, the danger is that the researcher might be unaware of the assumptions and limitations in the use and interpretation of a statistic.

Reporting the Results

The most important consideration in preparing any research report is the nature of the audience. The purpose is to communicate information, and therefore, the report should be prepared specifically for the readers of the report. Sometimes the format for the report will be defined for the researcher (e.g., a dissertation), while other times, the researcher will have complete latitude regarding the structure of the report. At a minimum, the report should contain an abstract, problem statement, methods section, results section, discussion of the results, and a list of references.

Validity and Reliability

Validity refers to the accuracy or truthfulness of a measurement. Are we measuring what we think we are? "Validity itself is a simple concept, but the determination of the validity of a measure is elusive".

Face validity is based solely on the judgment of the researcher. Each question is scrutinised and modified until the researcher is satisfied that it is an accurate measure of the desired construct. The determination of face validity is based on the subjective opinion of the researcher.

Content validity is similar to face validity in that it relies on the judgment of the researcher. However, where face validity only evaluates the individual items on an instrument, content validity goes further in that it attempts to determine if an instrument provides adequate coverage of a topic. Expert opinions, literature searches, and pretest open-ended questions help to establish content validity.

Criterion-related validity can be either predictive or concurrent. When a dependent/independent relationship has been established between two or more variables, criterion-related validity can be assessed. A mathematical model is developed to be able to predict the dependent variable from the independent variable(s). *Predictive validity* refers to the ability of an independent variable (or group of variables) to predict a future value of the dependent variable. *Concurrent validity* is concerned with the relationship between two or more variables at the same point in time.

Construct validity refers to the theoretical foundations underlying a particular scale or measurement. It looks at the underlying theories or constructs that explain a phenomena. This is also quite subjective and depends heavily on the understanding, opinions, and biases of the researcher.

Reliability is synonymous with repeatability. A measurement that yields consistent results over time is said to be reliable. When a measurement is prone to random error, it lacks reliability. The reliability of an instrument places an upper limit on its validity. A measurement that lacks reliability will necessarily be invalid. There are three basic methods to test reliability : test-retest, equivalent form, and internal consistency.

A *test-retest* measure of reliability can be obtained by administering the same instrument to the same group of people at two different points in time. The degree to which both administrations are in agreement is a measure of the reliability of the instrument. This technique for assessing reliability suffers two possible drawbacks. First, a person may have changed between the first and second measurement. Second, the initial administration of an instrument might in itself induce a person to answer differently on the second administration.

The second method of determining reliability is called the *equivalent-form* technique. The researcher creates two different instruments designed to measure identical constructs. The degree of correlation between the instruments is a measure of equivalent-form reliability. The difficulty in using this method is that it may be very difficult (and/or prohibitively expensive) to create a totally equivalent instrument.

The most popular methods of estimating reliability use measures of *internal consistency*. When an instrument includes a series of questions designed to examine the same construct, the questions can be arbitrarily split into two groups. The correlation between the two subsets of questions is called the *split-half* reliability. The problem is that this measure of reliability changes depending on how the questions are split. A better statistic, known as Chronbach's alpha, is based on the mean (absolute value) interitem correlation for all possible variable pairs. It provides a conservative estimate of reliability, and generally represents "the lower bound to the reliability of an unweighted scale of items". For dichotomous nominal data, the KR-20 is used instead of Chronbach's alpha.

Variability and Error

Most research is an attempt to understand and explain *variability*. When a measurement lacks variability, no statistical tests can be (or need be) performed. Variability refers to the dispersion of scores.

Ideally, when a researcher finds differences between respondents, they are due to true difference on the variable being measured. However, the combination of systematic and random errors can dilute the accuracy of a measurement. *Systematic error* is introduced through a constant bias in a measurement. It can usually be traced to a fault in the sampling procedure or in the design of a questionnaire. *Random error* does not occur in any consistent pattern, and it is not controllable by the researcher.

11

Forecasting Methodology

Many scholars have proposed a variety of ways to categorise forecasting methodologies. The following classification is a modification of the schema developed by Gordon over two decades ago:

Genius Forecasting

This method is based on a combination of intuition, insight, and luck. Psychics and crystal ball readers are the most extreme case of genius forecasting. Their forecasts are based exclusively on intuition. Science fiction writers have sometimes described new technologies with uncanny accuracy.

There are many examples where men and women have been remarkable successful at predicting the future. There are also many examples of wrong forecasts. The weakness in genius forecasting is that its impossible to recognise a good forecast until the forecast has come to pass.

Some psychic individuals are capable of producing consistently accurate forecasts. Mainstream science generally ignores this fact because the implications are simply to difficult to accept. Our current understanding of reality is not adequate to explain this phenomena.

Trend Extrapolation

These methods examine trends and cycles in historical data, and then use mathematical techniques to extrapolate to the future. The assumption of all these techniques is that the forces responsible for creating the past, will continue to operate in the future. This is often a valid assumption when forecasting short term horizons, but it falls short when creating medium and long term forecasts. The further out we attempt to forecast, the less certain we become of the forecast.

The stability of the environment is the key factor in determining whether trend extrapolation is an appropriate forecasting model. The concept of "*developmental inertia*" embodies the idea that some items are more easily changed than others. Clothing styles is an example of an area that contains little inertia. It is difficult to produce reliable mathematical forecasts for clothing. Energy consumption, on the other hand, contains substantial inertia and mathematical techniques work well. The developmental inertia of new industries or new technology cannot be determined because there is not yet a history of data to draw from.

There are many mathematical models for forecasting trends and cycles. Choosing an appropriate model for a particular forecasting application depends on the historical data. The study of the historical data is called exploratory data analysis. Its purpose is to identify the trends and cycles in the data so that appropriate model can be chosen.

The most common mathematical models involve various forms of *weighted smoothing* methods. Another type of model is known as *decomposition*. This technique mathematically separates the historical data into trend, seasonal and random components. A process known as a "turning point analysis" is used to produce forecasts. *ARIMA* models such as adaptive filtering and Box-Jenkins analysis constitute a third class of mathematical model, while *simple linear regression and curve fitting* is a fourth.

The common feature of these mathematical models is that historical data is the only criteria for producing a forecast. One might think then, that if two people use the same model on the same data that the forecasts will also be the same, but this is not necessarily the case. Mathematical models involve smoothing constants, coefficients and other parameters that must decided by the forecaster. To a large degree, the choice of these parameters determines the forecast.

It is vogue today to diminish the value of mathematical extrapolation. Makridakis (one of the gurus of quantitative forecasting) correctly points out that judgmental forecasting is superior to mathematical models, however, there are many forecasting applications where computer generated forecasts are more feasible. For example, large manufacturing companies often forecast inventory levels for thousands of items each month. It would simply not be feasible to use judgmental forecasting in this kind of application.

Consensus Methods

Forecasting complex systems often involves seeking expert opinions from more than one person. Each is an expert in his own discipline, and it is through the synthesis of these opinions that a final forecast is obtained.

One method of arriving at a consensus forecast would be to put all the experts in a room and let them "argue it out". This method falls short because the situation is often controlled by those individuals that have the best group interaction and persuasion skills.

A better method is known as the Delphi technique. This method seeks to rectify the problems of face-to-face confrontation in the group, so the responses and respondents remain anonymous. The classical technique proceeds in well-defined sequence. In the first round, the participants are asked to write their predictions. Their responses are collated and a copy is given to each of the participants. The participants are asked to comment on extreme views and to defend or modify their original opinion based on what the other participants have written. Again, the answers are collated and fed back to the participants. In the final round, participants are asked to reassess their original opinion in view of those presented by other participants.

The Delphi method general produces a rapid narrowing of opinions. It provides more accurate forecasts than group discussions. Furthermore, a face-to-face discussion following the application of the Delphi method generally degrades accuracy.

Simulation Methods

Simulation methods involve using analogs to model complex systems. These analogs can take on several forms. A *mechanical analog* might be a wind tunnel for modeling aircraft performance. An equation to predict an economic measure would be a *mathematical analog.* A *metaphorical analog* could involve using the growth of a bacteria colony to describe human population growth. *Game analogs* are used where the interactions of the players are symbolic of social interactions.

Mathematical analogs are of particular importance to futures research. They have been extremely successful in many forecasting applications, especially in the physical sciences. In the social sciences however, their accuracy is somewhat diminished. The extraordinary complexity of social systems makes it difficult to include all the relevant factors in any model.

Clarke reminds us of a potential danger in our reliance on mathematical models. As he points out, these techniques often begin with an initial set of assumptions, and if these are incorrect, then the forecasts will reflect and amplify these errors.

One of the most common mathematical analogs in societal growth is the S-curve. The model is based on the concept of the logistic or normal probability distribution. All processes experience exponential growth and reach an upper asymptopic limit. Modis has hypothesized that chaos like states exist at the beginning and end of the S-curve. The disadvantage of this S-curve model is that it is difficult to know at any point in time where you currently are on the curve, or how close you are to the asymtopic limit. The advantage of the model is that it forces planners to take a long-term look at the future.

Another common mathematical analog involves the use of multivariate statistical techniques. These techniques are used to model complex systems involving relationships between two or more variables. Multiple regression analysis is the most common technique. Unlike trend extrapolation models, which only look at the history of the variable being forecast, multiple regression models look at the relationship between the variable being forecast and two or more other variables.

Multiple regression is the mathematical analog of a systems approach, and it has become the primary forecasting tool of economists and social scientists. The object of multiple regression is to be able to understand how a group of variables (working in unison) affect another variable.

The multiple regression problem of *collinearity* mirrors the practical problems of a systems approach. Paradoxically, strong correlations between predictor variables create unstable forecasts, where a slight change in one variable can have dramatic impact on another variable. In a multiple regression (and systems) approach, as the relationships between the components of the system increase, our ability to predict any given component decreases.

Gaming analogs are also important to futures research. Gaming involves the creation of an artificial environment or situation. Players (either real people or computer players) are asked to act out an assigned role. The "role" is essentially a set of rules that is used during interactions with other players. While gaming has not yet been proven as a forecasting technique, it does serve two important functions. First, by the act of designing the game, researchers learn to define the parameters of the system they are studying. Second, it teaches researchers about the relationships between the components of the system.

Cross-impact Matrix Method

Relationships often exist between events and developments that are not revealed by univariate forecasting techniques. The cross-impact matrix method recognises that the occurrence of an event can, in turn, effect the likelihoods of other events. Probabilities are assigned to reflect the likelihood of an event in the presence and absence of other events. The resultant inter-correlational structure can be used to examine the relationships of the components to each other, and within the overall system. The advantage of this technique is that it forces forecasters and policy-makers to look at the relationships between system components, rather than viewing any variable as working independently of the others.

Scenario

The scenario is a narrative forecast that describes a potential course of events. Like the cross-impact matrix method, it recognises the interrelationships of system components. The scenario describes the impact on the other components and the system as a whole. It is a "script" for defining the particulars of an uncertain future.

Scenarios consider events such as new technology, population shifts, and changing consumer preferences. Scenarios are written as long-term predictions of the future. A most likely scenario is usually written, along with at least one optimistic and one pessimistic scenario. The primary purpose of a scenario is to provoke thinking of decision makers who can then posture themselves for the fulfillment of the scenario(s). The three scenarios force decision makers to ask: 1) Can we survive the pessimistic scenario, 2) Are we happy with the most likely scenario, and 3) Are we ready to take advantage of the optimistic scenario?

Decision Trees

Decision trees originally evolved as graphical devices to help illustrate the structural relationships between alternative choices. These trees were originally presented as a series of yes/no (dichotomous) choices. As our understanding of feedback loops improved, decision trees became more complex. Their structure became the foundation of computer flow charts.

Computer technology has made it possible create very complex decision trees consisting of many subsystems and feedback loops. Decisions are no longer limited to dichotomies; they now involve assigning probabilities to the likelihood of any particular path.

Decision theory is based on the concept that an *expected value* of a discrete variable can be calculated as the average value for that variable. The expected value is especially useful for decision makers because it represents the most likely value based on the probabilities of the distribution function. The application of Bayes' theorem enables the modification of initial probability estimates, so the decision tree becomes refined as new evidence is introduced.

Utility theory is often used in conjunction with decision theory to improve the decision making process. It recognises that dollar amounts are not the only consideration in the decision process. Other factors, such as risk, are also considered.

Combining Forecasts

It seems clear that no forecasting technique is appropriate for all situations. There is substantial evidence to demonstrate that combining individual forecasts produces gains in forecasting accuracy. There is also evidence that adding quantitative forecasts to qualitative forecasts reduces accuracy. Research has not yet revealed the conditions or methods for the optimal combinations of forecasts.

Judgmental forecasting usually involves combining forecasts from more than one source. Informed forecasting begins with a set of key assumptions and then uses a combination of historical data and expert opinions. Involved forecasting seeks the opinions of all those directly affected by the forecast (e.g., the sales force would be included in the forecasting process). These techniques generally produce higher quality forecasts than can be attained from a single source.

Combining forecasts provides us with a way to compensate for deficiencies in a forecasting technique. By selecting complementary methods, the shortcomings of one technique can be offset by the advantages of another.

Difficulties in Forecasting Technology

Clarke describes our inability to forecast technological futures as a failure of nerve. When a major technological breakthrough does occur, it takes conviction and courage to accept the implications of the finding. Even when the truth is starring us in the face, we often have difficulty accepting its implications.

Clark refers to this resistance to change as cowardice, however, it may be much deeper. Cognitive dissonance theory in psychology has helped us understand that resisiance to change is a natural human characteristic. It is extremely difficult to venture beyond our latitudes of acceptance in forecasting new technologies.

Clarke states that knowledge can sometimes clog the wheels of imagination. He embodied this belief in his self-proclaimed law:

"When a distinguished but elderly scientist states that something is possible, he is almost certainly right. When he states that something is impossible, he is very probably wrong."

Nearly all futurists describe the past as unchangeable, consisting as a collection of knowable facts. We generally perceive the existence of only one past. When two people give conflicting stories of the past, we tend to believe that one of them must be lying or mistaken.

This widely accepted view of the past might not be correct. Historians often interject their own beliefs and biases when they write about the past. Facts become distorted and altered over time. It may be that past is a reflection of our current conceptual reference. In the most extreme viewpoint, the concept of time itself comes into question.

The future, on the other hand, is filled will uncertainty. Facts give way to opinions. As de Jouvenel points out, the facts of the past provide the raw materials from which the mind makes estimates of the future. All forecasts are opinions of the future (some more carefully formulated than others). The act of making a forecast is the expression of an opinion. The future, as described by de Jouvenel, consists of a range of possible future phenomena or events. These *futuribles* are those things that *might* happen.

Defining a Useful Forecast

Science fiction novelist Frederik Pohl has suggested that the "only time a forecast has any real utility is when it is not totally reliable". He proposes a thought experiment where a Gypsy fortune teller predicts that we will be run over and killed when we leave the tea room. If we know that the Gypsy's predictions are one hundred percent accurate, then Pohl states that the fortune is useless, because we would be unable to alter the forecast. In other words, predictions only become useful when they are not completely reliable.

The apparent paradox created by Pohl's thought experiment is only a function of the particular situation. The paradox exists only when 1) we want the future to be different than the prediction, and 2) when we believe that there is no way for us to adapt to or affect the forthcoming changes. Pohl's thought experiment actually doesn't even meet that criteria, since one could present a convincing argument that it is more desirable to spend the rest of our lives confined to the comfort of a tea room than to leave and meet certain death. Obviously, our new life would be difficult to accept and adapt to, but it could be done. Prisoners do it all the time.

A forecast can be one hundred percent accurate and still be useful. For example, suppose our Gypsy had told us that after leaving her tea room we would safely return home. Again, since we know that her forecasts are completely accurate, we would receive emotional comfort from her predictions. In a more tangible example, suppose the prediction is that our manufacturing company will receive twice as many orders for widgets as we had anticipated. Since the forecast is one hundred percent accurate, we would be wise to order more raw materials and increase our production staff to meet the coming demand.

Pohl is wrong. The goal of forecasting is to be as accurate as possible. In the case of business demand forecasting, it is naive to suggest that an accurate forecast is useless. On the contrary, a more accurate forecast enables us to plan the use our resources in a more ecological fashion. We can minimise waste by adapting to our expectations of the future.

It is sometimes useful in thought experiments to look at the situation from the opposite perspective. Suppose we know that our Gypsy is always wrong in her predictions. Her accuracy is guaranteed to be zero. Note that this is different than random forecasts, where she might *hit the mark* once in a while. The Gypsy sighs with relief and says that there is no fatal accident in store for us today. According to Pohl's reasoning, this should provide the most useful forecast because it has the least accuracy. It's obvious, though, that this fortune is as useless as the one where she is completely accurate. Leaving the Gypsy's tea-room is not something we would want to do.

If we view accuracy as a continuum, it may be that the antonym of accuracy is randomness (instead of inaccuracy). In this case, Pohl's theory would suggest that random forecasts are more useful than accurate forecasts. In demand forecasting, the degree of over- and under-utilisation of our resources is proportional to the difference between the observed and predicted values. Random forecasts are entirely unacceptable for this type of application.

Pohl's thought experiment is very important because it forces us to look at the theoretical foundations of forecasting. First, Pohl's experiment may not be valid because it violates a basic assumption of forecasting (i.e., we cannot predict the future with one hundred percent accuracy). Second, the usefulness of a forecast does not always seem to be related to its accuracy. Both extremes (completely accurate and completely inaccurate) can produce useful or useless forecasts.

The *usefulness* of a forecast is not something that lends itself readily to quantification along any specific dimension (such as accuracy). It involves complex relationships between many things, including the type of information being forecast, our confidence in the accuracy of the forecast, the magnitude of our dissatisfaction with the forecast, and the versatility of ways that we can adapt to or modify the forecast. In other words, the usefulness of a forecast is an application sensitive construct. Each forecasting situation must be evaluated individually regarding its usefulness.

One of the first rules of doing research is to consider how the results will be used. It is important to consider who the readers of the final report will be during the initial planning stages of a project. It is wasteful to expend resources on research that has little or no use. The same rule applies to forecasting. We must strive to develop forecasts that are of maximum usefulness to planners. This means that each situation must be evaluated individually as to the methodology and type of forecasts that are most appropriate to the particular application.

Do Forecasts Create the Future

A paradox exists in preparing a forecast. If a forecast results in an adaptive change, then the accuracy of the forecast might be modified by that change. Suppose the forecast is that our business will experience a ten percent drop in sales next month. We adapt by increasing our promotion effort to compensate for the predicted loss. This action, in turn, could affect our sales, thus changing the accuracy of the original forecast.

Many futurists (de Jouvenel, Dublin, Pohl, and others) have expressed the idea that the way we contemplate the future is an expression of our desire to create that future. Physicist Dennis Gabor, discoverer of holography, claimed that the future is invented, not predicted. The implication is that the future is an expression of our present thoughts. The idea that we create our own reality is not a new concept. It is easy to imagine how thoughts might translate into actions that affect the future.

Biblical records speak of faith as the force that could move mountains. Recent research in quantum mechanics suggests that this may be more than just a philosophical concept. At a quantum level, matter itself might simply be a manifestation of thought. Electrons and other subatomic particles seem to exist only when physicists are looking for them, otherwise, they exist only as energy.

An incredible discovery was made at the University of Paris in 1982. A team of researchers lead by Alain Aspect found that under certain conditions, electrons could instantaneously communicate with each other across long distances. The results of this experiment have been confirmed by many other researchers, although the implications are exceedingly hard to accept. Three explanations are possible: 1) information can be transferred at speeds exceeding the speed of light, 2) the passage of time is an illusion, 3) the distance between the electrons is an illusion. All three explanations rock our perception of reality.

David Bohm has explained Aspect's experiment by hypothesizing a holographic universe in which reality is essentially a projection of some deeper dimension that we are not able to comprehend. Instantaneous communication is possible because the distance between the particles is an illusion. Neurophysiologist Karl Pribram has also theorised about the holographic nature of reality. His theory is based on a study of the way that the brain recalls memory patterns, but the implications are the same. Reality is a phantasm. If reality is an illusion, then the future is also an illusion.

The phenomena of being able to see the future is known as precognition. Most people believe that (to some degree) they can predict the future. Fortune-tellers, however, believe they can view the future. There is a major difference. We predict the future based on knowledge, intuition and logic. Precognitive persons claim to "see" the future. Knowledge and logic are not involved.

Throughout history, there have been many reports of gifted psychics with precognitive powers. Through some unknown mechanism, these people are able predict things that will happen in the future. If we admit that even a single person in history has possessed this capability, then we must accept the fact that our concept of reality needs dramatic alteration. Time itself may not exist as we currently perceive it. Forecasting may be a method of creating illusions.

Forecasting can, and often does, contribute to the creation of the future, but it is clear that other factors are also operating. A holographic theory would stress the interconnectedness of all elements in the system. At some level, everything contributes to the creation of the future. The degree to which a forecast can shape the future (or our perception of the future) has yet to be determined experimentally and experientially.

Sometimes forecasts become part of a creative process, and sometimes they don't. When two people make mutually exclusive forecasts, both of them cannot be true. At least one forecast is wrong. Does one person's forecast create the future, and the other does not? The mechanisms involved in the construction of the future are not well understood on an individual or social level.

Modis believes that the media provides the mechanism by which social forecasts take on a creative context. In this theory, extensive media coverage acts as a resonating cavity for public opinion, and creates a "*cultural epidemic*" that modifies social behavior.

Dublin points out that the "future has become so integral to the fabric of modern consciousness that few people feel compelled to question it...". Because of the power of a prediction to affect the future, he goes on to state that prophesy is usually a self-interest quest for power.

Ethics of Forecasting

Are predictions of the future a form of propaganda, designed to evoke a particular set of behaviors? Dublin states that the desire for control is implicit in all forecasts. Decisions made today are based on forecasts, which may or may not come to pass. The forecast is a way to control today's decisions.

Dublin is correct. The purpose of forecasting is to control the present. In fact, one of the assumptions of forecasting is that the forecasts will be used by policy-makers to make decisions. It is therefore important to discuss the ethics of forecasting. Since forecasts can and often do take on a creative role, what right do we have to make forecasts that involve other peoples futures?

Nearly everyone would agree that we have the right to create our own future. Goal setting is a form of personal forecasting. It is one way to organise and invent our personal future. Each person has the right to create their own future. On the other hand, a social forecast might alter the course of an entire society. Such power can only be accompanied by equivalent responsibility.

There are no clear rules involving the ethics of forecasting. In *Future Shock*, Toffler discussed the importance of value impact forecasting, the idea that social forecasting must involve physical, cultural and societal values. It is doubtful that forecasters can leave their own personal biases out of the forecasting process. Even the most mathematically rigorous techniques involve judgmental inputs that can dramatically alter the forecast.

Many futurists have pointed out our obligation to create socially desirable futures. Unfortunately, a socially desirable future for one person might be another person's nightmare. For example, modern ecological theory says that we should think of our planet in terms of sustainable futures. The finite supply of natural resources forces us to reconsider the desirability of unlimited growth. An optimistic forecast is that we achieve and maintain an ecologically balanced future. That same forecast, the idea of zero growth, is a catastrophic nightmare for the corporate and financial institutions of the free world. Our Keynesian system of profit depends on continual growth for the well-being of individuals, groups, and institutions.

Desirable futures is a subjective concept. It can only be understood relative to other information. The ethics of forecasting certainly involves the obligation to create desirable futures for the person(s) that might be affected by the forecast. If a goal of forecasting is to create desirable futures, then the forecaster must ask the ethical question of "desirable for whom?".

To embrace the idea of liberty is to recognise that each person has the right to create their own future. Forecasters can promote libertarian beliefs by empowering people that might be affected by the forecast. Involving these people in the forecasting process, gives them the power to become co-creators in their futures.

12

Dialectical Inquiry in Political Research

The purpose of this chapter is to present and exemplify Dialectical Inquiry (DI) as a useful structured qualitative research method for studying organisational sense making processes as they are understood by participants.

Organisational sense making presents a challenge to the researcher. Gareth Morgan has classified the multiple models, metaphors, and constructs we impose on organisational phenomena in our efforts to gain valid scientific understandings. Taken together, our models and theories are inconsistent, incommensurate, and paradoxical. They seek to answer the question, "How are we to understand, as scientists, organisational phenomena?" A related question is to ask how organisational actors understand the same phenomena. Kaplan argues that we must distinguish between the meaning of an act to the actor and it's meaning to scientists taking that act as subject matter. We presume that those understandings are similar, but that is only a presumption. "Observational data have no more validity than attaches to that presumption". That suggests that the relationship between our models and theories, and those in use by organisational actors, are problematic. We should not impose our constructs as valid representations of the understandings of organisational actors.

Managerial understandings about organisational functioning must make sense, even if such functioning appears unreasonable and irrational at times. There must be "method to the madness." Ethnomethodology assumes as much, referring to "the availability...of common sense knowledge of...society" or to "the grasp of what were...adequate methods for dealing with...matters." Sensibility, thus, implies theory building. There must be a model, or models, that grant structure to experience, and reduce equivocality by distilling events into recognisable patterns. Discovery of such theories implies a grounded theory perspective as opposed to the imposition of rational academic models.

Purposeful actors whose actions are guided by their own particular understandings of the processes in which they participate constitute organisations. If we assume that actors have choices, *their* categories and meanings become necessary, complementary elements in a valid representation of those processes. Furthermore, those processes "make sense" to participants. They represent a more or less coherent representation of how their organisations function. However, most of this knowledge and understanding is tacit, communicated in anecdotes, narratives, and stories. It should be clear that the discovery and explication of tacit knowledge necessarily calls for qualitative research methods.

The research opportunity sets up a strategic choice for the researcher. We can review the literature, accepted constructs and theories, and the various instruments available to measure and verify aspects of these models and theories. In effect, we would be imposing the understandings of researchers on to the experiences of organisational actors. Alternatively, we can assume that organisational actors are competent in their work, that is, that their successful functioning indicates effective theories of action. In that case, we cannot impose our constructs or instruments. We must search the qualitative content of narrations and interviews to discover meanings and theories-in-use. The constructs, to be measured, are not yet available. The assumption of purposefulness and competence requires, at this stage of the research, qualitative methods.

Development of Dialectical Inquiry

The development of Dialectical Inquiry as a method of qualitative research derives from the work of C. West Churchman, as further developed by R. O. Mason. In his book, *The Design of Inquiring Systems*, Churchman compares several competing scientific approaches to testing the truth content of statements including those of Locke, Leibniz, Kant, and Hegel. The purpose was a philosophical analysis of a practical question, "Could a computer determine whether there was life on Mars?"

The dialectic assumes that a thesis and its antithesis can be developed to explain any set of facts and data. This is a strong epistemological assumption. Conflicting models can emerge from facts and data, and both models have valid claims to truth. The conflicts derive from differing interpretative assumptions actors apply to facts and data. Paul Feyerabend applies these principles to science, arguing that the relationship between theory and data is incestuous; theory defines what will be called data, and data, in turn, verifies the theory. Theories should be tested against radically antithetical theories. The point of the dialectic is to posit antithetical theories and models as a method of elucidating the assumptions underpinning those theories and models.

Richard Mason used dialectical modeling to support decision making for a firm faced with two antithetical strategic plans for its future. There has been an extensive debate on its utility in support of effective decision-making in the pages of the *Academy of Management Review*. Given that our focus is on discovery, not decision-making, the benefits with respect to decision processes are not a concern.

The dialectic is clearly a qualitative research method. Its focus is on the content and meaning of models and theories in use. As will be demonstrated in this research, the number of subjects evoking particular models of technology transfer is irrelevant to discovering their meaning. Indeed, one subject richly described all three models that emerged from the research. The significance of each model is its utility in understanding the alternative models.

Logic of Dialectical Discovery

The focus on discovery forces us to abandon some of the assumptions noted in the above discussion. We cannot assume the availability of competing models; they must emerge from the data. Nor can we arbitrarily limit the number of competing models to two. In principle, there are no limits to the number of potential models. Nevertheless, Dialectical Inquiry does impose a structure on the qualitative research process.

DI imposes a meta-theoretical framework on the research process. It parallels the efforts of others to better structure grounded theory methods, and reduces the "magical moments" that are needed to bridge between emergent theories and data. DI makes the ontological assumption that organisational actors can operate on the basis of multiple implicit models. While the dialectic implies two models, grounded research principles suggest that we do not limit the number of models in use. That becomes an empirical question. Furthermore, DI assumes that such models, upon analysis, will prove to be in conflict. This does not mean that decisions and processes are necessarily inconsistent or incoherent. Given that these models are tacit, organisational actors will be unaware of inconsistencies. Rather, the DI framework requires that emergent models be distilled so that underlying assumptions, counter assumptions, and contradictions become evident.

The meta-theoretical framework imposed by DI is not about the content of managerial models, but their structure taken as a set. The point is that by juxtaposing tacit models within an imposed structure, their content and meaning will become evident. The logic of DI is an example of Sheffield's notion of a philosophic method. A philosophical perspective is utilised explicitly to frame inquiry.

These distinctions might be better grasped metaphorically. Imagine organising processes as a shared *fabric cognitive map* of understandings overlaid in a multiplicity of patterns. As organisational history accumulates and evolves, much of that understanding becomes tacit. The map appears as a dense mass of meanings created by the folding over, under, and into of understandings and interpretations, a wadded ball without beginning or end. The logic of processes becomes obscure. Processes appear to work even if they are poorly understood. Rules of thumb evolve to guide actions encoded in anecdotes, stories, and myths. These may be understood as "scripts". According to Lord and Kernan, scripts are the cognitive knowledge structures that are held in people's memory. In this sense, scripts describe the sequencing of events in conventional or familiar situations.

Scripts work whether they are well understood or not. Moreover, there is no requirement that scripts be consistent. In the case studied, this was the situation that confronted expert managers when they interviewed colleagues across their company. Anecdotal data revealed no apparent logic or pattern. There was nowhere to grasp the *fabric* in the ball; the *map* could not be read.

DI can be used to identify and make explicit models that stretch out the *fabric map* and expose both patterns and interpretations. Imagine each model as a stake stretching its corner of the fabric, exposing part of the *map*. To achieve this stretching, each model must be distilled to an extreme formulation (i.e., to the point where it becomes almost dysfunctional). Practical scripts are composites of these extreme models. Thus, inconsistent models can become the basis for what appears as coherent purposeful action.

Method of Dialectical Inquiry

The logical structure imposed by DI requires the researcher to identify competing models and explore them in depth. It must be emphasized that these models must emerge from respondents. They should not be controlled by the questions of the interviewer or by categories suggested by the interviewers. In this particular research, the interviewers were themselves unaware of technology transfer models. They asked respondents to explain how technology transfer worked from their experience. The results were anecdotes, narratives, and a variety of assertions. The record of these interviews was the data that we analysed.

The method was to identify particular themes that seemed to be recurring across interviews. For example, someone claimed that you do not transfer technology. You get the expert. The theme is people. A second theme was about information. Once identified, it becomes possible to document the many instances when a theme is expressed across the interviews. Following the identification of common themes, each was defined as a model that excluded the others.

Conceptual clarity allows the researcher to expose the assumptions that drive the model. Each model incorporates ontological assumptions about organisational functioning. Exclusive models suggest conflicting assumptions and counter assumptions, all of which expose the tacit understandings of how each model "works." If we assume that each model represents some organisational truth and that they are in conflict, it follows that each is incomplete with respect to the truths of competing models. Forcing each model to its extreme stretches the *fabric cognitive map,* making it intelligible.

It must be noted that the identified models are subject to whatever biases interviewers, interviewees, and researchers bring to bear. Alternative sets of models, in dialectical relationships, could also be postulated. We can assume that each model can be a basis for finer distinctions, and the exposure of other models collapsed under a single model. DI provides an initial map that is useful to practitioners and a point of departure for further research.

Our purposes in this research, then, were to apply Dialectical Inquiry as a method of discovery of explicit models shared among competent professionals and managers in organisations, and to demonstrate the efficacy of DI as a qualitative research methodology. The methodological hypothesis is: The imposition of a dialectical structure will distill emergent theories in use by organisational actors that validly represent their tacit understandings.

Discovery versus Imposition

Discovery and imposition suggest conflicting modes of inquiry. The first implies "inquiry from the inside," while the second implies *a priori* categories. Glaser and Strauss suggest that theory should emerge from data. In this research we decided, *a priori*, that a dialectical pattern would be discovered in the interview data. Such believing should result in seeing what researchers expect. Nevertheless, this application of DI seeks to bridge the conflict between these approaches.

The *content* of organisational enactments of technology transfer is emergent (i.e., the product of interview data), while the *form* in which they are interpreted is dialectical. In essence, we are saying that while content may not be predictable, the relationship between various scripts, their conflicts, and contradictions are predictable. This imposition of dialectic order may be understood both epistemologically and ontologically. The former assumes that the dialectic structures our ways of knowing the world. The latter assumes that the world is necessarily dialectical and paradoxical.

Research Setting

ABC is a large aerospace firm with significant resources invested in research and development (R&D), and general dissatisfaction with the effectiveness of technology transfer (or *infusion* as they called it) between R&D units and project groups. An Engineering Management Quality Improvement Team (Management Team or interviewing team), made up of high-level engineers and engineering managers, was chartered by the company to investigate the poor rate of technology infusion. "Why isn't technology infusion more effective" was their concern. The problems appeared to span the entire company and appeared generic to the industry, given many years of public discussion of the issues.

The Management Team interviewed 55 top engineering managers across the company in many geographical locations. Interviewees understood the charter of the Management Team. Individual team members asked interviewees to reflect upon their years of managerial experience, and explain how technology transfer works at ABC. Technology transfer obviously made sense to respondents, no matter how ineffective it was. Yet, the Management Team could not draw useful general conclusions from their highly anecdotal data. The Management Team's report provided a rich and complex picture of technology transfer across the firm. Interviews between competent professionals with shared, but tacit, understandings did not yield a coherent model of technology transfer.

This is a strange outcome for a group of experienced managers in dialog with expert colleagues. The norms of rationality and the presumption of logic should preclude such outcomes. It was to be expected that when managers assume the roles of practitioner-researchers, studying their own organisational processes, they would impose order on the data in a process of socially constructing a reasonable reality. Chenail and Maione raise the question of how practitioner-researchers conceptualise and "evaluate their qualitative research projects in light of their already knowing too much ...without being totally overwhelmed by it." Clearly, the ABC Management Team was overwhelmed by the data they collected.

The ABC Management Team, subsequently, turned to the first author for help in "making sense of the data." The challenge for the researcher was to *explain* to the team what they already knew. In other words, to discover patterns and meanings within the anecdotal data they had collected. At no point were the researchers in contact with any of the interviewees. Given that the researcher was not part of the interview process, the authors did not determine the conditions of the Management Team's research. Given that the interviews were conducted between employees of a single firm, it is doubtful that any human subject protections were in place. Indeed, the identities of all of the interviewees were part of the published interview record.

Technology Transfer

Perhaps the outcome should not be surprising. The

management of technology has become an area of increasing concern for government and industry, and an emerging domain of academic research. The rate of development and implementation of new technologies is seen as an indicator of industry competitiveness in international markets, and the performance of research and development organisations is considered critical to competitive success. Considerable government resources are being devoted to R&D to support both defense and commercial technological development. Of particular concern have been the processes of technology transfer.

A characteristic of much research on the processes of technology transfer has been to take technology for granted, while studying organisational variables as determinants of the success or failure of technology transfer efforts. O'Connor, Parsons, Liden, and Herold suggest that "technology will readily cross boundaries," while human resources practices are not easily transferable. Wilkof develops a socio-technical analysis of a technological innovation that focuses almost entirely on organisational, social, and cultural factors. In a later paper O'Connor, Parsons and Liden argue for greater attention to attitudinal and behavioral responses to new technologies. The technology management literature is replete with many models of technology transfer, developed as extensions of more or less rational models of organisational processes. There is a tendency to impose academic models upon the phenomena, even at this necessarily preliminary stage of inquiry.

New technologies are equivocal, poorly understood, and necessarily incomplete. Arguing they are transferable, but for organisational constraints, assumes away their uncertainties and shifts the focus towards attitudes, beliefs, and culture. Several questions are confounded in current research efforts on technology transfer. For example, "Are the issues technological, organisational, resistance to change, motivational, or cultural?" This study suggests that even when there are strong organisational and individual motives for the adoption and implementation of new technologies, and when such technology transfers are intra-organisational among units within the same organisation who enjoy proximity, technology transfer can be problematic.

Process of Dialectical Inquiry

The focus of the research is on the underdeveloped "technology of technology transfer," to use Tornatsky's perceptive term. Our research purpose was to develop models of technology transfer grounded in the experience of ABC's managers (i.e., make their "technology of technology transfer" explicit). This process involved four distinct steps, each of which is discussed below.

Step 1: Identifying Scripts and Models

Making sense of printed interview notes is necessarily a creative endeavor. The reconstructed logic of the dialectical presentation does not mirror sense-making as it unfolds. The research process required several readings for immersion, familiarity, and note taking. Script search commenced with the fourth reading to seek strong exclusive images that might typify models.

We should differentiate three terms to make the research process more transparent. We see "themes" as a common thread of ideas that suggests a script. A script is a cognitive knowledge structure about how processes work in organisations. Since scripts are poorly understood, we differentiate them from a "model." The model is characterised by logical coherence (i.e., an understanding of how it works). Thus, the research process is to seek themes in the interview data, infer from these themes a shared script, and develop the implicit model by examining its underlying assumptions. Given that the framework is dialectical, we expect each of these models to contradict the others.

Themes are first identified by a strong unequivocal assertion in the interview notes that purports to exclude alternative assertions. For example, "The best way to transfer technology is to transfer people." Among the many lesser assertions and anecdotes, this assertion stands out as a potential theme. It suggests a strong script. Taking this theme as a potential theme, the interviews were again reviewed seeking to find further similar statements. It quickly became apparent that many managers shared this view of technology transfer. People spoke of it in many ways. For examples, "People you know," "old boy contacts," "technology exists as good people," and "transfer of technology is essentially the transfer of people." The evidence of this theme could fill pages with quotes from the interviews. It was, by far, the most frequent of the technology transfer models discussed by the interviewed managers. This model, or script, was tentatively labeled the "people-mover model".

Once the first script had been verified with a plethora of quotations from the interviews, a similar search was conducted for a second model. The dialectic framework was used as a heuristic. Specifically, we sought a strong assertion that, in some way, excluded the first script. Did any interviewee deny the first theme? Again, a strong assertion triggered recognition of a potential second theme, "We need directives to force projects to... document..." Note that the subject is information. People are not mentioned, signaling an alternative theme. This theme was initially narrowly labeled the "documentation model". However, further review of the interviews suggested a more inclusive label, the "*communication model,*" to include references to documentation, symposia, seminars, bulletins, databases, etc... The references to this model, less frequent than the "people-mover model" took many forms. Examples include, "We need more corporate memory," "more communication," "projects should be briefed," and "total lack of documentation." There were also many references to journals, updates, briefings, meetings, seminars, symposia, and the need for databases. This clearly qualified as an important and frequent theme in the interviews.

The third model proved more elusive. The most frequent references were to the first two models. Furthermore, while DI implies at least two models, there is no requirement for more to emerge. Statements, that implicitly denied both these models, yielded two more "scripts." Examine the following statement: "For a technology to be ABC on-the-shelf, ABC must put it on the shelf." There is no mention of people, communication, or documentation. A different theme is signaled here. We tentatively labeled this third theme the "on-the-shelf model."

The discovery of the "on-the-shelf model" required some reflection about the first two models. The first model was emphatically about people, while the second was clearly about information. The third had to relate to some other domain. It took some imagination to parse a set of quotes that seemed to suggest a similar script. Paraphrased, the following are examples.

— Program requirements call for the utilisation of a proven concept... implies the availability of appropriate specifications, allowables and design manual information...

— Not enough data exists to assure low risk.

— Risk avoidance [guides selection].

— Allowables did not exist.

— A need exists for rigorous and objective classification of the maturity of a technology.

The term "allowables" is retained because it signaled the concerns of the engineers. "Allowables" refers to the design limits of a new technology. To jump ahead, they are about the conditions where the new technology will NOT work.

This script clearly, refers to aspects of the technology itself and not to experts or the means used to convey knowledge to others. Conceptually, each of these scripts is quite different. One is about people, the second is about information, and the third is about the technology. The last quote captured the essence of the model. It was about the maturity of the technology. It should be noted that the first author's engineering background allowed him to discover the script suggested by this last group of quotations. This third model was relabeled as the "maturity of technology model" to reflect its content more explicitly.

Step 2: Defining the Models

The next step in the process was for the researcher to invent definitions of each model. The model is not a scientific construct. It is a theory-in-use by organisational members. While evidence will be offered that it may be generalisable to other organisations, it is not connected to academic organisational theories. The purpose of these definitions was to provide a basis for developing a set of assumptions that explicate each model. The definitions provide tentative formal meaning to the metaphorical labels that derived from the subjective analysis and coding of the interview data.

The process of defining each model is iterative. A definition based on the interview data is ventured and its assumptions are made explicit. These assumptions are tested against the definitions and assumptions of competing models. Each definition is honed so that it is consistent with its own assumptions and opposed to those of competing models. This creates a dialectic structure where each model anchors an extreme position.

This structure, anchored by extreme conflicting models, creates a framework of understanding within which the interviewing team could make sense of their findings.

We must emphasize that this structure represents a framework for thought, not action. Practical actors draw from all of these models without understanding their explicit content. The research goal was to make that content explicit, so that actors could more intelligently deal with the challenges of technology transfer.

We begin with model definitions that emerged from the process.

A. The people-mover model

Technology transfer occurs when a person expert in an advanced technology is assigned to a program and produces outcomes in that program that utilise that technology.

B.The communication model

Technology transfer is essentially a communication process affected through the documentation of research and development and dissemination through the media of documents, databases, seminars and presentations.

The definition developed for the maturity of technology model demonstrates the iterative nature of the process. We cannot simply label and define a model. We must test it against the other models and for consistency with the interview data. We, first, ventured the following definition.

C.The maturity of technology model – Tentative definition

Technology transfer takes place when results, data, and specifications are sufficiently complete to allow a designer to apply the technology and such applications have occurred.Is it about the technology or the designer? If the R&D experts are the designers, the model collapses into the people-mover model. The dialectic requires a sharper differentiation. The definition did not carefully relate to the maturity of the technology. A second definition proved more explicit. The notion of maturity is anchored to the ability to utilise the technology. Even this definition is somewhat problematic because of the overlap with the communication model. However, as a basis for testing assumptions and counter-assumptions, it proved adequate.

C2 The maturity of technology model

Technology transfer takes place when a technology is mature and sufficiently complete knowledge has been communicated to designers and engineers to utilise that technology practically and effectively.

A possible fourth model

A fourth script hinted at in the data argued that technologies are purchased from suppliers, and thereby developed for engineers and designers. Typical of the type of assertion indicative of this script was "It is more prudent to put risk for technology infusion on the shoulders of suppliers." The problem with this model is that technology refers to knowledge that can be used predictably. Given this recognition, suppliers do not transfer technology: They simply provide hardware or related supplies. They may learn a new technology in producing their products, but their knowledge remains with them. This model was rarely mentioned in the interviews. Given the charter of the interviewers and the specific focus on technology transfer within the company, this model was not explored.

Upon further reflection, exploration of this model might have yielded interesting results. Some managers appear to be too risk averse to engage the challenges of technology development and transfer. That suggests that another barrier to technology transfer is risk avoidance. It would have been difficult, given the paucity of responses, to explore this model. Moreover, the focus of the interviewing team may have suppressed the expression of risk avoidance. It may have been very significant, but that could not be inferred from the interview data.

Step 3: Assumptions and Counter Assumptions

The meaning of each model is further clarified by inferring the assumptions underpinning each model. In this qualitative methodology, researchers maintain relative freedom in developing their taxonomy from the interview data. The models become the objects of further conceptual inquiry. In seeking assumptions, researchers escape the limitations of the anecdotal data.

This is, therefore, a creative and iterative process. The assumptions of each model are tested against competing models to reveal counter assumptions. These, in turn, force further clarification of the original assumptions. The purpose is to make salient the differences between models and sharply distinguish between them.

Step 4. Identify and Define Contradictions

This process forces each model into its extreme interpretation further illuminating differences. Conflicting models suggest that effective technological transfer is necessarily a paradoxical process. This suggests a hypothesis that goes beyond current DI practice.

Given that each model has relevance and validity, and given that they are in conflict, then, necessarily, each model is limited and incomplete. It follows that each model is self-contradictory if pushed to an extreme.

If each model grasps an essential truth, and each is in conflict with the others, then each model is necessarily incomplete. It follows that attempting to apply any of these models, while ignoring the others, will lead to failure.

So clarified, the models developed through the DI process can better serve as a basis for parsing discussions on such broad concepts as technology transfer. More important, pushing each technology transfer model to the point of self-contradiction unambiguously establishes its meaning. This appears to liberate it from a host of other organisational variables creating a basis for generalising each model to other organisational settings. We would expect all aerospace firms engaged in research to face similar technology transfer challenges. Research interpretations of contradictions inherent in each of the three models developed from DI analysis of the interview data follow.

People-mover model contradiction

Clearly, experts moved to projects to develop applications increase their knowledge of a new technology, but do they transfer that knowledge to others? More likely, it remains with the expert. Thus, this model can collapse into a supplier model. Experts return to research facilities, and only project hardware and software remain after them. The interviews provided ample evidence for this outcome, for example, "We do not manage to capture our past knowledge and experience" and "Old boy' contacts... will present difficulties when we lose older people." In short, without a mechanism for teaching and learning, technology will not be transferred.

The contradiction, then, of the people-mover model is: Simply employing the expert to solve a specific problem may assure that he or she learns more about a technology. Without provision for teaching and learning, the technology will not be available to others.

The communications model contradiction

The contradiction relates to the content of the knowledge required for effective technology transfer and to learning processes. Advanced technologies are necessarily incomplete and untried. We may know how they work. Without application, we are unlikely to know their design limits (i.e., the conditions when they will not work).

Thus, it is what is unknown about an immature technology that may be more important than the known. The contradiction inherent in the *communication model is:* The expectation that researchers can document and communicate what they do not know.

The maturity of technology model contradiction

The primary contradiction is the process of putting a technology on-the-shelf. An immature technology must be applied to develop the design parameters and limitations of its utilisation. The maturity of technology model requires exactly this information as a precondition for such applications. In effect, the model calls for technologies to be transferred before they will be applied; to "bootstrap" themselves.

Therefore, the contradiction inherent in the maturity of technology model is: An immature technology must be applied to develop its design parameters and limitations. Yet, the model requires exactly such information as a condition for such applications.

The Requirements for Effective Technology Transfer

The three models suggest particular requirements for the successful transfer of technology from research and development to utilisation in practical designs.

— Experts knowledgeable in the technology must work with designers and engineers. It is clear that too much of the knowledge in new technologies is implicit and untested for, to be utilised without expert direction and experience.

— The new technology must be tested to establish its design limitations. The process of utilisation creates the conditions for testing a new technology and discovering its design limits. Experts will learn from both designers and testing of new designs. Until design limits are verified, the new technology will be considered immature and problematic.

— The process of application and testing must be sufficiently documented for the technology to be useable for other designers.

It is not sufficient to successfully utilise a new technology in a particular application. It is necessary to document the design, the variables, and the nature of the tests. The technology will not have been transferred unless there is sufficient documentation to attest to its maturity and inform its utilisation.

In effect, a technology will have been transferred when project engineers have mastered it well enough to teach it to others and do so, it is well enough documented so that others can learn it, and it has been applied and tested sufficiently for its limitations to be understood.

Methodological Reflections

Recognition of each of these tentative models was triggered by strong negative constraints on technology transfer. "We do not transfer technology, we get the expert." "They don't document." "It must be on the shelf." "We don't transfer technology, we purchase hardware." While the models seem self-evident from the data, they are, nevertheless, the interpretations of the researcher, not the subjects. "The laws of science may thus be *descriptions* of how the world looks... or *prescriptions* for how to look at the world. We really have no way of knowing which". The dialectic was imposed on the data as a prescription for discovery. To be valid as descriptions of technology transfer, their validity had to be tested.

With the framework complete and appearing to encompass all of the interview data, and the cognitive maps implicit in the data stretched, to reveal competing perspectives, all of the data and analysis (enriched by many quotations from the management team interview notes) were presented to the management team, who had conducted the interviews. The presentation took over four hours and proceeded in exactly the order presented here. Much time was devoted to exemplifying the models and their assumptions with interview data. Given that the researchers' interpretive processes moved them well beyond the interview data, it was necessary to test the validity of their models and assumptions.

Internal Validity

Once assumptions, counter assumptions, and contradictions are explicit, it is important to perform reality checks on the findings. Argyris and Schon have argued that subjects should test valid information. Weick sets some criteria for the validation of theories that are as appropriate for manager's theories as those of scientists. The foremost criterion is "plausibility." This is especially important if the object of inquiry is sense-making enactments. Aubusson also argues that interpretations should be checked with those who have direct knowledge of the phenomena.

At the end of the presentation, two questions were asked of the management team. The first was a test of internal validity, "Do the findings conform to your experience of the practices of technology transfer in ABC and do they constitute a reasonable interpretation of the interview data?"

The management team, of course, had conducted all of the interviews. They had access to all the company data, and constituted a panel of experts on technology transfer in the organisation. The management team's response was remarkably positive. It was asserted that the models represented the interviews well, albeit with different labels and images. Indeed, one member expressed his relief that someone had finally made sense of their findings. Furthermore, the management team found the models *interesting* and *believable*, two other criteria set by Weick.

The following question was a test of *internal* validity, "How consistent were the results in representing the interview data?" Given the rich debates on the validity of qualitative findings, it is important to define what the researchers meant by validity. DI, in this research, was employed as a method of *discovery*, not measurement. Internal validity, in this case, meets the criteria suggested by Winter, in so far as it represents the meanings and experiences of individuals, and a group of knowledgeable professionals. The three models of technology transfer were an interesting, useful, believable, representation of the data gathered by a team of subject matter experts. It made sense to them.

Internal validity does not imply an exclusive frame of reference. It is certainly possible that a set of alternative models might also demonstrate their validity and provide other insights into the complexities of technology transfer.

External Validity

A more important test is external validity. Winter argues that external validity is not usually important to qualitative researchers. "Qualitative findings are best generalisable to the development of theories and not wider populations." We disagree; external validity, as we define it, proved to be very important in this research. Given the characterisation of technology transfer, in terms of ideal types of models, the models may be generalisable across many organisations.

That is, the challenges represented by these models may be inherent in the field of advanced technological development, independent of particular organisations and their practices. They may be formulated differently if examined from a different perspective, but they cannot be avoided.

Distilled to their essentials and stripped of the accretions of particular organisational cultures and practices, ideal models should be valid for all large organisations faced with the challenges of technology transfer. It was important to test this conclusion leading to a second question. "Can any aerospace organisations of similar size and complexity escape the implications of the three models derived from the analysis?"

The management team had rich industry experience, and had interacted with colleagues across the industry for many years. They were asked to reflect on whether these models were not inherent in the technology transfer enterprise, a valid characterisation of technology transfer processes across many different firms.

Note what is and is not implied by the question. The question does not suggest that other organisations conduct technology transfer efforts in a way similar to ABC. It does not specify particular practices. It asks whether the practices or understandings of other firms could be mapped on the basis of these models.

Again, the management team concluded that the proposed models were valid. In their experience, and on the basis of their many contacts in the industry, they saw these models as reflecting industry wide issues. The models appeared "generic," although many other such models might have been developed.

External validity has particular organisational relevance. If the models are "generic," they are not a function of personalities, local organisational cultures, structures, or management styles. Recall that these are the variables in most research on technology transfer. Most of the models discussed in the literature were developed as extensions of theories and models of organisational processes. Generic models should lead us to question much of this quantitative research on technology transfer.

The recognition of generic challenges and models of technology transfer change the discourse within the organisation. The issues are not leadership, personalities, culture, or organisational structure. They are inherent in the endeavor. Even if every unit is effective and competent, these challenges will remain. That creates an opportunity to collaborate across units rather than fight about responsibility for failure, and enables the organisation to transcend disruptive conflict at least with respect to technology transfer issues.

13

Case Study Research in Political Science

The meaning of case study in political science draws on earlier meanings in other fields. One such is psychology, where case studies have been used since the mid-1800s to capture *details* that provide *insight into human behavior*, as well as to develop clinical *methods*. Medical cases are used in similar ways. In social work, "casework", developed in the 1920s, entails the *detailed reporting* of a client's history and needs as a way to support analysis for intervening through the helping process. Another historical source is the Harvard Business School's development in the 1950s of "cases" as a method of instruction based on *real-life contexts* to encourage *active learning*, a usage developed further at the Maxwell and Kennedy Schools. These italicised features can be found in earlier political case studies, including Peter Blau's 1955 *The Dynamics of Bureaucracy* and Graham Allison's 1971 *Essence of Decision*, both of which serve as classic examples of case studies that demonstrate theorising that is situated in real-life historical and contextual details of human action. How to access or generate such data details and how to establish and evaluate their scientific standing is the focus of debate over "case study method."

To understand the role and meaning of case study within political science today, one needs to know something of its internal disciplinary organisation; and this varies by both department and country. North American political science typically has four sub-fields: political theory, national government (e.g., American, Canadian), comparative politics, and international relations (including security studies); public policy and public administration, to the extent that they are still part of political science departments, are either separate or treated as part of national government studies. In Europe, political science is commonly referred to as politics or government studies and is only occasionally divided into subfields, such as European Politics, International Relations or European Public Administration. With the exception of political theory, all subfields draw on the case study as a method of analysis, but with different interpretations of what it means and how to do it.

Whereas textbooks describe "the case study" as the most common method of analysis in political science, these words are then used to refer to a range of meanings and usages that vary from specific methods to a research approach. Those advancing "case study" as a set of *methods* — the predominant meaning — engage the concept as a specific form of research involving multi-site studies aimed at establishing causal inferences and hypothesis-testing. Those taking the second perspective typically treat "case study" as part of a broader *methodology* that emphasizes human meaning and reflexivity. These scholars more often engage in single-site research aimed at detailing the lived experiences of persons in that setting.

Despite their distinctive histories and occasionally competing ontological and epistemological presuppositions, the discipline's sub-fields share a widespread agreement associating case studies closely with qualitative research. This comes from the fact that case studies rest on the intense study of lived human experiences by means of on-site fieldwork and some combination of (participant) observation, (in-depth) interviews, and/or document analysis. The two perspectives described above each place a different accent on case study methodology. The intra-disciplinary divide concerns the extent to which case study research is perceived as becoming more and more detached from its human-, meaning-centered origins, along with a judgment on the desirability of that detachment. What began in the 1950s as the investigation of unique practices in socio-political life (the second perspective) has increasingly in the last quarter century been expected to change that approach, situating it instead in a methodological playing field that takes one understanding of natural science methods and techniques as the requirement for studies of the political to be seen as scientific.

Recent textbooks formalising case study research in political science in ways consistent with that understanding have contributed to the development of intra-disciplinary disagreements over the character of case study research.

Single-Site Studies

Early case studies, and many done today, consist of largely single site-studies that allow researchers to immerse themselves in the uniqueness of real-life events in what might be called a traditional Chicago-School-type approach. The analysis is inductive and human-centered and is driven by a desire to learn about the potentially multiple social realities that characterise the setting and its "actors" (or "members"). In this form, the case study is perhaps the most archetypal qualitative methodology of all, paralleling Chicago School participant observation in sociology, especially the community and occupational studies, and ethnographic study in anthropology characteristic of the1930s-1960s.

The meaning-centered case study perspective is rooted in single-site studies. "Single-site" has been equated by some methodologists with single "n" studies, a point that is important for understanding contemporary disagreements about the value of case study research. Simply stated, a *single-site* study refers to research carried out in one relatively bounded setting (e.g., a governmental organisation, a community), whereas a single *"n"* study refers to the number of observations conducted as part of experimental research. "Observation" means different things. Field research-based case studies engage in observation understood in an ethnographic sense, meaning that the number of "observations" – persons spoken with, conversations conducted, events and/or interactions seen and/or participated in, documents read, etc. – is not co-terminous with the number of locations in which the case study is carried out. From this perspective, a single-site case study generates a multitude of qualitative-interpretive, within-case "observations" reflecting patterns of interaction, organisational practices, social relations, routines, actions, and so on. And when "setting" is understood from an open systems perspective, the number of sites may also multiply, especially as one traces the focus of study – say, a policy being implemented – across the full range of actions entailed. Observation as treated in an experimental sense – the source of single "n" terminology – is based on the principle that a larger number of cases subjected to analysis yields more valid general principles, another logic altogether.

In the national government subfield, for example, a case study might analyse an institution, such as the courts or political leadership. Richard Fenno's 1978 case study of US Members of Congress involved "soaking and poking," accompanying and interviewing them as they traveled about their districts. While the single site was the Congress, Fenno investigated the tactics, perceptions, and overall political behavior of the elected representatives in multiple home sites. Case study research has also been used for exploring local government and/or agency levels, especially within public policy and administration subfields. Herbert Kaufman's 1960 case study of the US Forest Service examined the practices of management strategies for shaping the behavior of its far-flung employees – a single agency, but multiple geographic sites. Jeffrey Pressman and Aaron Wildavsky's 1973 case study on the local implementation of US economic development policies identified the twists and turns in multi-level decision-making as the reason that agreeing on policy objectives was a lot less complicated than implementing them – another single case, here with multiple organisational and departmental settings.

These three case studies offer contextualised insights into the unique, situated practices of human political life. They represent a period in political science when "single-site" case studies were common. As qualitative researchers have come under increasing pressure, especially following the publication of Gary King, Robert Keohane, and Sidney Verba's 1994 *Designing Social Inquiry*, to conform their research more and more to large "n" studies, they have increased their attention to theorising about case study methodology, particularly within the subfield of comparative politics, with a noticeable recent growth in methods books and a turn toward analytic approaches aspiring to match the logic of quantitative research. This marks one of the intra-disciplinary splits, between those "qualitative" researchers who accept this approach and those "interpretive" researchers who follow less realist approaches under a broader understanding of science.

Multi-Site Studies

Multi-site case study analysis is a hallmark of the

comparative politics subfield, which has, to a large extent, laid claim to comparative case study research as its own, unique method. Like single-site case study scholars, multi-site comparativists draw upon case studies to explore human diversity, although they are perhaps more inclined to use them to establish general propositions about human conditions and interactions. In some instances, comparative case studies are used as a way to focus on detailed analysis of human diversity with the aim of revealing uniqueness. Theda Skocpol's 1979 comparative historical case analysis of the unique social revolutions in France, Russia, and China aimed at general theoretical understanding concerning what leads to political revolution. Robert Putnam's 1994 comparative case study of regional government in Italy analysed the significance of civic community for thriving democratic government.

Adding "comparative" to "case study" brings additional methodological requirements concerning project design and research objectives. By identifying and distinguishing between dependent and independent variables, comparative case studies examine co-variation across case data, by contrast with single case studies done from a qualitative approach which typically search out congruence between theory and data, looking for theory-driven within-case expectations, *and* with single case studies done from an interpretive approach which are more likely today to appear as ethnographic or participant-observer studies and which often use case material to explore particular theoretical issues. Comparison is treated as a "controlled" approach to research whereby the researcher is said to systematically explore similarities and differences based on a predetermined classification of cases. Research design, then, puts great emphasis on the criteria for comparability as the force driving case selection. Most qualitative comparative case study scholars make reference to small "n" comparative studies; most speak of variables, about inference and control, classification and typology. The aim of controlled study – generalisation – is advocated, on the whole, by case study scholars following positivist ontological and epistemological presuppositions and their associated methods of inquiry. This variables- and causal inference-centered approach parallels the work associated with large 'n', statistics-based research. The focus on law-like generalisations that this entails runs counter to a more interpretive approach that focuses, instead, on *verstehen*, thick description, reflexivity, and other such elements for establishing the trustworthiness of the research. Proponents of qualitative comparative case study research differ from their quantitative colleagues in that they limit the number of sites they study (fewer than 6 seems to be the rule of thumb), and they mix numerical and word forms of reporting in an effort to combine generalisation and uniqueness. This latter idea is one largely advanced by Charles Ragin, who claims that comparative case studies not only assess general causal relationships but also have the ability to generate in-depth, contextual understanding. Looking from the outside, the methodological views of these qualitative scholars appear to be merging with quantitative researchers, both of them advancing a shared notion of science.

A 1971 article by political scientist Arend Lijphart sheds some light on these developments. Lijphart used natural science logic in assessing methods of scientific inquiry for conducting political research. He prescribed a general set of methods ranked by scientific value aimed at generalisation and causation with the goal of producing scientific explanations. He listed experimentation as the first and most desirable method for scientific inquiry, followed by the statistical method, the comparative case method, and, lastly, the (single) case study method (which is albeit closely connected to the comparative method). Lijphart's hierarchy is based on the degree of control, the manifestation of time order, and the presence and strength of association, all of which are marshaled in support of causal inference. According to this ranking, a method becomes less "scientific" as it digresses from an experimental research design. This hierarchy of scientific methods and tradition of privileging methods that establish causality are carried through to today's methodological debates concerning the scope and methods of analysis that are to characterise the political science discipline, including the place of case study among them.

Scientific Environment for Political Science Research

At the moment, that form of case study research that places case studies squarely among other methods aiming for causal explanations is on the rise. This is evident in the considerable attention given to developments in and applications of techniques such as Qualitative Comparative Analysis (QCA), optimal sequence matching, necessary condition arguments, and typological methods for analysing cases. Textbooks single these out as advancements in case study research, on the argument that they provide a step towards a desired methodological "rigor" while safeguarding traditional case study features. Contemporary methodologists like Andrew Bennett, Henry Brady, David Collier, Alexander George, John Gerring, and Gary King have worked to develop case study research in these ways in response to critiques concerning what they have perceived as the limitations of more meaning-focused, traditional forms of case studies. While these developments encourage reflection on the character of the method, the changes reflect a narrow understanding of science that rests on such terminology as selection bias, (internal) validity, reliability, and generalisation. A technical, detached, and often complex language recurs in the wealth of case study textbook chapters dedicated to presenting methodological safeguards for case study research. Entire chapters engage such procedures as "process-tracing" (within-case analysis to track links between likely causes and outcomes), "typological theorising" (contingent generalisations based on systematic comparison and case selection), and "path dependency" (time reference used to explain causes and choices). All of these are intended to refute challenges to internal validity and selection bias attributed to case study research. This language assumes ontological and epistemological presuppositions associated with positivist and sometimes critical realist philosophies, at the expense of engaging with case study methods informed by interpretive philosophical presuppositions that would emphasize such criteria as thickly described narratives of situated lived experience, research positionality and reflexivity, and the multiple possible meanings of political language, acts, and physical artifacts.

These trends might be understood as a commitment to ensuring a competitive position for case study research in contemporary political science by updating earlier case study notions with newer, more effective tools. Alternatively, the trends could be interpreted as a defensive posture—the aftermath of a lingering 1963 remark by Donald Campbell and Julian Stanley about how single case studies had *no* scientific value. The King, Keohane, and Verba advocacy of a single approach to scientific inference for both the natural and the social sciences might also be understood to play a role. Either interpretation is indicative of a decisive turn towards the systemisation of case study procedures in a particular direction, and this is portrayed in textbooks as a way forward for qualitative case study scholars.

Evaluating Case Studies

Many of the aforementioned contemporary case study scholars explicitly promote combining quantitative and qualitative methods and devote considerable attention to issues of design as a way of assuring scientific rigor. Their methodological writings focus on orderly, systemised, and verifiable case study procedures. Case study's use for a more interpretive understanding of social and human life is increasingly less visible. While it is still possible to find some references to the advantages of case study research for offering real-life insight into social phenomena, flexibility of methods, and sensible translations of theory, as in Bent Flyvbjerg's 2001 work, it is by far more common to find references to its (newfound) potential for testing hypotheses, examining causal mechanisms in detail, assessing the reliability of inferences, or developing internally valid measures of concepts.

A fair amount of discussion, especially in comparative politics, has focused on concept formation and definition and the extent to which the operationalisation of concepts needs to be grounded in the case study at hand. This point lies at the heart of the differences between qualitative and interpretive case study research design and methods. The debate concerns a priori versus situated concept formation; that is, the stipulation of concept meanings that are defined prior to the research versus "meanings-in-use" that are allowed to emerge during fieldwork in the course of the research. A priori concept formation is prominent in comparative or multi-site case study research and goes hand-in-hand with a "controlled" case study research design. The argument for such an approach is that even though concepts may have different meanings in use, this is a matter of degrees of difference rather than differences in type of concept, making comparison possible. Other scholars argue that conceptual meanings cannot be fixed in the abstract, that they are highly contextualised. In such an approach, the uses of terms and definitions are linked to unique experiences and embedded in time and space; influenced by linguistic, country and/or regional, organisational, and/or communal history and situation. The argument emphasizes the need to understand concepts as rooted each in its own particular setting. Frederic Schaffer's 1998 *Democracy in Translation* studying the meaning of "democracy" to the people of Ṣenegal is an example. The general claim that case study research is a qualitative method remains, but scholars differ on the meaning of this label in the argumentation for case study research.

Critical Assessment

Case study research remains a central method of analysis in contemporary political science research, despite periods of more and less acceptance and the rupture between those who wish to preserve its earlier form and those trying to bring it closer to quantitative modes. Growing attention to methods and methodology in the context of particular meanings of "science" is also reflected in the textbooks. Until fairly recently, case study methods textbooks were rare, and for a while, Robert Yin's 1984 text (in various editions) was the only one available. It was an influential piece, but it has taken case study's traditionally more interpretive focus in decidedly realist, positivist directions.

A large part of today's methodological treatments of case study research in political science comes from comparative politics scholars, and that sub-field is currently providing significant impetus in the direction of multi-sited, comparative case study research. Those methodologists are making every effort to articulate what comprises a case study in order to increase its acceptance in a wider, largely quantitatively-oriented methodological playing field. More and more, case studies are being described as ranging between little detail across many cases and a lot of detail for a few or a single case. Prior notions of meaning-giving inquiry are either being bypassed or overshadowed by specific terms and methods that ignore interpretive inquiry in favor of attention to variables-based causal inferences. While it is difficult to anticipate the future of case study research in political science, it can be said that much depends on how present methodological debates unfold and how intensely political scientists hold on to earlier forms of case study research as a legitimate way of doing science.

14

Comparative Research Method

In the literature of comparative politics, a wide variety of meanings is attached to the terms "comparison" and "comparative method." The comparative method is defined here as one of the basic methods—the others being the experimental, statistical, and case study methods—of establishing general empirical propositions. It is, in the first place, definitely a *method,* not just "a convenient term vaguely symbolising the focus of one's research interests." Nor is it a special set of substantive concerns in the sense of Shmuel N. Eisenstadt's definition of the comparative approach in social research; he states that the term does not "properly designate a specific method..., but rather a special focus on cross-societal, institutional, or macrosocietal aspects of societies and social analysis."

Second, the comparative method is here defined as *one* of the basic scientific methods, not *the* scientific method. It is, therefore, narrower in scope than what Harold D. Lasswell has in mind when he argues that "for anyone with a scientific approach to political phenomena the idea of an independent comparative method seems redundant," because the scientific approach is "unavoidably comparative." Likewise, the definition used here differs from the very similar broad interpretation given by Gabriel A. Almond, who also equates the compar-ative with the scientific method: "It makes no sense to speak of a comparative politics in political science since if it is a science, it goes without saying that it is comparative in its ap-proach."

Third, the comparative method is here re-garded as a *method of discovering empirical re-lationships among variables,* not as a method of measurement. These two kinds of methods should be clearly distinguished. It is the latter that Kalleberg has in mind when he discusses the "logic of comparison." He defines the comparative method as "a form of measurement"; comparison means "nonmetrical ordering," or in other words, ordinal measurement. Similarly, Sartori is thinking in terms of measurement on nominal, ordinal (or comparative), and cardinal scales when he describes the conscious thinker as "the man that realises the limitations of not having a thermometer and still manages to say a great deal simply by saying hot and cold, warmer and cooler." This important step of measuring variables is logically prior to the step of finding relationships among them.

Finally, a clear distinction should be made between *method* and *technique.* The comparative method is a broad-gauge, general method, not a narrow, specialised technique. In this vein, Gunnar Heckscher cautiously refers to "the method (or at least the *procedure)* of comparison," and Walter Goldschmidt prefers the term comparative *approach,* because "it lacks the preciseness to call it a method." The comparative method may also be thought of as a basic research *strategy,* in contrast with a mere tactical aid to research. This will become clear in the discussion that follows.

Experimental, Statistical, and Comparative Methods

The nature of the comparative method can be understood best if it is compared and contrasted with the two other fundamental strategies of research; these will be referred to, following Neil J. Smelser's example, as the *experimental* and the *statistical* methods. All three methods (as well as certain forms of the case study method) aim at scientific explanation, which consists of two basic elements: (1) the establishment of general empirical relationships among two or more variables, while (2) all other variables are controlled, that is, held constant. These two elements are inseparable: one cannot be sure that a relationship is a true one unless the influence of other variables is controlled. The *ceteris paribus* condition is vital to empirical generalisations.

The experimental method, in its simplest form, uses two equivalent groups, one of which (the experimental group) is exposed to a stimulus while the other (the control group) is not. The two groups are then compared, and any difference can be attributed to the stimulus. Thus one knows the relationship between two variables—with the important assurance that no other variables were involved, because in all respects but one the two groups were alike. Equivalence—that is, the condition that the *cetera* are indeed *paria*—can be achieved by a process of deliberate randomisation. The experimental method is the most nearly ideal method for scientific explanation, but unfortunately it can only rarely be used in political science because of practical and ethical impediments.

An alternative to the experimental method is the statistical method. It entails the conceptual (mathematical) manipulation of empiricially observed data—which cannot be manipulated situationally as in experimental design—in order to discover controlled relationships among variables. It handles the problem of control by means of *partial correlations*. For instance, when one wants to inquire into the relationship between political participation and level of education attained, one should control for the influence of age because younger generations have received more education than older generations. This can be done by partialing—dividing the sample into a number of different age groups and looking at the correlations between participation and education within each separate age group. Paul F. Lazarsfeld states that this is such a basic research procedure that it "is applied almost automatically in empirical research. Whenever an investigator finds himself faced with the relationship between two variables, he immediately starts to 'cross-tabu-late,' i.e., to consider the role of further variables."

The statistical method can be regarded, therefore, as an approximation of the experimental method. As Ernest Nagel emphasizes, "every branch of inquiry aiming at reliable general laws concerning empirical subject matter must employ a procedure that, if it is not strictly controlled experimentation, has the essential logical functions of experiment in inquiry." The statistical method does have these essential logical functions, but it is not as strong a method as experimentation because it cannot handle the problem of control as well. It cannot control for all other variables, merely for the other *key* variables that are known or suspected to exert influence. Strictly speaking, even the experimental method does not handle the problem of control perfectly, because the investigator can never be completely sure that his groups are actually alike in every respect. But experimental design provides the closest approximation to this ideal. The statistical method, in turn, is an approximation—not the equivalent—of the experimental method. Conversely, one can also argue, as Lazarsfeld does, that the experimental method constitutes a special form of the statistical method, but only if one adds that it is an especially potent form.

The logic of the comparative method is, in accordance with the general standard expounded by Nagel, also the same as the logic of the experimental method. The comparative method resembles the statistical method in all respects except one. The crucial difference is that the number of cases it deals with is too small to permit systematic control by means of partial correlations. This problem occurs in statistical operations, too; especially when one wants to control simultaneously for many variables, one quickly "runs out of cases." The comparative method should be resorted to when the number of cases available for analysis is so small that cross-tabulating them further in order to establish credible controls is not feasible. There is, consequently, no clear dividing line between the statistical and comparative methods; the difference depends entirely on the number of cases. It follows that in many research situations, with an intermediate number of cases, a combination of the statistical and comparative methods is appropriate. Where the cases are national political systems, as they often are in the field of comparative politics, the number of cases is necessarily so restricted that the comparative method has to be used.

From the vantage point of the general aims and the alternative methods of scientific inquiry, one can consider the comparative method in proper perspective and answer such questions as the following, raised by Samuel H. Beer and by Harry Eckstein: Can comparison be regarded as "the social scientist's equivalent of the natural scientist's laboratory?" and: "Is the comparative method in the social sciences... really an adequate substitute for experimentation in the natural sciences, as has sometimes been claimed?" The answer is that the comparative method is not the equivalent of the experimental method but only a very imperfect substitute. A clear awareness of the limitations of the comparative method is necessary but need not be disabling, because, as we shall see, these weaknesses can be minimised. The "conscious thinker" in comparative politics should realise the limitations of the comparative method, but he should also recognise and take advantage of its possibilities.

Comparative Method: Weaknesses and Strengths

The principal problems facing the comparative method can be succinctly stated as: many variables, small number of cases. These two problems are closely interrelated. The former is common to virtually all social science research regardless of the particular method applied to it; the latter is peculiar to the comparative method and renders the problem of handling many variables more difficult to solve.

Before turning to a discussion of specific suggestions for minimising these problems, two general comments are in order. First, if at all possible one should generally use the statistical (or perhaps even the experimental) method instead of the weaker comparative method. But often, given the inevitable scarcity of time, energy, and financial resources, the intensive comparative analysis of a few cases may be more promising than a more superficial statistical analysis of many cases. In such a situation, the most fruitful approach would be to regard the comparative analysis as the first stage of research, in which hypotheses are carefully formulated, and the statistical analysis as the second stage, in which these hypotheses are tested in as large a sample as possible.

In one type of comparative cross-national research, it is logically possible and may be advantageous to shift from the comparative to the statistical method. Stein Rokkan distinguishes two aims of cross-national analysis. One is the testing of "*macro* hypotheses" concerning the "interrelations of structural elements of total systems"; here the number of cases tends to be limited, and one has to rely on the comparative method. The other is "*micro* replications," designed "to test out in other national and cultural settings a proposition already validated in one setting." Here, too, one can use the comparative method, but if the proposition in question focuses on individuals as units of analysis, one can also use the statistical method; as Mer-ritt and Rokkan point out, instead of the "one-nation, one-case" approach, nationality can simply be treated as an additional variable on a par with other individual attributes such as occupation, age, sex, type of neighbourhoods, etc.

Terence K. Hopkins and Immanuel Wallerstein make a similar distinction between truly "cross-national studies" in which total systems are the units of analysis, and "multi-national but *cross-individual* research."

The second general comment concerns a dangerous but tempting fallacy in the application of the comparative method: the fallacy of attaching too much significance to negative findings. The comparative method should not lapse into what Johan Galtung calls "the traditional quotation/ illustration methodology, where cases are picked that are in accordance with the hypothesis—and hypotheses are rejected if one deviant case is found." All cases should, of course, be selected systematically, and the scientific search should be aimed at probabilistic, not universal, generalisations. The erroneous tendency to reject a hypothesis on the basis of a single deviant case is rare when the statistical method is used to analyse a large sample, but in the comparative analysis of a small number of cases even a single deviant finding tends to loom large. One or two deviant cases obviously constitute a much less serious problem in a statistical analysis of very many cases than in a comparative study of only a few —perhaps less than ten—cases. But it is nevertheless a mistake to reject a hypothesis "because one can think pretty quickly of a contrary case." Deviant cases weaken a probabilistic hypothesis, but they can only invalidate it if they turn up in sufficient numbers to make the hypothesized relationship disappear altogether.

After these introductory observations, let us turn to a discussion of specific ways and means of minimising the "many variables, small N" problem of the comparative method. These may be divided into four categories:

(1) *Increase the number of cases as much as possible.* Even though in most situations it is impossible to augment the number of cases sufficiently to shift to the statistical method, any enlargement of the sample, however small, improves the chances of instituting at least some control. Modern comparative politics has made great progress in this respect as a result of the efforts of the field's innovators to fashion universally applicable vocabularies of basic politically relevant concepts, notably the approaches based on Parsonian theory and Gabriel A. Almond's functional approach. Such a restatement of variables in comparable terms makes many previously inaccessible cases available for comparative analysis. In addition to extending the analysis geographically, one should also consider the possibilities of "longitudinal" (cross-historical) extension by including as many historical cases as possible. It was the promise of discovering universal laws through global and longitudinal comparisons that made Edward A. Freeman enthusiastically espouse the comparative method almost a century ago. In his *Comparative Politics,* published in 1873, he called the comparative method "the greatest intellectual achievement" of his time, and stated that it could lead to the formulation of "analogies... between the political institutions of times and countries most remote from one another." Comparative politics could thus discover "a world in which times and tongues and nations which before seemed parted poles asunder, now find each one its own place, its own relation to every other." The field of comparative politics has not yet achieved—and

may never achieve—the goals that Freeman set for it with such optimism. But his words can remind us of the frequent utility of extending comparative analyses both geographically and historically.

(2) *Reduce the "property-space" of the analysis.* If the sample of cases cannot be increased, it may be possible to combine two or more variables that express an essentially similar underlying characteristic into a single variable. Thus the number of cells in the matrix representing the relationship is reduced, and the number of cases in each cell increased correspondingly. Factor analysis can often be a useful technique to achieve this objective. Such a reduction of what Lazarsfeld calls the "property-space" increases the possibilities of further cross-tabulation and control without increasing the sample itself. It may also be advisable in certain instances to reduce the number of classes into which the variables are divided (for instance, by simplifying a set of several categories into a dichotomy), and thus to achieve the same objective of increasing the average number of cases per cell. The latter procedure, however, has the disadvantage of sacrificing a part of the information at the investigator's disposal, and should not be used lightly.

(3) *Focus the comparative analysis on "comparable" cases.* In this context, "comparable" means: similar in a large number of important characteristics (variables) which one wants to treat as constants, but dissimilar as far as those variables are concerned which one wants to relate to each other. If such comparably cases can be found, they offer particularly good opportunities for the application of the comparative method because they allow the establishment of relationships among a few variably while many other variables are controlled. As Ralph Braibanti states, "the movement from hypothesis

> to theory is contingent upon analysis of the total range of political systems," but it is often more practical to accord priority to the focus on a limited number of comparable cases and the discovery of *partial* generalisations.

Whereas the first two ways of strengthening the comparative method were mainly concerned with the problem of "small N," this third approach focuses on the problem of "many variables." While the total number of variables cannot be reduced, by using comparable cases in which many variables are constant, one can reduce considerably the number of *operative* variables and study their relationships under controlled conditions without the problem of running out of cases. The focus on comparable cases differs from the first recommendation not only in its preoccupation with the problem of "many variables" rather than with "small N," but also in the fact that as a by-product of the search for comparable cases, the number of cases subject to analysis will usually be *decreased.* The two recommendations thus point in fundamentally different directions, although both are compatible with the second (and also the fourth) recommendation.

This form of the comparative method is what John Stuart Mill described as the "method of difference" and as the "method of concomitant variations." The method of difference consists of "comparing instances in which [a] phenomenon does occur, with instances in other respects similar in which it does not." The method of concomitant variations is a more sophisticated version of the method of difference: instead of observing merely the presence or absence of the operative variables, it observes and measures the quantitative variations of the operative variables and relates these to each other. As in the case of the method of difference, all other factors must be kept constant; in Mill's words, "that we may be warranted in inferring causation from concomitance of variations, the concomitance itself must be proved by the Method of Difference."

Mill's method of concomitant variations is often claimed to be the first systematic formulation of the modern comparative method. It should be pointed out, however, that Mill myself thought that the methods of difference and of concomitant variations could not be applied in the social sciences because sufficiently slimier cases could not be found. He stated that their application in political science was "completely out of the question" and branded any attempt to do so as a "gross misconception of the mode of investigation proper to political phenomena." Durkheim agreed with Mill's negative judgment: "The absolute elimination of adventitious elements is an ideal which cannot really be attained;... one can never be even approximately certain that two societies agree or differ in all respects save one." These objections are founded on a too exacting scientific standard—what Sartori calls "over-conscious thinking." It is important to remember, however, that in looking for comparable cases, this standard should be approximated as closely as possible.

The area approach appears to lend itself quite well to this way of applying the comparative method because of the cluster of characteristics that areas tend to have in common and that can, therefore be used as controls. But opinions on the utility of the area approach differ sharply: Gunnar Heckscher states that "area studies are of the very essence of comparatively government," and points out that "the number of variables, while frequently still very large, is at least reduced in the case of a happy choice of area." Roy C. Macridis and Richard Cox also argue that if areas are characterised by political as well as non-political uniformities, "the area concept will be of great value, since certain political processes will be compared between units within the area against a common background of similar trait configuration"; they cite Latin America as an example of an area offering the prospect of "fruitful intra-area comparison." On the other hand, Dank-wart A. Rustow declares in a recent article that area study is "almost obsolete," and he shows little faith in it as a setting for "manageable comparative study." He argues that "mere geographic proximity does not necessarily furnish the best basis of comparison," and furthermore that "comparability is a quality that is not inherent in any given set of objects; rather it is a quality imparted to them by the observer's perspective." This is a compelling argument that should be carefully considered.

It is not true that areas reflect merely geographic proximity; they tend to be similar in many other basic respects. By means of an inductive process—a factor analysis of 54 social and cultural variables on 82 countries—Bruce M. Russett discovered socio-culturally similar groupings of countries, which correspond closely to areas or regions of the world as usually defined. Comparability is indeed not inherent in any given area, but it is more likely within an area than in a randomly selected set of countries. It seems unwise, therefore, to give up the area approach in comparative politics. But two important provisos should be attached to this conclusion. First, the area approach can contribute to comparative politics if it is an aid to the comparative method, not if it becomes an end in itself. Otherwise, area study may indeed become "a form of imprisonment." It is against this danger that the thrust of Rustow's argument is directed. Second, the area approach should not be used indiscriminately, but only where it offers the possibility of establishing crucial controls. In this respect, some of the smaller areas may offer more advantages than the larger ones—Scandinavia, for example, which has barely been exploited in this manner, or the Anglo-American countries, which have received greater comparative attention (but which do not constitute an area in the literal sense).

An alternative way of maximising comparability is to analyse a single country diachronically. Such comparison of the same unit at different times generally offers a better solution to the control problem than comparison of two or more different but similar units (e.g., within the same area) at the same time, although the control can never be perfect; the same country is not really the same at different times. A good example of diachronic comparative analysis is Charles E. Frye's study of the empirical relationships among the party system, the interest group system, and political stability in Germany under the Weimar and Bonn Republics. Frye argues that "for the study of these relationships, Weimar and Bonn make a particularly good case [strictly speaking, *two* cases] because there are more constants and relatively fewer variables than in many cross-national studies. Yet the differences could hardly be sharper."

Unless the national political system itself constitutes the unit of analysis, comparability can also be enhanced by focusing on intranation instead of internation comparisons. The reason is again the same: comparative intranation analysis can take advantage of the many similar national characteristics serving as controls. Smelser illustrates the utility of this strategy with the example of a hypothetical research project on industrialisation in Germany and Italy: "For many purposes it would be more fruitful to compare northern Italy with southern Italy, and the Ruhr with Bavaria, than it would be to compare Germany as a whole with Italy as a whole. These two countries differ not only in level of industrialisation, but also in cultural traditions, type of governmental structure, and so on." The advantage of intra-unit comparison is that inter-unit differences can be held constant. "Then, having located what appear to be operative factors in the in-tra-unit comparisons, it is possible to move to the inter-unit comparisons to see if the same differences hold in the large."

As Juan J. Linz and Amando de Miguel point out, a particularly promising approach may be the combination of intranation and in-ternation comparisons: 'The comparison of those sectors of two societies that have a greater number of characteristics in common while differing on some crucial ones may be more fruitful than overall national comparisons." An illustrative example of this approach in the political realm is suggested by Raoul Naroll: "If one wishes to test theories about the difference between the cabinet and the presidential systems of government... one is better advised to compare Manitoba and North Dakota than to compare Great Britain and the United States, since with respect to all other variables Manitoba and North Dakota are very much alike, while Great Britain and the United States have many other differences."

(4) *Focus the comparative analysis on the "key" variables.* Finally, the problem of "many variables" may be alleviated not only by some of the specific approaches suggested above but also by a general commitment to theoretical parsimony. Comparative analysis must avoid the danger of being overwhelmed by large numbers of variables and, as a result, losing the possibility of discovering controlled relationship, and it must therefore judiciously restrict itself to the really key variables, omitting those of only marginal importance. The nature of the comparative method and its special limitations constitute a strong argument against what Lass-well and Braibanti call "configurative" or "contextual" analysis: "the identification and interpretation of factors in the whole social order which appear to affect whatever political functions and their institutional manifestations have been identified and listed for comparison" (Braibanti's definition). Lasswell

> argues that the comparative method as usually applied has been insufficiently configurative, and calls for the exploration of more variables: the entire context—past, present, and future—"must be continually scanned."

Scanning all variables is not the same as including all variables, of course, as long as one is on one's guard against an unrealistic and eventually self-defeating perfectionism. Comparatively politics should avoid the trap into which the decision-making approach to the study of international politics fell, of specifying and calling for the analysis of an exhaustive list of all variables that have any possible influence on the decision-making process. Parsimony suggests that Joseph LaPalombara's call for a "segmented approach" aiming at the formulation of middle-range propositions concerning partial systems makes a great deal of sense. Similarly, Eckstein's urgent call for greater manageability of the field should be carefully heeded: "The most obvious need in the field at present is simplification-and simplification on a rather grand scale-for human intelligence and scientific method can scarcely cope with the large numbers of variables, the heaps of concepts, and the mountains of data that seem at present to be required, and indeed to exist, in the field."

It is no accident that the most fruitful applications of the comparative method have been in anthropological research. In primitive societies, the number of variables is not as bewilderingly large as in more advanced societies. All relevant factors can therefore be more easily surveyed and analysed. In this respect, anthropology can be said to provide "almost a laboratory for the quasi-experimental approach to social phenomena." Political science lacks this advantage, but can approximate it by focusing attention on the key variables in comparative studies.

A final comment is in order about the relationship of comparative politics as a substantive field and comparison as a method. The two are clearly not coterminous. In comparative politics, other methods can often also be employed, and the comparative method is also applicable in other fields and disciplines. A particularly instructive example is James N. Rosenau's study of the relative influence of individual variables (personal policy beliefs and "personalising tendencies") and role variables (party role and committee role) on the behavior of United States senators during two similar periods: the "Acheson era," 1949-1952, and the "Dulles era," 1953-1956. Rosenau argues that these two eras were characterised by a generally similar international environment and that the two secretaries of state conducted similar foreign policies and also resembled each other in personal qualities. He terms the method that he uses in his analysis the method of "quantitative historical comparison." One of its basic characteristics is the testing of hypotheses by comparing two eras (cases) that are "essentially comparable... in all respects except for the... variables being examined." The method is called "quantitative" because the variables are operationally defined in quantitative terms, and "historical" because the two cases compared are historical eras. The method is, therefore, a special form of the comparative method. It illustrates one of very many ways in which an imaginative investigator can devise fruitful applications of the comparative method.

Comparative and Case Study Method

The discussion of the comparative method is not complete without a consideration of the case study method. The statistical method can be applied to many cases, the comparative method to relatively few (but at least two) cases, and the case study method to one case. But the case study method can and should be closely connected with the comparative method (and sometimes also with the statistical method); certain types of case studies can even be considered implicit parts of the comparative method.

The great advantage of the case study is that by focusing on a single case, that case can be intensively examined even when the research resources at the investigator's disposal are relatively limited. The scientific status of the case study method is somewhat ambiguous, however, because science is a generalising activity. A single case can constitute neither the basis for a valid generalisation nor the ground for disproving an established generalisation.

Indirectly, however, case studies can make an important contribution to the establishment of general propositions and thus to theory-building in political science. Six types of case studies may be distinguished. These are ideal types, and any particular study of a single case may fit more than one of the following categorise:

(1) Atheoretical case studies;

(2) Interpretative case studies;

(3) Hypothesis-generating case studies;

(4) Theory-confirming case studies;

(5) Theory-inflrming case studies;

(6) Deviant case studies.

Cases may be selected for analysis because of an interest in the case *per se* or because of an interest in theory-building. The first two types of cases belong to the former category. *Atheoretical case studies* are the traditional single-country or single-case analyses. They are entirely descriptive and move in a theoretical vacuum: they are neither guided by established or hypothesized generalisations nor motivated by a desire to formulate general hypotheses. Therefore, the direct theoretical value of these case studies is nil, but this does not mean that they are altogether useless. As

LaPalombara emphasizes, the development of comparative politics is hampered by an appalling lack of information about almost all of the world's political systems. Purely descriptive case studies do have great utility as basic data-gathering operations, and can thus contribute indirectly to theory-building. It can even be claimed that "the cumulative effect of such studies will lead to fruitful generalisation," but only if it is recognised that this depends on a theoretically oriented secondary analysis of the data collected in atheoretical case studies.

As indicated earlier, the atheoretical case study and the other types of case studies are ideal types. An actual instance of an theoretical case study probably does not exist, because almost any analysis of a single case is guided by at least some vague theoretical notions and some anecdotal knowledge of other cases, and usually results in some vague hypotheses or conclusions that have a wider applicability. Such actual case studies fit the first type to a large extent, but they also fit one or more of the other types (particularly the third, fourth, and fifth types) at least to some extent.

Interpretative case studies resemble theoretical case studies in one respect: they, too, are selected for analysis because of an interest in the case rather than an interest in the formulation of general theory. They differ, however, in that they make explicit use of established theoretical propositions. In these studies, a generalisation is applied to a specific case with the aim of throwing light on the case rather than of improving the generalisation in any way. Hence they are studies in "applied science." Since they do not aim to contribute to empirical generalisations, their value in terms of theory-building is nil. On the other hand, it is precisely the purpose of empirical theory to make such interpretative case studies possible. Because of the still very limited degree of theoretical development in political science, such case studies are rare. One interesting example is Michael C. Hudson's imaginative and insightful case study of Lebanon in the light of existing development theories, in which he discovers a serious discrepancy between the country's socio-economic and political development.

The remaining four types of case studies are all selected for the purpose of theory-building. Hypothesis-generating case studies start out with a more or less vague notion of possible hypotheses, and attempt to formulate definite hypotheses to be tested subsequently among a larger number of cases. Their objective is to develop theoretical generalisations in areas where no theory exists yet. Such case studies are of great theoretical value. They may be particularly valuable if the case selected for analysis provides what Naroll calls a sort of "crucial experiment" in which certain variables of interest happen to be present in a special way.

Theory-confirming and *theory-inarming case studies* are analyses of single cases within the framework of established generalisations. Prior knowledge of the case is limited to a single variable or to none of the variables that the proposition relates. The case study is a test of the proposition, which may turn out to be confirmed or inflrmed by it. If the case study is of the theory-confirming type, it strengthens the proposition in question. But, assuming that the proposition is solidly based on a large number of cases, the demonstration that one more case fits does not strengthen it a great deal. Like-wise, theory-infirming case studies merely weaken the generalisations marginally.. The theoretical value of both types of case studies is enhanced, however, if the cases are, or turn out to be, extreme on one of the variables: such studies can also be labeled "crucial experiments" or crucial tests of the propositions.

Deviant case analyses are studies of single cases that are known to deviate from established generalisations. They are selected in order to reveal why the cases are deviant—that is, to uncover relevant additional variables that were not considered previously, or to refine the (operational) definitions of some or all of the variables. In this way, deviant case studies can have great theoretical value. They weaken the original proposition, but suggest a modified proposition that may be stronger. The validity of the proposition in its modified form must be established by further comparative analysis.

Of the six types of case studies, the hypothesis-generating and the deviant case studies have the greatest value in terms of their contribution to theory. Each of these two types, however, has quite different functions in respect to theory-building: The hypothesis-generating case study serves to generate new hypotheses, while the deviant case study refines and sharpens existing hypotheses. The deviant case study—as well as the theory-confirming and theory-infirming case studies—are implicitly comparative analyses. They focus on a particular case which is singled out for analysis from a relatively large number of cases and which is analysed within the theoretical and empirical context of this set of cases. The deviant case may be likened to the "experimental group" with the remainder of the cases constituting the "control group." Just as the analytical power of the comparative method increases the closer it approximates the statistical and experimental methods, so the analytical power of the case study method increases the more it approximates the comparative method in the form of deviant case analysis. Such case analysis requires, of course, that the position of the deviant case on the variables under consideration, and consequently also its position relative to the other cases, are clearly defined.

The different types of cases and their unequal potential contributions to theory-building should be kept in mind in selecting and analysing a single case. Some of the shortcomings in Eckstein's otherwise insightful and thought-provoking case study of Norway may serve as instructive examples. Eckstein argues that the Norwegian case deviates from David B. Truman's proposition concerning "overlapping memberships," because Norway is a stable democracy in spite of the country's deep and non-overlapping geographic, economic, and cultural cleavages. But he fails to place the case of Norway in relation to other cases. In fact, although he describes Norway's divisions as "astonishingly great, sharp, and persistent," he explicitly rules out any comparison with the cleavages in other countries. This exclusion seriously weakens the case study. Furthermore, instead of trying to refine Truman's proposition with the help of the deviant findings, Eckstein simply drops it. In terms of the sixfold typology of case studies discussed above, his analysis of the Norwegian case is only a theory-infirming one and is not made into a deviant case study.

From then on, the case study becomes a theory-confirming one. Eckstein finds that the Norwegian case strikingly bears out his own "congruence" theory, which states that governments tend to be stable if there is considerable resemblance (congruence) between governmental authority patterns and the authority patterns in society. He demonstrates persuasively that both governmental and social patterns of authority are strongly democratic in Norway and thus highly congruent. The problem here is not that the Norwegian facts do not fit the theory, but that they fit the theory too perfectly. The perfect fit strengthens the theory marginally, but does not contribute to its refinement.

Bibliography

Almond, Gabriel Abraham (2002). *Ventures in political science.* Lynne Rienner Publishers. p. 29.

Bealey, Frank; Chapman, Richard A.; Sheehan, Michael (1999). *Elements in political science.* Edinburgh University Press. pp. 3–4.

Berg, B.L. (1995). *Qualitative research methods for the social sciences* (2nd ed.). Boston: Allyn and Bacon.

Bositis, D.A. (1990). *Research designs for political science: contrivance and demonstration in theory and practice.* Carbondale: Southern Illinois University Press.

Coffey, A., & Atkinson, P. (1996). *Making sense of qualitative data.* Thousand Oaks, CA: Sage.

Farr, James; Seidelman, Raymond (1993). *Discipline and history: political science in the United States.* University of Michigan Press. pp. 230–233.

Girden, E.R. (1996). *Evaluating research articles from start to finish.* Thousand Oaks, CA: Sage.

Goel, M.L. (1988). *Political science research: a methods handbook.* Ames: Iowa State University Press.

Hakim, C. (1987). *Research design: strategies and choices in the design of social research.* Boston: Allen & Unwin.

Johnson, J.B., & Joslyn, R.A. (1995). *Political science research methods* (3rd ed.). Washington, DC: CQ Press.

Kinder, D.R., & Palfrey, T.R. (Eds.). (1993). *Experimental foundations of political science.* Ann Arbor: University of Michigan Press.

Klingemann, Hans-Dieter, ed. (2007) *The State of Political Science in Western Europe.* Opladen: Barbara Budrich Publishers.

Lane, Ruth (1996). *Political science in theory and practice: the 'politics' model.* M. E. Sharpe. p. 89.

Lyberg, L. et al. (Eds.). (1997). *Survey measurement and process quality*. New York: Wiley.

Marshall, C., & Rossman, G.B. (1995). *Designing qualitative research* (2nd ed.). Newbury Park, CA: Sage.

Muhsin, Mahdi (2001). *Alfarabi and the foundation of Islamic political philosophy*. p. 35.

Nachmias, C., & Nachmias, D. (1992). *Research methods in the social sciences* (4th ed.). New York: St. Martin's Press.

Reid. S. (1987). *Working with statistics: an introduction to quantitative methods for social scientists*. Totowa, N.J.: Rowman & Littlefield.

Robson, C. (1993). *Real world research: a resource for social scientists and practitioner-researchers*. Oxford; Cambridge, MA: Blackwell.

Schramm, S. F.; Caterino, B., eds. (2006). *Making Political Science Matter: Debating Knowledge, Research, and Method*, New York and London: New York University Press. Making Political Science Matter. *Google Books*. 4 Feb. 2009.

Seidman, I.E. (1991). *Interviewing as qualitative research: a guide for researchers in education and the social sciences*. New York: Teachers College Press.

Shaffir, W.B., & Stebbins, R.A. (1991). *Experiencing fieldwork: an inside view of qualitative research*. Newbury Park, CA: Sage.

Silverman, D. (1993). *Interpreting qualitative data: methods for analysing talk, text. and interaction*. London: Thousand Oaks, CA: Sage.

Spoull, N.L. (1995). *Handbook of research methods: a guide for practitioners and students in the social sciences*. (2nd ed.). Metuchen, NJ: Scarecrow Press.

Stern, P.C., & Kalof, L. (1996). *Evaluating social science research*. New York: Oxford University Press.

Tausch, A.; Prager, F. (1993). *Towards a Socio-Liberal Theory of World Development*. Basingstoke: Macmillan; New York: St. Martin's Press.

Tesch, R. (1990). *Qualitative research: analysis types and software tools*. New York: Falmer Press.

Wilcox, R.R. (1987). *New statistical procedures for the social sciences· modern solutions to basic problems*. Hillsdale, N.J.: Erlbaum.

Yin, R.K. (1994). *Case study research: design and methods* (2nd ed.). Newbury Park, CA: Sage.

Index